Does Inequality Matter?

HOW PEOPLE PERCEIVE ECONOMIC DISPARITIES AND SOCIAL MOBILITY

OECD
BETTER POLICIES FOR BETTER LIVES

Please cite this publication as:
OECD (2021), *Does Inequality Matter? How People Perceive Economic Disparities and Social Mobility*, OECD Publishing, Paris, *https://doi.org/10.1787/3023ed40-en*.

ISBN 978-92-64-77595-4 (print)
ISBN 978-92-64-87200-4 (pdf)

Photo credits: Cover © Adeline Marchal.

Corrigenda to publications may be found on line at: *www.oecd.org/about/publishing/corrigenda.htm*.

Foreword

Most people in OECD countries are concerned about high and increasing inequality and the lack of equal opportunities. Indeed, in the past decades the income gap between rich and poor has widened and social mobility has stagnated in many OECD countries, as documented by in-depth OECD analysis over the past years. *Does Inequality Matter? How People Perceive Economic Disparities and Social Mobility* is the sixth in a series of OECD flagship publications on the trends, causes and consequences of inequality and the remedies needed to address them. *Growing Unequal? (2008)* and *Divided we Stand (2011)* analysed the key features and causes of rising inequality. *In it Together (2015)* extended the evidence and showed that rising inequality harms economic growth by constraining the opportunities of the worse-off. *The Broken Social Elevator (2018)* highlighted that sticky floors and sticky ceilings limit social mobility and opportunities for low- and middle-income families to move up the social ladder. The OECD's most recent report in this series *Under Pressure: The Squeezed Middle Class (2019)* documented the three main challenges for the middle class: unfairness, uncertainty, and affordability. The present report *Does Inequality Matter?* turns the attention to how people *perceive* inequality and social mobility, and why analysing people's views helps design successful inequality-reducing policies.

This report is the outcome of a collective effort with contributions from a team of policy analysts from the OECD Centre on Well-Being, Inclusion, Sustainability and Equal Opportunity (WISE) and the Directorate for Employment, Labour and Social Affairs (ELS). The main authors of the report are Emanuele Ciani (WISE) for Chapters 2, 3, 4 and 5; Thomas Manfredi (ELS at the time of writing) for Chapters 2 and 4; Kamil Kouhen (WISE) for Chapter 4. Thomas Manfredi and Kamil Kouhen contributed to all chapters and provided statistical and research assistance, together with Federico Attili (WISE) and Louis Fréget (ELS at the time of writing).

Michael Förster (WISE) led the team and supervised the project and the publication, as well as co-authoring Chapter 1 with Emanuele Ciani. Anne-Lise Faron (WISE) prepared the manuscript for publication along with Carmen Fernandez Biezma (PAC) who led the production process. Martine Zaïda, Julia Carro (WISE) and Paul Gallagher provided support and advice on communication aspects, along with Kate Lancaster, France Charlet and Spencer Wilson (PAC). Ken Kincaid contributed to editing the report.

We are very grateful to Romina Boarini (Director of WISE), Marco Mira D'Ercole (Counsellor of WISE), Stefano Scarpetta (Director of ELS), Mark Pearson (Deputy Director of ELS) and Stephane Carcillo (Head of the Jobs and Income Division in ELS) for their guidance and extensive comments on various versions of the report. We gratefully acknowledge the many suggestions provided by members of the Working Party on Social Policy and the Employment, Labour and Social Affairs Committee of the OECD as well as by experts of the European Commission.

The OECD work on perceptions of inequality and preferences for redistribution was carried out with the financial assistance of the European Union, DG Employment, and the OECD would like to thank them for their support.

We also thankfully acknowledge the comments and suggestions on earlier drafts of the report provided by colleagues from the OECD Centre on Well-Being, Inclusion, Sustainability and Equal Opportunity, the

Directorate for Employment, Labour and Social Affairs and the Directorate for Public Governance (GOV). These include Carlotta Balestra (WISE), Monica Brezzi (GOV), Chris Clarke (WISE), Valerie Frey (ELS), Santiago Gonzalez (GOV), Sebastian Königs (ELS), Neil Martin (WISE) and Fabrice Murtin (WISE). Finally, we are indebted to Marco Colagrossi (Joint Research Centre), Stefano Filauro (European Commission), Sébastian Lechevalier (École des Hautes Études en Sciences Sociales), Johanna Mollerstrom (George Mason University), Jonas Pontusson (University of Geneva), Panu Poutvaara (University of Munich) and David Rueda (University of Oxford) for their comments and suggestions on the initial results of this report.

This document was produced with the financial assistance of the European Union. The views expressed herein can in no way be taken to reflect the official opinion of the OECD member countries or the European Union.

Table of contents

FIGURES

TABLES

Follow OECD Publications on:

http://twitter.com/OECD_Pubs

http://www.facebook.com/OECDPublications

http://www.linkedin.com/groups/OECD-Publications-4645871

http://www.youtube.com/oecdilibrary

http://www.oecd.org/oecddirect/

This book has...

StatLinks

A service that delivers Excel® files from the printed page!

Look for the *StatLinks* at the bottom of the tables or graphs in this book. To download the matching Excel® spreadsheet, just type the link into your Internet browser, starting with the ***https://doi.org*** prefix, or click on the link from the e-book edition.

ISO country codes

AUS	Australia	**JPN**	Japan
AUT	Austria	**KOR**	Korea
BEL	Belgium	**LVA**	Latvia
CAN	Canada	**LTU**	Lithuania
CHL	Chile	**LUX**	Luxembourg
COL	Colombia	**MEX**	Mexico
CRI	Costa Rica	**NLD**	Netherlands
CZE	Czech Republic	**NZL**	New Zealand
DNK	Denmark	**NOR**	Norway
EST	Estonia	**POL**	Poland
FIN	Finland	**PRT**	Portugal
FRA	France	**SVK**	Slovak Republic
DEU	Germany	**SVN**	Slovenia
GRC	Greece	**ESP**	Spain
HUN	Hungary	**SWE**	Sweden
ISL	Iceland	**CHE**	Switzerland
IRL	Ireland	**TUR**	Turkey
ISR	Israel	**GBR**	United Kingdom
ITA	Italy	**USA**	United States

Executive summary

Through extensive cross-country evidence, previous OECD reports have shown that income inequality has increased in most OECD countries over the last thirty years or so and that social mobility stagnated or worsened in some countries. The present report turns the attention to how people *perceive* inequality and social mobility.

In the recovery after the COVID-19 crisis, gathering public support is key to sustain the momentum for reforms that tackle inequalities and promote equal opportunities. Understanding how people form their perceptions and opinions about inequality can help understand the public support for such reforms. The report finds that there is increasing consensus that inequality is a problem, but there are increasing divisions about its extent and what to do about it.

Do people care about inequality? Most people are concerned about inequality. Four in five people in the OECD feel income disparities are too large in their country. People care about inequality of both outcomes and opportunities, as they perceive high income and earnings disparities as well as low social mobility. The average OECD citizen believes that slightly more than 50% of the national income goes to the 10% richest households and that only 4 out of 10 poor children make it out of poverty once they become adult. Concern over income and earnings disparities has risen in the last three decades, in line with the increase in income inequality measured by conventional statistical indicators: while in the 1980s the median individual believed that top earners earn 5 times as much as bottom earners, this perceived top-to-bottom earnings ratio has increased to 8 today. However, also tolerance for inequality increased: today the median person believes that top earners should earn 4 times as much as the bottom earners, up from 3 times in the late 1980s.

Are perceptions disconnected from reality? Even if most people do not have a full set of information, perceptions do reflect real-life evidence of economic inequality in the society. Indeed, even if there is no full match, perceptions and conventional estimates are correlated across countries: people perceive higher income disparities and lower social mobility where conventional estimates are also higher and lower, respectively. Furthermore, concern over income disparities and conventional estimates of inequality have moved in line over time: in countries where statistical indicators of income inequality grew the most, so did people's concern over inequality. For each point increase in the Gini index – a conventional indicator of income inequality – there is almost a 2-percentage point increase in the share of people who strongly agree that income disparities are too wide. Experimental evidence also shows that people incorporate information about inequality consistently in their beliefs. When confronted with information about the actual extent of economic disparities and social mobility, people become more aware of inequality and more concerned about it.

Does high concern imply widespread support for government intervention? In general, the more people are concerned about inequality, the higher their demand for redistribution, but in some countries support for government intervention falls short of concern. Across the OECD, 80% of people who find income disparities to be too large think that it is the responsibility of the government to reduce them. However, in 1/5 of the countries this fraction is below 60%. Furthermore, over time preferences for income redistribution in OECD countries have, on average, risen less than concerns. Besides perceptions of and concern over inequality, demand for inequality-reducing policies is driven by beliefs around what drives inequality, in particular whether access to opportunities is widespread and hard work brings success: across the OECD, demand for more progressive taxation is lower where people believe that poverty is due mostly to lack of personal effort. Furthermore, people's support for specific policies depends on whether those policies are perceived to be effective in reducing inequality. In fact, people are less likely to demand more redistribution if they believe that benefits are mistargeted. On the same line, they are less in favour of progressive taxation if they believe that petty corruption is widespread among public officials, prompting the misuse and misallocation of public benefits. Experimental evidence shows that informing people about the redistributive impact of policies and their effectiveness in addressing inequalities helps raise support.

How divided is public opinion within countries? Despite a growing concern about inequality, there are increasing differences about its extent and what to do about it. Within a given country, most people would like to live in a more equal society. However, they disagree on the extent of inequality and social mobility. Within the average OECD country, one person in four thinks that more than 70% of the national income goes to the 10% richest households, contrary to another fourth of individuals who think that less than 30% goes to the richest households. As a consequence, people disagree with each other as to by how much inequality should be reduced, but mostly because they perceive different levels of inequality, rather than because they have different preferred levels. This division of public opinion has grown in the last three decades, showing signs of polarization: in most OECD countries there is an increasing gap between those who believe inequality is high and those who believe it is low. Interestingly, disagreements over the extent of inequality are wide even among people with similar socio-economic characteristics. In fact, the increased level of disagreement over the last three decades is mostly explained by increased disagreement *within* socio-economic groups, rather than between them.

How can people's perceptions of and concern over inequality inform policy? Despite people's concern over inequality, public support in favour of inequality-reducing policies cannot be taken for granted. Getting citizens and governments on the same page when it comes to policies reducing inequality and promote social mobility requires understanding how people form their perceptions and opinion. The report highlights the importance of:

- *Better understanding of public support for reform*: People care about inequality of both outcomes and opportunities, hence reform packages that tackle both aspects are more likely to gain support. Policy makers should nonetheless take into account people's preferences for specific policy mixes, which may be more opportunity enhancing or focusing more on equalising outcomes. They may also focus on specific aspects of inequality more than on others (e.g. disparities at the top versus bottom). Furthermore, as disagreement is strong also between people with similar socio-economic characteristics, policies that are limited to just one main group might fail to reach sufficient consensus even within that target group.
- *Better understanding of the effectiveness of policies*: People's support for specific policies is higher when those policies are perceived to be effective in reducing inequality. This reinforces the need for evaluating the effectiveness of policies in a transparent way, to gain people's confidence. Such evaluation should be coupled with increased effort to facilitate people's understanding of the functioning and, in particular, the impact of the policies.
- *Better information on inequality and equality of opportunities*: Providing high-quality information about inequality can help reduce the widespread dispersion of perceptions that leads to a divided public opinion. It has the potential for providing common ground for public debate even if it would not necessarily reduce the differences in opinion about policies.

1. Overview

Although the post-COVID-19 recovery will afford the opportunity to introduce reforms that address high levels of inequality, implementation will require widespread support from the public. To better understand what factors drive public support, the report conducts a detailed cross-country analysis of people's perceptions of and concern about inequality of outcomes and opportunities. It documents how concern over income disparities have risen in OECD countries over time, mirroring the rise of income inequality measured by conventional indicators like those derived from household statistics. In most countries a large majority of the population now believes that income disparities are too wide and that intergenerational mobility is weak. Yet, sufficient support for inequality-reducing policies may not materialise if people fail to agree on concrete policy options or doubt their effectiveness. Moreover, even when the majority demands more equality, a strongly divided public opinion complicates the introduction of reforms. Indeed, the report highlights how people within the same country are often divided over whether inequality is too great and, if so, what governments should do to address the challenge. This chapter also looks at how the findings from analyses of perceptions and concern can inform policy making.

1.1. The COVID-19 crisis has opened a window of opportunity for addressing inequalities

The COVID-19 crisis has exposed and accentuated inequalities, although the short-term effect on income inequality are mixed thanks to governments' interventions. The shocks it has dealt to the labour-market have caused highly asymmetrical effects across the population (OECD, 2020[1]; OECD, 2021[2]). However, governments across the OECD have moved swiftly with measures that eased the impact of the shock on vulnerable workers and households. As a result, inequality in disposable income has not risen by much and may have even declined in some countries (Brewer and Gardiner, 2020[3]; Chetty et al., 2020[4]; Almeida et al., 2020[5]; Clark, D'Ambrosio and Lepinteur, 2020[6]; European Commission, 2020[7]; Carta and De Philippis, 2021[8]).

The pandemic has lent weight to the argument in favour of offsetting unequal shocks in order to prevent social tensions (Baldwin, 2020[9]). Inequalities were already high before the pandemic, and COVID-related measures did not enough to address them. Almost all OECD countries have experienced rises in income inequality in the last 30 years (OECD, 2015[10]; OECD, 2011[11]), social mobility has stalled (OECD, 2018[12]), and the middle class has been squeezed by rising costs, employment uncertainty and stagnating income (OECD, 2019[13]). Equality of opportunity has come under pressure with many children of low-earning parents enjoying less opportunities to realize their full potential (OECD, 2018[12]).

Recovery packages offer a great chance to introduce reforms that address the long-standing disparities and lack of opportunities which affect many in the population (Boone et al., 2020[14]; OECD, 2020[1]; OECD, 2020[15]). The successful implementation of such reforms requires strong buy-in from citizens. Support should be wide enough to sustain the momentum of reform over time and achieve long-term objectives.

Even prior to the crisis, a large majority of OECD citizens were indeed concerned about economic disparities and demanded more equal distribution of income. Approximately 80% of people living in OECD countries felt that income disparities in their country were too wide, according to 2017 data from the International Social Survey Programme (ISSP) and the Eurobarometer. Seven in ten users of the OECD's Compare Your Income (CYI) web-tool consider that the income share which goes to the richest 10% is five or more percentage points larger than it should be.[1]

There are also indications that the ongoing crisis has heightened awareness of inequality. Respondents to the 2020 OECD Risks that Matter survey (OECD, 2021[16]) who have experienced health-related problems or economic hardship during the pandemic perceive income inequality to be greater and social mobility lower than other respondents. They are also more likely to want more government intervention and more progressive taxation to narrow the differences between rich and poor. Similarly, respondents affected by job loss during the crisis demand higher public spending on social protection (OECD, 2021[16]).

People from OECD countries are generally in favour of interventions that would reduce current levels of inequality. Most respondents (slightly more than 6 out of 10) to the 2020 OECD Risks that Matter survey believe their government should do more to reduce income differences between rich and poor by collecting taxes and providing social benefits (Figure 1.1). Furthermore, a similar share also believe that, to support the poor, governments should tax the rich more than they currently do. Demand for such redistributive policies is particularly strong in countries where people perceive that income inequality is high and social mobility low.

Figure 1.1. People are supportive of interventions to reduce income differences, particularly where they perceive high inequality and low social mobility

Demand for more government intervention to reduce income differences versus perceptions of income inequality and social mobility

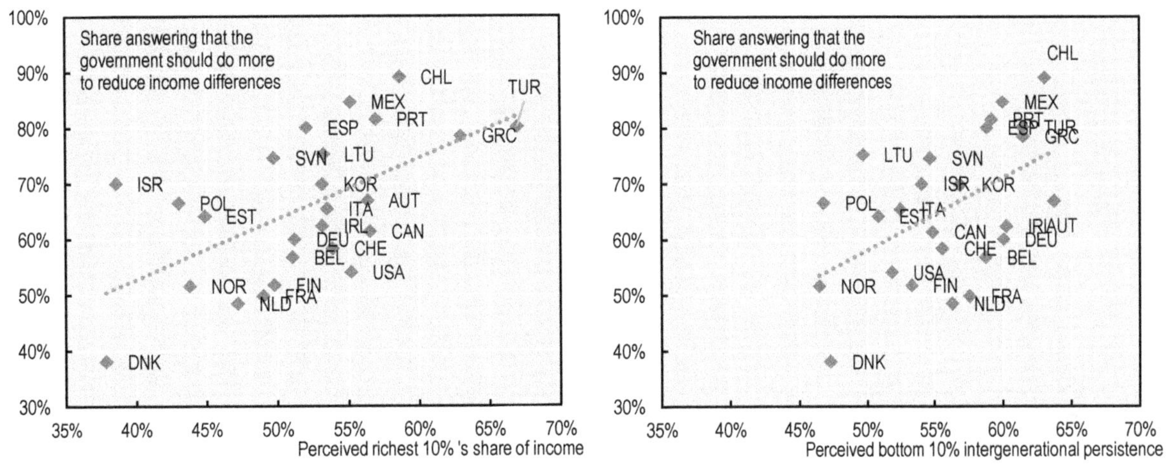

Note: Blue lines are linear fit. The shares on the y axis refer to answers to the question "Governments can reduce income differences between the rich and the poor by collecting taxes and providing social benefits. In your country. Do you think the government should do more or less to reduce income differences?" The shares are calculated excluding respondents who answer "can't choose".

Source: OECD calculations from the 2020 Risks that Matter Survey (Section 3.1).

StatLink https://stat.link/16hj83

Yet public support in favour of inequality-reducing policies cannot be taken for granted. Does the widespread demand for more equality imply demand for any government intervention? Which concrete policies are people more likely to support? How people's concern about inequality and demand for redistribution have evolved over the last three decades offers important insights into those questions. Since the late 1980s, concern over income disparities has generally risen across the OECD, mirroring the rise in income inequality recorded by conventional, or "objective", statistical indicators.[2] However, support for redistributive government interventions has not risen to the same extent. In fact, in several countries, a sizeable share of people is concerned about income disparities, but does not think that it is the state's responsibility to tackle them (Figure 1.2).

Figure 1.2. People's demand for redistribution is less than their concern for income disparities

Fraction of people who believe it is the responsibility of the government to reduce income differences, among those who think that such disparities are too large, 2017

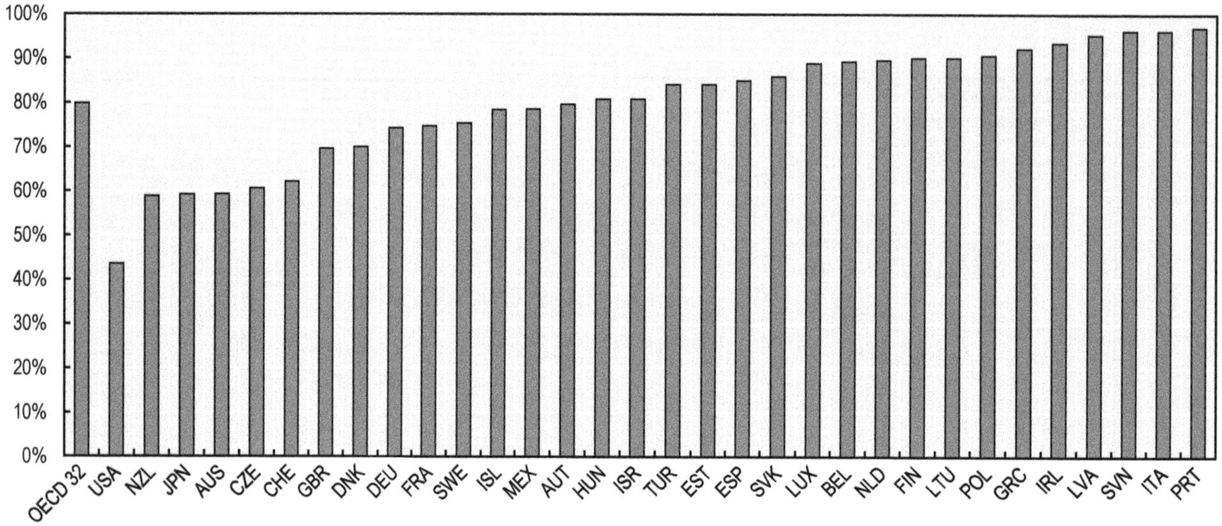

Note: Respondents are asked their opinion about the statements "Differences in income in [country] are too large" and "It is the responsibility of the government to reduce the differences in income between people with high incomes and those with low income". In Eurobarometer the statements are slightly different: "Nowadays in [our country] differences in people's incomes are too great" and "The government in [our country] should take measures to reduce differences in income levels", but the response scale is identical. For consistency, this figure uses data from ISSP where available.

Source: OECD calculations from ISSP 2017, apart from Belgium, Estonia, Greece, Ireland, Italy, Luxembourg, Latvia, Netherlands, Poland, Portugal, Slovenia whose data are from Eurobarometer 471/2017.

StatLink https://stat.link/qker74

Analysing concern over inequality and demand for redistribution may help design widely supported reforms that tackle long-standing disparities. To do so, it is important to underpin concern and demand to act. National support for inequality-reducing reforms stems from both people's concern over inequality and their preferences as to the extent and forms of such reforms (Box 1.1).

On the one hand, concern depends on both perceived and preferred levels of inequality.[3] On the other hand, people's support for redistributive policies depends on their view of the role governments should play in reducing economic disparities. Such views differ extensively across countries. Furthermore, different combinations of perceptions of income or earnings inequality and intergenerational mobility might prompt support for different policy mixes. Perceptions of greater income or earnings inequality could give more weight to policies that directly affect outcomes, such as unemployment benefit, while perceived intergenerational persistence might boost support for pro-opportunity action such as educational policies.

Furthermore, people within the same country often hold different views on what to do about inequality. Even if emergency welfare measures in the wake of the pandemic currently enjoy a rather broad consensus, recent years have seen polarisation in opinions of redistributive and welfare policies (Alesina, Miano and Stantcheva, 2020[17]), with different groups in society expressing views that are hard to conciliate. And even when most people evince concern over inequality, country averages mask wide differences in perceived and preferred levels of inequality among citizens. Analysing the distribution of perceptions and how it evolves over time helps shed light on the polarisation of public debate.

Box 1.1. What shapes demand for inequality-reducing policies?

People's demand for redistribution depends on their concern about current levels of inequality and on their views about the role of government and its policies. These two factors – concern over inequality and opinions of the state – determine not only people's preferences for more or less redistribution, but also the type of state intervention they would support. Apart from redistribution through tax and benefit systems, people might support policies aimed at fostering equal opportunities, such as educational programmes for disadvantaged students, or action to directly limit market disparities, such as introducing the minimum wage. In fact, people in a country may not share the same views on what policies are best suited to tackling economic disparities. Such disagreements affect how people's concern over income disparities translate into different demands for redistribution.

People's concern about inequality depends on the level they perceive (what they *think* it is) and the level they prefer, i.e. what they think it *should* be (for a more detailed discussion see Annex 1.A). Cross-country differences in the average level of concern may not therefore match those measured by conventional inequality indicators. On the one hand, people might perceive a different level of inequality than what those statistical indicators record. On the other hand, the preferred level of inequality also differs across countries, and therefore two societies with similar levels of inequality might differ in the level of concern because they have different tolerance of disparities. It should be noted that "conventional" statistical indicators of inequality reflect a specific evaluation, which might not correspond to the individuals' evaluation.[1] In the report, "conventional indicators" refer to statistical indicators of inequality derived from household income data (such as the Gini index of disposable income inequality from the *OECD Income Distribution Database*). Such measures are based on a set of conventions specifying the way income is defined, the components it includes, how it is adjusted for household size, etc.[2] The term "conventional", albeit imprecise, denotes such indicators as opposed to people's perceptions, which are subjective estimates.

Policy preferences depend also on whether individuals believe they would personally gain or lose from redistributive policies. Such gains and costs hinge on whether they perceive to be in the top of the income distribution – so that they would likely incur in personal costs (e.g. through higher top income taxes) – or in the bottom – so that they would likely gain. However, people's perceived relative income position is not always consistent with their actual position.

The impact of an increase in inequality on people's concern depends on how their perceptions, views and preferences interact. When inequality grows, perceptions might shift accordingly, causing an increase in concern (Figure 1.3). Concern may also diminish because people become more tolerant of inequality – if, for example, they adjust their preferred level thereof in response to their current experience.

Perceptions of inequality are multi-faceted (Table 1.1).[3] People form views about inequality through information they have on various outcomes, like earnings or household incomes, but also on the extent of social mobility. Equally, they may come to believe that inequality is attributable to individual effort or circumstances beyond an individual's control. **These perceptions and beliefs shape their concern over inequality and are strongly interconnected.** One example is the relation between the perceived richest 10's share of income and the perceived chances that children born into poor families will be in the same income bracket as their parents when they grow up. These perceptions are in line with the so-called "Great Gatsby Curve" (OECD, 2018[12]), i.e. the stylised fact that higher income inequality goes hand in hand with weak upward social mobility.

Figure 1.3. How preferences for redistribution are shaped by people's concern over inequality and their views of government and policies

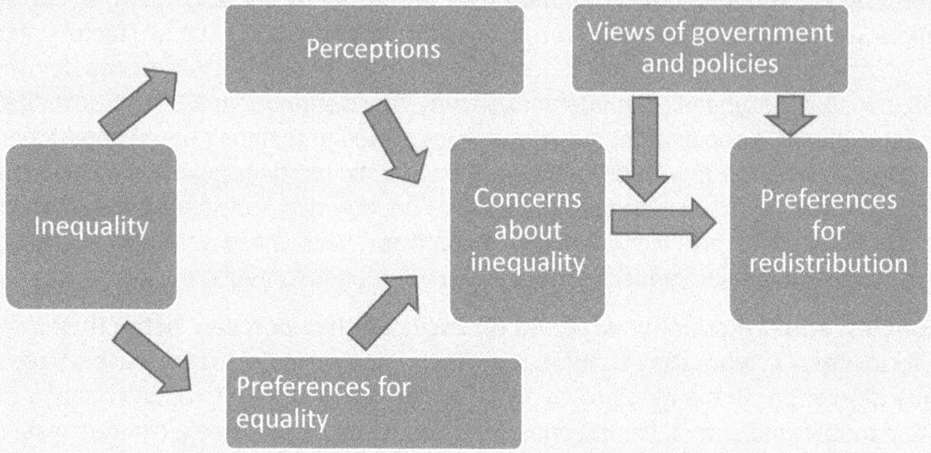

Table 1.1. Glossary of key concepts

List of the main concepts used in the report (section of first use in parentheses)

Type of subjective factors	Domain	
	Inequality of outcomes	Inequality of opportunities
Perceptions	Perceived richest 10%'s share of income (Section 2.2). Perceived top-bottom earnings ratio: what people believe that top and bottom earners earn – what the top 10% earn compared to what the bottom 10% earn (Section 2.2). Perceived personal position in the income distribution (Section 3.3).	Importance of coming from a wealthy family / having educated parents / hard work to get ahead in life (Sections 2.1 and 2.2) Perceived intergenerational persistence: see qualitative index (Section 2.2). Perceived intergenerational income persistence among the bottom 10%: perceived share of children from the poorest 10% of households who remain in the poorest 10% once adults (Section 2.2).
Preferences	Preferred richest 10%'s share of income: the share of national income that people believe should go to the top 10% richest households (Section 2.3) Preferred top-bottom earnings ratio: what people think that top and bottom earners should earn (Section 2.3).	
Concern	Concern over income disparities: agreement or strong agreement with the statement that income disparities are too great (Section 2.1). Concern over earnings disparities: estimated gap between perceived and preferred top-bottom earnings ratio (Section 2.3). Concern over income disparities (alternative measure): gap estimated between perceived and preferred top income shares of the 10% (Section 2.3).	

Notes

1. As put by Kolm (1976, p. 416[18]): "I can take (...) any two countries and prove that inequality is higher in the one or in the other, by choosing different inequality measures." To take this into account, the Atkinson index explicitly incorporates a parameter that captures aversion towards inequality, and therefore its value changes with the level of aversion.

2. Alternatively, these measures could be described as "objective" measures, as opposed to the "subjective" estimates of people's perceptions. The term "objective", however, would neglect the fact that each single inequality indicator, such as the Gini index, is based on a set of conventions and has a normative interpretation.

3. This report analyses these indicators separately, although it highlights how they strongly interrelate. Bavetta, Li Donni and Marino (2017[19]) suggest an alternative multidimensional approach, based on latent variables, to combine different indicators relating to multiple dimensions. Such method requires observing all the indicators within the same survey.

1.2. People's average perceptions of inequality tend to mirror conventional statistical indicators, although with some differences

Average perceptions of inequality correlate with conventional estimates of income disparities and intergenerational persistence

Across countries, where indicators from the OECD and other sources show higher income inequality and less social mobility, people also generally perceive greater inequality and lower mobility (Table 1.2 and Chapter 2). The finding suggests that perceptions, despite being based on incomplete information, do reflect real evidence of economic inequality in the society.

Nevertheless, perceptions and conventional indicators may differ widely in some countries. Some countries rank lower in terms of perceptions than conventional indicators – i.e. people perceive to live in a more equal society than they actually are – either with regards to income inequality (Israel, Lithuania and the Netherlands), intergenerational persistence (Canada, Switzerland and the United States), or both (France and Italy). In other countries the ranking in terms of perceptions outstrips the one in conventional indicators – i.e. people perceive to be in a less equal society than they actually are – either for income inequality (Austria, Belgium, Canada and Finland), intergenerational persistence (Turkey and Spain), or both (Greece).

Table 1.2. Most countries rank similar in perceived and conventionally measured levels of income inequality of intergenerational persistence, but for some there are important differences

	Income inequality		Intergenerational persistence	
	Income share that goes to the 10% richest, measured by conventional indicators	Perceived income share that goes to the top 10% richest	Intergenerational earnings persistence, measured by conventional indicators	Perceived intergenerational income persistence in the bottom 10% poorest
Slovenia	Low	Low	-	-
Belgium	Low	Medium	Medium	Medium
Norway	Low	Low	Low	Low
Estonia	Low	Low	-	-
Denmark	Low	Low	Low	Low
Poland	Low	Low	-	-
Austria	Low	High	High	High
Finland	Low	Medium	Low	Low
Netherlands	Medium	Low	Medium	Medium
Canada	Medium	High	Medium	Low
Germany	Medium	Medium	High	High
Greece	Medium	High	Low	High
Ireland	Medium	Medium	Medium	High
Switzerland	Medium	Medium	High	Medium
Spain	Medium	Medium	Low	Medium
France	Medium	Low	High	Medium
Korea	Medium	Medium	Medium	Medium
Portugal	High	High	Medium	Medium
Italy	High	Medium	High	Low
Israel	High	Low	-	-

	Income inequality		Intergenerational persistence	
Lithuania	High	Medium	-	-
United States	High	High	Medium	Low
Turkey	High	High	Low	High
Mexico	High	High	-	-
Chile	High	High	High	High

Note: Countries are ranked low/medium/high depending on the distribution of the indicator among the countries observed; for example, "High" for estimated top 10% income share refers to the eight countries with the highest values. The estimated intergenerational earnings persistence refers to the elasticity between the earnings of sons observed late 2000s and the earnings of their fathers when they were approximately of the same age. The ranking for intergenerational persistence is calculated only for those countries for which the intergenerational earnings elasticity is available in OECD (2018[12]), *A Broken Social Elevator? How to Promote Social Mobility.*

Source: OECD calculations from the 2020 Risks that Matter Survey; *OECD Income Distribution Database* (https://stats.oecd.org/Index.aspx?DataSetCode=IDD) for top income shares, OECD (2018[12]), *A Broken Social Elevator? How to Promote Social Mobility*, for intergenerational earnings persistence (Section 2.2).

StatLink https://stat.link/70efdo

In recent decades, as income inequality has risen in many OECD countries, so has people's concern over income disparities

Concern over income disparities and conventional estimates of inequality have moved consistently over time. The share of people who strongly agree that income disparities are too wide has risen at least since the late 1980s (Figure 1.4), in line with the increase in income inequality measured by conventional statistical indicators (OECD, 2011[11]). In countries where conventional estimates of income inequality grew the most, so did people's concern over inequality. The trend suggests that people have generally incorporated into their perceptions the factual information about trends in income disparities.

Figure 1.4. Concern over income disparities has increased in recent decades

Share of people who strongly agree that income differences in their country are too large, OECD averages

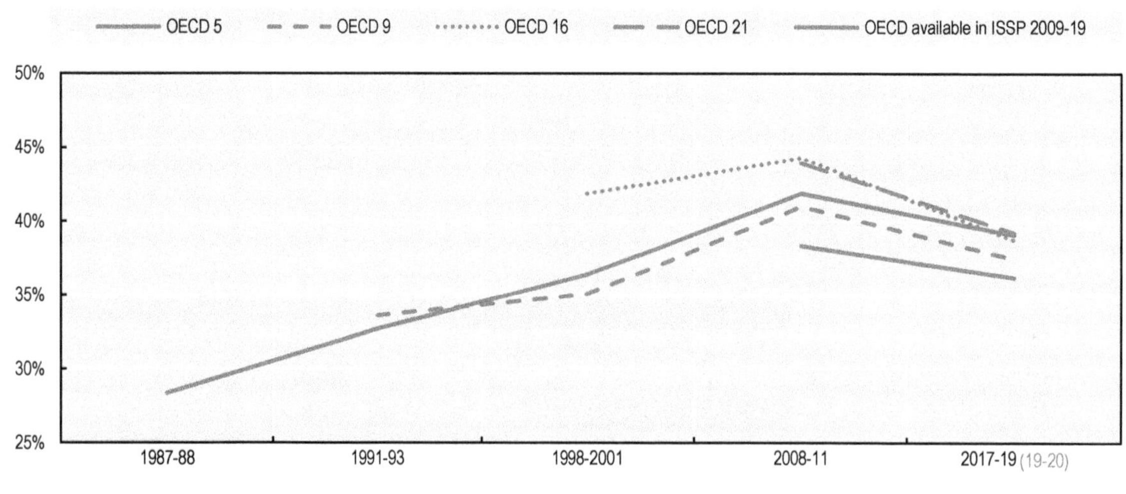

Note: Unweighted average across countries.

OECD 5: Austria, Australia, United Kingdom, Hungary, United States; OECD 9: plus Germany, New Zealand, Slovenia, Sweden; OECD 16: plus Czech Republic, Denmark, Spain, France, Israel, Japan, Slovakia; OECD 21: plus Switzerland, Finland, Iceland, Lithuania, Turkey.

OECD available in ISSP 2009-19 refers to the countries present in both ISSP 2009 and 2019, for which trends are more fully comparable. They include Australia, Switzerland, Chile, Czech Republic, Germany, Denmark, Finland, United Kingdom, Italy, Japan, New Zealand, Norway, Slovenia.

Source: OECD calculations from ISSP 1987, 1992, 1999, 2009, 2017 and 2019; Australian Survey of Social Attitudes 2019; Norwegian part of ISSP 2019; British Social Attitudes 2019 (Section 2.1).

StatLink https://stat.link/8lg32n

The rise in concern has been driven by the rise in perceived disparities. Perceived top-bottom earnings disparities – for which data are available on a long period of time – have widened substantially in recent decades in the countries studied. In 2019-20, people perceived top earners – doctors and CEOs of large national corporations – as earning an average of eight times more than bottom earners, i.e. unskilled workers in a factory (Figure 1.5). This perceived earnings ratio was a steep increase over the late 1980s and early 1990s, when it was around 5/1, before reaching its peak during the global financial crisis.

Figure 1.5. Perceived earnings disparities have increased substantially over time

Perceived and preferred top-bottom earnings ratios, averaged across eight OECD countries

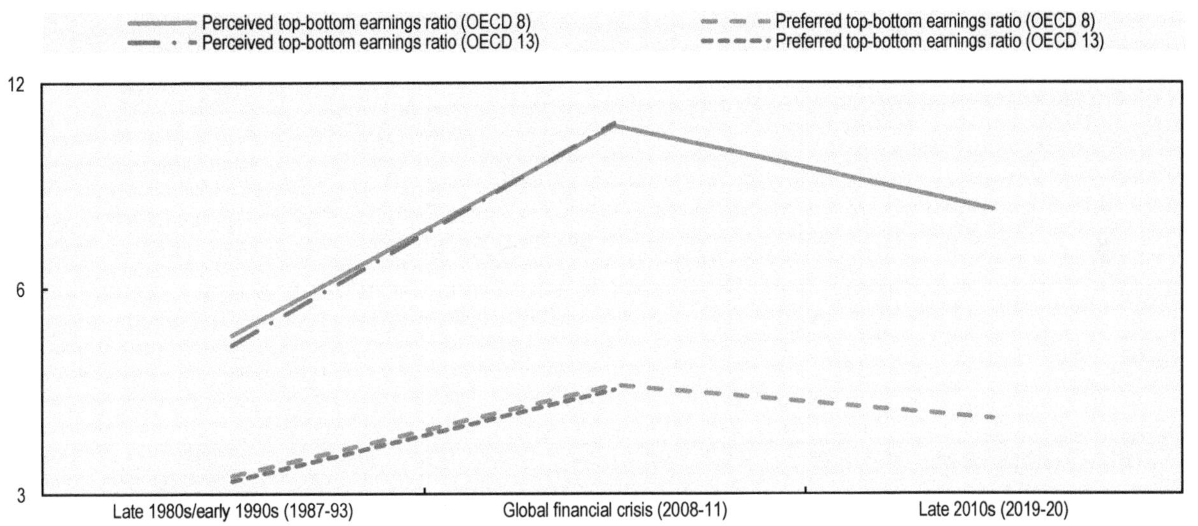

Note: The values are the average of the median values in logarithmic scale (base 2). OECD 13 includes Austria, Australia, Germany, Hungary, Italy, New Zealand, Norway, Poland, Slovenia, Sweden, Switzerland, United Kingdom and the United States. OECD 8 misses Austria, Hungary, Poland, Sweden, United States (for these countries, data is only available up to the global financial crisis).
Source: OECD calculations from ISSP 1987, 1992, 2009, 2019; Australian Survey of Social Attitudes 2019; Norwegian part of ISSP 2019; British Social Attitudes 2019 (Section 2.3).

StatLink https://stat.link/gp0xlu

Tolerance of earnings inequality increased slightly, as people adapted to higher levels of earnings inequality over time. Preferred levels of inequality are considerably lower than perceived levels in all OECD countries. However, preferences evolved over time: between the late 1980s and the global financial crisis preferred earnings disparities rose in all the countries studied, more steeply in those where perceived disparities grew the most. Preferred disparities then declined in the most recent decade, 2010-19, though they nevertheless remained wider than in the late 1980s and early 1990s.

On average, the increase in preferred earnings disparities offset the sharp growth in perceived disparities by almost one-half. As a consequence, rising perceived inequality in earnings did not fully translate into greater concern over inequality. Yet, despite the growing preference for wider earnings inequality, demand for greater earnings equality has also grown in recent years.

A rise in the perceived importance of hard work for getting ahead in life between the early 1990s and the global financial crisis may partly explain people's increased tolerance of inequality (Figure 1.6). People who believe that hard work matters more than luck or other circumstances beyond an individual's control for getting ahead in life are more accepting of income inequality, because they believe that high earning disparities are the reward for differences in individual effort. However, among the countries observed up to 2019, the perceived importance of hard work fell between the early and late

2010s. The trend suggests that people are becoming more unsure that differences in income and earnings are due to differences in individual effort.

Figure 1.6. The belief in hard work for getting ahead in life grew in the two decades up to the global financial crisis, but seems to be receding

Share of respondents who believe that hard work is very important or essential for getting ahead in life

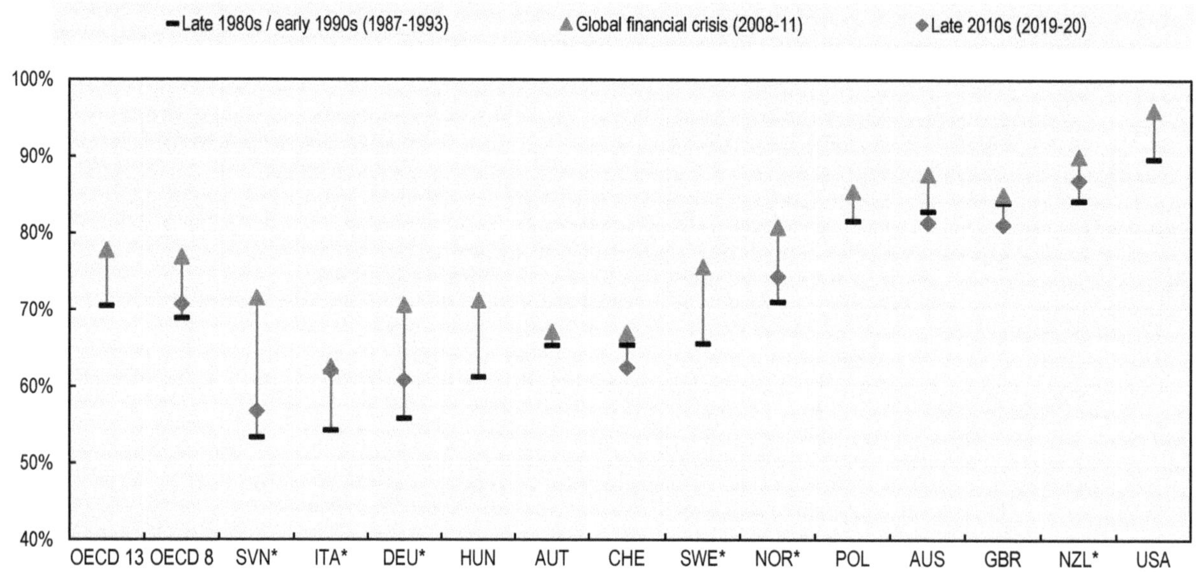

Source: OECD calculations from ISSP 1987, 1992, 2009 and 2019.

StatLink https://stat.link/4of8xw

1.3. Growing concern over inequality increases demand for redistribution, but do not necessarily spell widespread support for all policies

People's perceptions and concern determine their preferences for income redistribution

Perceptions of and concern over inequality are important drivers of demand for redistribution. Concern over income disparities in all countries correlates closely with the share of the population who agree that it is the state's responsibility to narrow income differences (Figure 1.7). Increases in inequality – as measured by conventional statistical indicators – are associated with greater demand for redistribution only insofar as people's concern about inequality rises accordingly (see Chapter 3).

Figure 1.7. Concern over income disparities correlates closely with demand for government redistribution

Shares of respondents who agree with either that is the government's responsibility to redistribute or that income disparities are too large

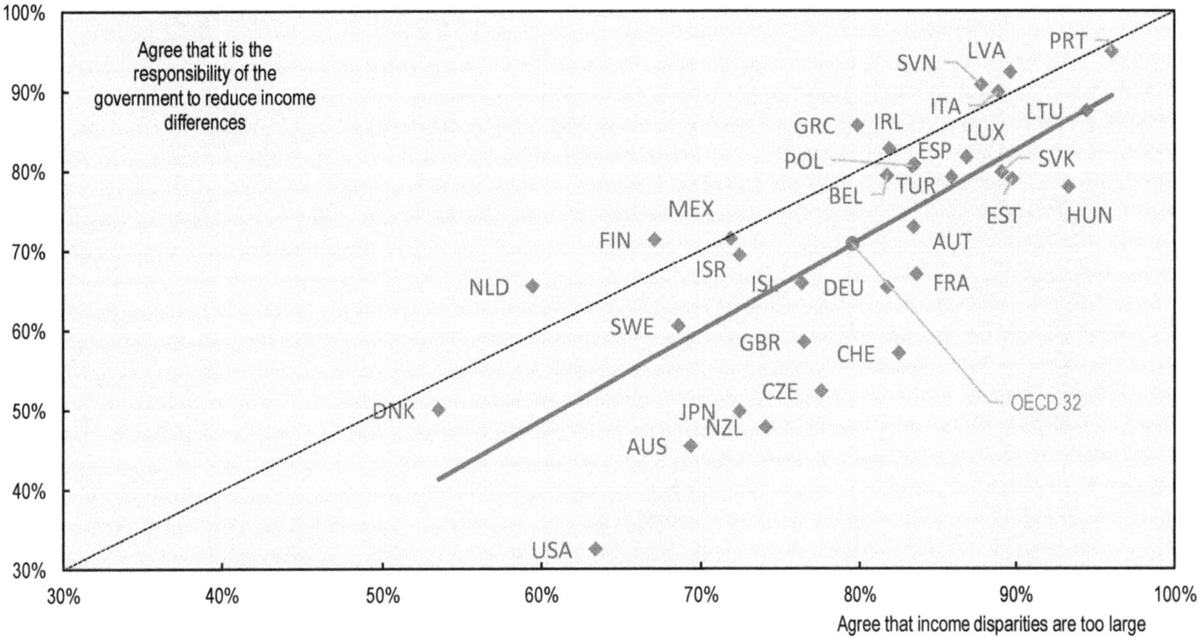

Source: OECD calculations from ISSP 2017 and Eurobarometer 471/2017 (Section 3.1).

StatLink https://stat.link/5p63sn

Both perceived inequality of outcomes and of opportunities drive preferences for inequality-reducing policies. Even when people believe that social mobility is high, greater perceived income inequality is associated with stronger demand for redistribution. However, perceptions of income inequality and social mobility can be associated with different policy preferences. Greater perceived income inequality, for example, is more closely associated with demand for more progressive taxation, as one would expect. On the other hand, perceived income inequality and intergenerational mobility influence to almost equal degrees demand for greater public expenditure on education system and healthcare (Figure 1.8).

Figure 1.8. The preferred type of inequality-reducing policies depends on combinations of perceptions over inequality and lack of equal opportunity

Impact of stronger perceptions on shares of respondents (percentage points) who support different policy interventions

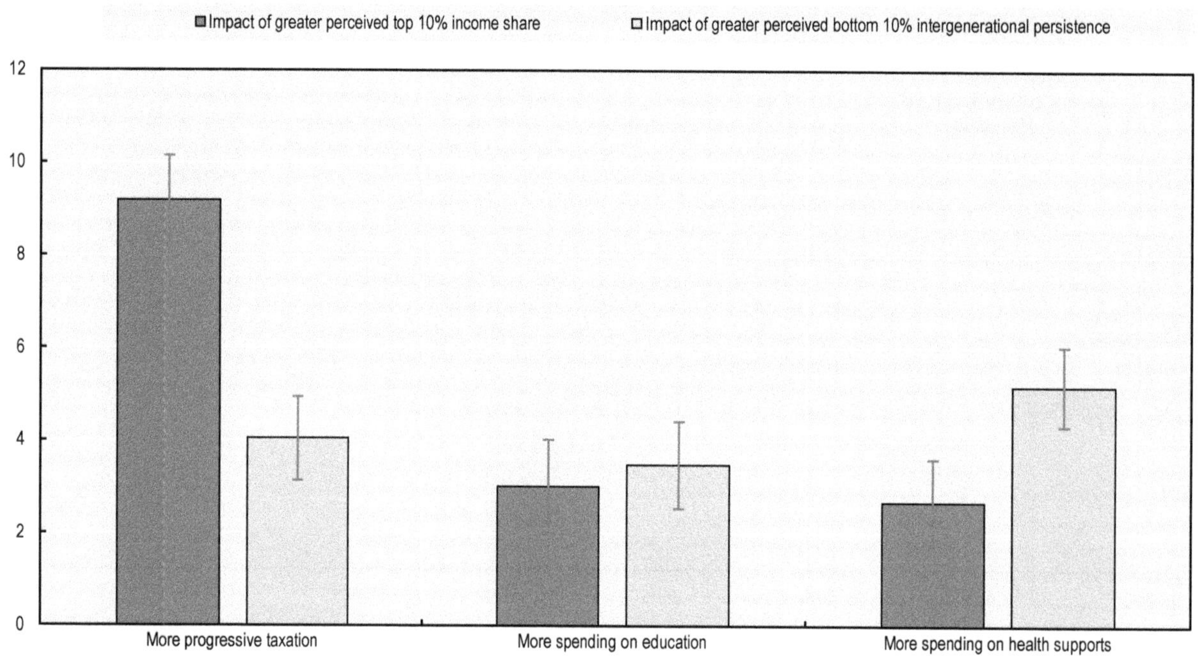

Note: "Stronger", or "higher" perceptions refer to an increase in either perception by 40 percentage points (approximately a shift from the 25th to the 75th percentile). The question on progressive taxation is "Should the government tax the rich more than they currently do in order to support the poor?" For the other categories, it follows the question "Thinking about the taxes you might have to pay and the benefits you and your family might receive, would you like to see the government spend less, spend the same, or spend more in each of the following areas?" Respondents answering "don't know" are not considered.
Source: OECD calculations from the 2020 Risks that Matter Survey (Section 3.4).

StatLink https://stat.link/fnmcp1

People's demand for inequality-reducing policies falls as own income rises: higher-income individuals prefer wider disparities, even if they perceive similar levels of inequality of outcomes and opportunities. Differences in preferences for inequality reflect "pocketbook considerations" – redistribution costs for the rich, but benefits the poor. The higher demand for redistribution among low-income individuals points to the fact that, when inequality rises, people who become poorer than the average increase their support for redistributive policies.

However, the link between own income and demand for inequality-reducing policies depends on people's perception of where they belong in the income distribution. Across OECD countries, a disproportionally high share of people believe they are part of the middle class. The experimental evidence suggests that giving people the facts increases demand for redistribution among those who discover that they are poorer than they thought, while it reduces it among those who find out that they are better-off (Ciani, Fréget and Manfredi, forthcoming[20]).

Yet, demand for redistribution also depends on people's social preferences and beliefs about the drivers of inequality. At the individual level, perceptions of the overall level of inequality and intergenerational mobility matter as much as own income for explaining preferences for redistribution. Furthermore, a climb in inequality also increases demand for redistribution among the rich: as inequality grows, their social preferences for narrower disparities outweigh their personal gains and losses from redistribution (Rueda and Stegmueller (2019[21]) and Section 3.3). In fact, although redistribution comes at a cost for them, the rich can still support it either because of purely altruistic motives or because they believe that higher inequality might harm them through other channels – e.g. through decreased national productivity or increased crime. Finally, independently from own income, people are more supportive of inequality-reducing policies if they believe that existing disparities are the result of circumstances outside an individual's control.

Beyond perceptions of inequality, people's views of the role of government and the effectiveness of policies matter

Even if perceptions of and concern over inequality are key drivers of redistributive preferences, stronger demand for more equality does not always spell widespread support for government intervention. Over time, preferences for income redistribution in OECD countries have, on average, risen less than concerns. Conventional statistical indicators also suggest they have also been less responsive to changes in observed income inequality (as tracked by conventional statistical indicators). In most countries, the share of respondents who believe that it is the state's duty to reduce income disparities is lower than the share who feel that such disparities are too wide (Figure 1.9). In some countries there is a sizeable share of respondents who believe it is the job of private companies, trade unions or individuals themselves to reduce income differences, rather than the government.

Figure 1.9. For some people, the greatest responsibility in reducing income differences lies with private companies, trade unions or individuals themselves

Shares of respondents by answer to the question: "Who do you think should have the greatest responsibility for reducing differences in income between people with high incomes and people with low incomes?" among those who think that such differences are too large

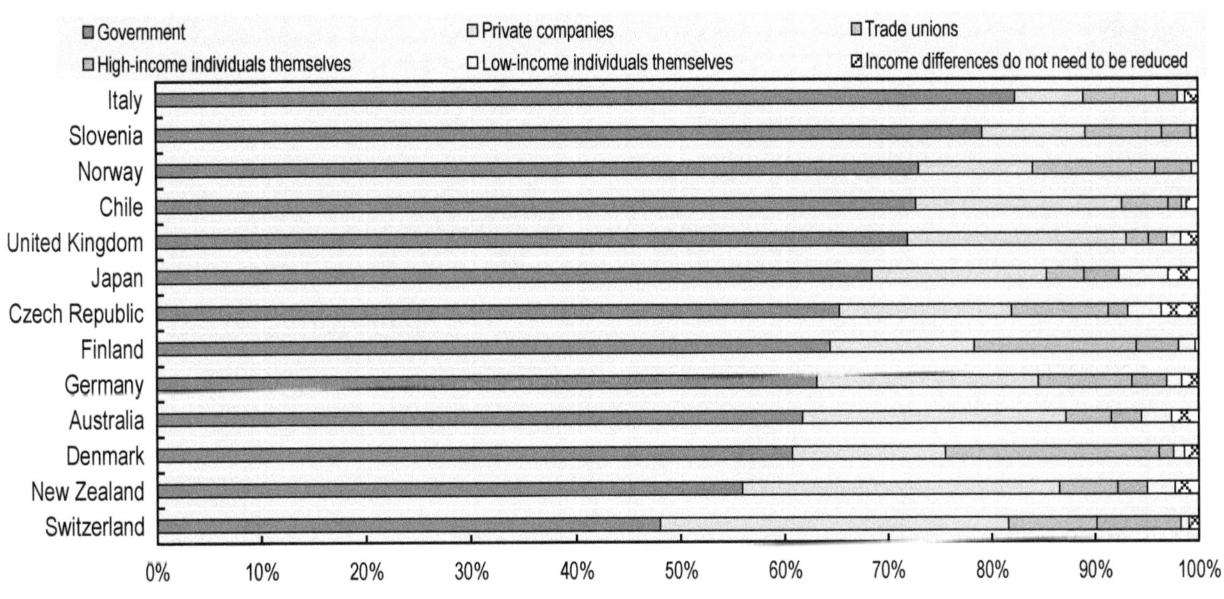

Source: OECD calculations from ISSP 2019.

StatLink https://stat.link/47c2pm

The perceived effectiveness of policies drives support for inequality-reducing policies. People demand more redistribution through the tax and benefit system if they believe that the benefits are effective and well targeted. Indeed, evidence from the OECD Trustlab survey shows that people are less in favour of progressive taxation if they believe that petty corruption is widespread among public officials, prompting the misuse and misallocation of public benefits. By contrast, experimental evidence shows that they do support redistributive policies if they perceive that those policies effectively reduce inequality and poverty.

Even if people agree on the need for policy action, they may disagree on what measures to take. Countries – and people – differ as to their perceptions of the scale of inequality of outcomes (bottom or top inequality) and obstacles to intergenerational mobility, like parental education or wealth. Similarly, people in different countries associate "redistribution" with different types of intervention, ranging from progressive taxation and income support to increased government expenditure on housing and healthcare.

1.4. In most countries, public opinion on inequality is divided

People's perceptions of current levels of income inequality may also vary widely within countries, with some people perceiving it as fairly low and others extremely high (Figure 1.10). In some countries – as in the OECD average – there is no single prevailing perception, but a wide variation. In others, like the United States, perceptions tend to polarise in groups with starkly different views. In only a few countries do most people tend to perceive broadly similar levels of income inequality – either low, as in Denmark, or high, as in Greece. Perceptions of earnings disparities and social mobility are similarly dispersed (see Chapter 4).

Figure 1.10. People's perceptions of income inequality are widely dispersed

Estimated distribution of perceived shares of total income going to the 10% richest households, OECD average and selected countries, 2020

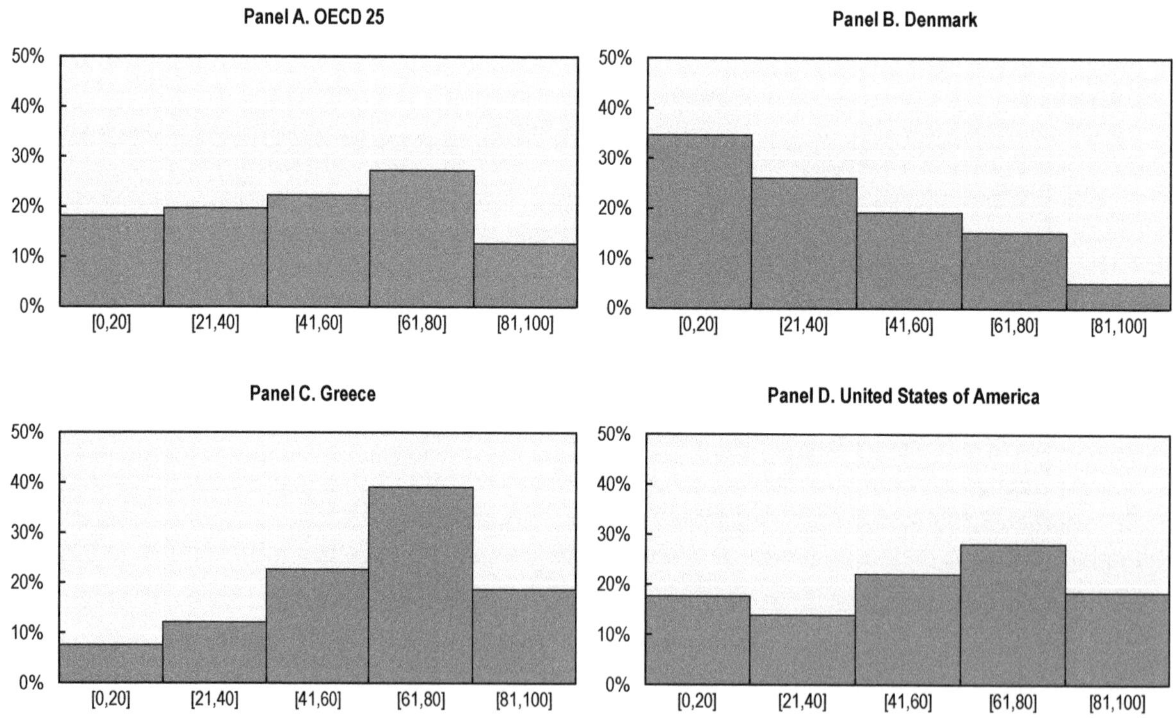

Note: The bars give the distribution of respondents' estimates of the richest 10%'s share of income in their country (where the bar is higher, more respondents answered in the displayed range).
Source: OECD calculations based on (OECD, 2021[16]), *Main Findings from the 2020 Risks that Matter Survey* (Section 4.1).

StatLink https://stat.link/bgm8ps

Different individuals are more likely to agree on the "ideal" level of income inequality than on what they think the current level of income inequality actually is. In fact, in all countries, the preferred share of income held by the top 10% vary less than perceived levels. People disagree with each other as to how much income inequality should be reduced, but mostly because they perceive different levels of inequality, rather than because they have different preferred levels.

Perceptions and preferences about earnings disparities have become considerably more dispersed in recent decades (Figure 1.11), indicating increased levels of disagreement. In some countries, there are also signs of mounting polarisation. Two schools of opinion have emerged: one believes current earnings disparities are more acceptable, and the other that they are extremely wide. People tend to disagree particularly about what levels of top earnings are and should be. Their steep rise in the last three decades, as documented by conventional statistical indicators (OECD, 2011[11]), is associated with a more divided public opinion.

Disagreements over the extent of inequality can be wide even among people with similar socio-economic characteristics. Such disagreements have increased over the years. Perceptions of income inequality and social mobility vary by income, educational attainment, employment status, gender, age, and household type, but those disparities are comparatively mild. No more than 10% of the total dispersion in perceptions reflects differences *between* socio-economic groups – the remaining 90% represents differences in perceptions among people with very similar profiles. Also the rise over time in the dispersion of perceptions of and concern over earnings disparities mostly reflects greater *within-group* dispersion.

Figure 1.11. People disagree more than 30 years ago on the extent of earnings disparities

10th and 90th percentiles of the perceived top-bottom earnings ratio, averaged across 8 OECD countries

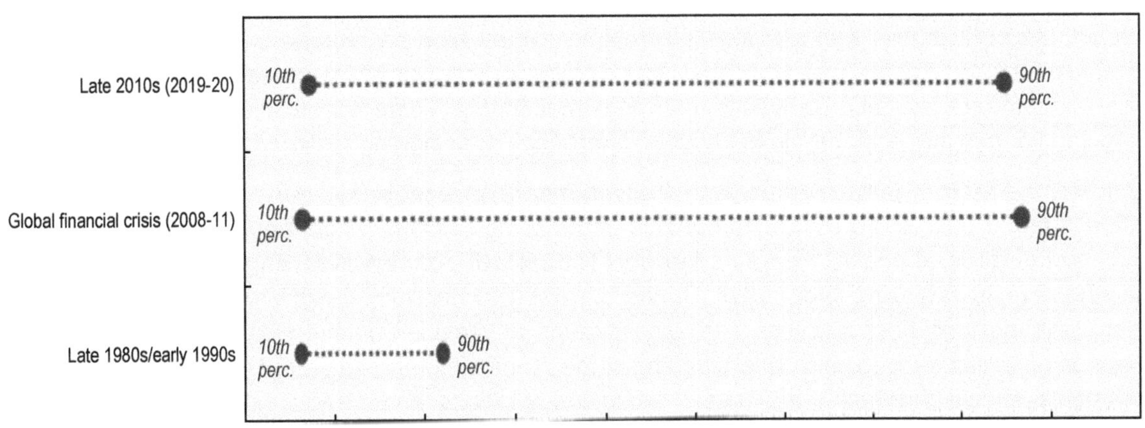

Note: The lines represent the difference between the bottom 10% of respondents and the top 10%, ranked by their view about the top-bottom earnings ratio. The values are the average of the values for Australia, Germany, Italy, New Zealand, Norway, Slovenia, Switzerland and the United Kingdom. Trends between the late 1980s and the global financial crisis are similar if countries observed only up to ISSP 2009 are included (Austria, Hungary, Poland, Sweden and the United States).
Source: OECD calculations from ISSP 1987, 1992, 2009, 2019; Australian Survey of Social Attitudes 2019; Norwegian part of ISSP 2019; British Social Attitudes 2019 (Section 4.2).

StatLink https://stat.link/r0obwc

1.5. Conclusion: understanding people's perceptions of and concern about inequality can help design the reforms that lie ahead

The COVID-19 crisis has exposed the vulnerability of large segments of the population in OECD countries. As emergency measures gradually fade, governments are set to implement reforms that will address that vulnerability and enhance equal opportunities. To that end, the report argues that getting citizens and governments on the same page when it comes to reducing inequality and promote social mobility requires understanding how people form their perceptions and opinions. Perceptions of, preferences for and concern over inequality all respond to changes in measured inequality. Eventually, however, it is how they combine that determines public support for reforms to tackle persistent disparities. Perceptions, preferences and concerns differ from one country to another and evolve over time. Data on people's views of inequality can, therefore, inform policy design and so increase the chances that proposed reforms garner the necessary public support.

Most people across the OECD believe that the current level of income inequality is too high. Perceptions of income inequality and low social mobility determine this concern. Furthermore, people are more concerned about income inequality when and where they believe that hard work is not a factor in getting ahead in life. In other words, they care about inequality of both outcomes and opportunities. They perceive them as interrelated, and both matter in demand for government intervention to reduce income differences. Reforms that tackle both are therefore more likely to receive support.

Nevertheless, the widespread demand for more equality **does not mean that people are in favour of any government intervention, as perceptions and preferences differ from country to country.** First, perceptions and preferences of outcomes and opportunities vary across societies. Consequently, how much importance people accord to outcomes rather than opportunities changes across countries, so influencing public support for policy mixes. Some focus on redistributing outcomes, like raising tax rates on high incomes, others on fostering equal opportunities, such as improving access to high-quality education. Second, people's perceptions and opinions may also be shaped by other considerations – whether top earnings are too high or bottom earnings are too low, or which obstacles to intergenerational mobility (like parental education or wealth) are more challenging. To garner sufficient public support, policy makers should take into account these national differences in designing reform packages.

Considering the scale of public resources that governments have mobilized during the pandemic, growing attention is being paid to the costs and benefits of incoming reforms. Importantly, **policy effectiveness matters to the general public. People's support for certain policies is stronger when they are seen to be effective in reducing inequality**. Hence the need to carefully design redistributive and welfare reforms, learning from best practices and assessments of previous action. However, it also shows the importance of facilitating people's understanding of the functioning and impact of the policies. To that end, governments should thoroughly evaluate existing interventions and clearly explain their redistributive effects, as well as collect the open data that would allow such an evaluation. They should draw on independent research from academia and non-governmental or international institutions, to guarantee transparency and facilitate people's confidence and trust.

Introducing reforms can be hard even when most people support them if different groups hold hard-to-reconcile views. In fact, public opinion is often divided about the extent of actual inequality and what to do about it. This division complicates the public debate around the need for inequality-reducing policies, because different groups often hold very different views. Importantly, such division goes past the class struggle: the strong division in the public opinion is only partly explained by differences in opinions between the rich and the poor or between socio-demographic groups. Policies focusing on just one main interest group – as defined along traditional lines (e.g. the young or the working class) – might fail to reach sufficient consensus even within that target group.

Experimental evidence shows that informing people about inequality changes their perceptions, although it has only a minor effect on redistributive preferences. **High-quality information about inequality of outcomes and opportunities could help lessen the widespread dispersion of perceptions across the population.** It could provide common ground for public debate, even if it would not necessarily ease differences of opinion about policies.

Lastly, the interpretation of data on people's perceptions requires careful analysis and measurement. **Improving comparability between countries and over time calls for standards and guidelines on how to measure perceptions, preferences and opinions pertaining to inequality**. The recently created OECD Expert Group on New Measures of the Public Acceptability of Reforms aims at contributing to this effort. This report also highlights a series of evidence gaps related to important factors that influence how people think about inequality.

References

Alesina, A. and N. Fuchs-Schündeln (2007), "Good-Bye Lenin (or Not?): The Effect of Communism on People's Preferences", *American Economic Review*, Vol. 97/4, pp. 1507-1528, http://dx.doi.org/10.1257/aer.97.4.1507. [31]

Alesina, A. and P. Giuliano (2011), "Preferences for Redistribution", in *Handbook of Social Economics*, Elsevier, http://dx.doi.org/10.1016/b978-0-444-53187-2.00004-8. [37]

Alesina, A., A. Miano and S. Stantcheva (2020), *The Polarization of Reality*, National Bureau of Economic Research, Cambridge, MA, http://dx.doi.org/10.3386/w26675. [17]

Almeida, V. et al. (2020), "Households´ income and the cushioning effect of fiscal policy measures during the Great Lockdown", *JRC Working Papers on Taxation and Structural Reforms*, No. 06/2020, European Commission, Joint Research Centre, Seville, https://ec.europa.eu/jrc/sites/default/files/jrc121598.pdf. [5]

Atkinson, A. (1970), "On the measurement of inequality", *Journal of Economic Theory*, Vol. 2/3, pp. 244-263, http://dx.doi.org/10.1016/0022-0531(70)90039-6. [41]

Baldwin, R. (2020), "https://voxeu.org/article/inequality-and-pandemic-make-explosive-mix", *VoxEU*, https://voxeu.org/article/inequality-and-pandemic-make-explosive-mix. [9]

Balestra, C. and G. Cohen (2021), "Income Inequality through People's Lenses: Evidence from the OECD Compare your Income Web-tool", *OECD Papers on Well-being and Inequalities*, forthcoming. [42]

Bavetta, S., P. Li Donni and M. Marino (2017), "An Empirical Analysis of the Determinants of Perceived Inequality", *Review of Income and Wealth*, Vol. 65/2, pp. 264-292, http://dx.doi.org/10.1111/roiw.12351. [19]

Benabou, R. and E. Ok (2001), "Social Mobility and the Demand for Redistribution: The Poum Hypothesis", *The Quarterly Journal of Economics*, Vol. 116/2, pp. 447-487, http://dx.doi.org/10.1162/00335530151144078. [39]

Benabou, R. and J. Tirole (2006), "Belief in a Just World and Redistributive Politics", *The Quarterly Journal of Economics*, Vol. 121/2, pp. 699-746, http://dx.doi.org/10.1162/qjec.2006.121.2.699. [32]

Boone, L. et al. (2020), *Building back better: enhancing equal access to opportunities for all*, https://oecdecoscope.blog/2020/07/21/building-back-better-enhancing-equal-access-to-opportunities-for-all/. [14]

Brewer, M. and L. Gardiner (2020), "The initial impact of COVID-19 and policy responses on household incomes", *Oxford Review of Economic Policy*, Vol. 36/Supplement_1, pp. S187-S199, http://dx.doi.org/10.1093/oxrep/graa024. [3]

Carta, F. and M. De Philippis (2021), "The impact of the COVID-19 shock on labour income inequality: Evidence from Italy", *Occasional Papers (Questioni di Economia e Finanza)*, No. 606, Bank of Italy, https://www.bancaditalia.it/pubblicazioni/qef/2021-0606/QEF_606_21.pdf?language_id=1. [8]

Chetty, R. et al. (2020), *The Economic Impacts of COVID-19: Evidence from a New Public Database Built Using Private Sector Data*, National Bureau of Economic Research, Cambridge, MA, http://dx.doi.org/10.3386/w27431. [4]

Ciani, E., L. Fréget and T. Manfredi (forthcoming), "Learning about inequality and preferences for redistribution: A meta-analysis of in-survey informational experiments". [20]

Clark, A. and C. D'Ambrosio (2015), "Attitudes to Income Inequality", in *Handbook of Income Distribution*, Elsevier, http://dx.doi.org/10.1016/b978-0-444-59428-0.00014-x. [29]

Clark, A., C. D'Ambrosio and A. Lepinteur (2020), "The Fall in Income Inequality during COVID-19 in Five European Countries", *ECINEQ Working Papers Series*, No. 565, Society for the Study of Economic Inequality, http://www.ecineq.org/milano/WP/ECINEQ2020-565.pdf. [6]

Corneo, G. and H. Grüner (2002), "Individual preferences for political redistribution", *Journal of Public Economics*, Vol. 83/1, pp. 83-107, http://dx.doi.org/10.1016/s0047-2727(00)00172-9. [25]

Cruces, G., R. Perez-Truglia and M. Tetaz (2013), "Biased perceptions of income distribution and preferences for redistribution: Evidence from a survey experiment", *Journal of Public Economics*, Vol. 98, pp. 100-112, http://dx.doi.org/10.1016/j.jpubeco.2012.10.009. [38]

Diermeier, M. et al. (2017), "Impact of inequality-related media coverage on the concerns of the citizens", *DICE Discussion Paper*, No. 258, Heinrich Heine University Düsseldorf, Düsseldorf Institute for Competition Economics (DICE), https://www.econstor.eu/bitstream/10419/162781/1/893307378.pdf. [26]

European Commission (2020), *Employment and Social Developments in Europe 2020*, Luxembourg: Publications Office of the European Union, http://dx.doi.org/10.2767/478772. [7]

Gärtner, M., J. Mollerstrom and D. Seim (2021), "Income Mobility, Luck/Effort Beliefs, and the Demand for Redistribution: Perceptions and Reality", *mimeo*. [24]

Giuliano, P. and A. Spilimbergo (2013), "Growing up in a Recession", *The Review of Economic Studies*, Vol. 81/2, pp. 787-817, http://dx.doi.org/10.1093/restud/rdt040. [35]

Hauser, O. and M. Norton (2017), "(Mis)perceptions of inequality", *Current Opinion in Psychology*, Vol. 18, pp. 21-25, http://dx.doi.org/10.1016/j.copsyc.2017.07.024. [22]

Hvidberg, K., C. Kreiner and S. Stantcheva (2020), *Social Position and Fairness Views*, National Bureau of Economic Research, Cambridge, MA, http://dx.doi.org/10.3386/w28099. [36]

Kolm, S. (1976), "Unequal inequalities. I", *Journal of Economic Theory*, Vol. 12/3, pp. 416-442, http://dx.doi.org/10.1016/0022-0531(76)90037-5. [18]

Luttmer, E. and M. Singhal (2011), "Culture, context, and the taste for redistribution", *American Economic Journal: Economic Policy*, Vol. 3/1, pp. 157-179, http://dx.doi.org/10.1257/pol.3.1.157. [30]

Mijs, J. (2019), "The paradox of inequality: income inequality and belief in meritocracy go hand in hand", *Socio-Economic Review*, http://dx.doi.org/10.1093/ser/mwy051. [34]

OECD (2021), *COVID-19 and Well-being: Life in the Pandemic*, OECD Publishing, Paris, https://doi.org/10.1787/1e1ecb53-en. [2]

OECD (2021), *Main Findings from the 2020 Risks that Matter Survey*, OECD Publishing, Paris, https://doi.org/10.1787/b9e85cf5-en. [16]

OECD (2020), "Building back better: A sustainable, resilient recovery after COVID-19", *OECD Policy Responses to Coronavirus (COVID-19)*, OECD Publishing, Paris, https://doi.org/10.1787/52b869f5-en. [15]

OECD (2020), *Enhancing Equal Access to Opportunities for All*, OECD Publishing, Paris, https://www.oecd.org/economy/enhancing-equal-access-to-opportunities-G20/. [1]

OECD (2019), *Under Pressure: The Squeezed Middle Class*, OECD Publishing, Paris, https://dx.doi.org/10.1787/689afed1-en. [13]

OECD (2018), *A Broken Social Elevator? How to Promote Social Mobility*, OECD Publishing, Paris, https://dx.doi.org/10.1787/9789264301085-en. [12]

OECD (2015), *In It Together: Why Less Inequality Benefits All*, OECD Publishing, Paris, https://dx.doi.org/10.1787/9789264235120-en. [10]

OECD (2011), *Divided We Stand: Why Inequality Keeps Rising*, OECD Publishing, Paris, https://dx.doi.org/10.1787/9789264119536-en. [11]

Osberg, L. and I. Bechert (2016), "Social values for equality and preferences for state intervention: Is the USA "Exceptional"?", *Working Paper*, No. 2016-03, Dalhousie University, Department of Economics, https://wp.economics.dal.ca/RePEc/dal/wpaper/DalEconWP2016-03.pdf. [40]

Perez-Truglia, R. (2019), *The Effects of Income Transparency on Well-Being: Evidence from a Natural Experiment*, National Bureau of Economic Research, Cambridge, MA, http://dx.doi.org/10.3386/w25622. [27]

Phillips, L. et al. (2020), *Inequality in People's Minds*, Center for Open Science, http://dx.doi.org/10.31234/osf.io/vawh9. [28]

Piketty, T. (1995), "Social Mobility and Redistributive Politics", *The Quarterly Journal of Economics*, Vol. 110/3, pp. 551-584, http://dx.doi.org/10.2307/2946692. [23]

Rueda, D. and D. Stegmueller (2019), *Who Wants What?*, Cambridge University Press, http://dx.doi.org/10.1017/9781108681339. [21]

Trump, K. (2018), "Income Inequality Influences Perceptions of Legitimate Income Differences", *British Journal of Political Science*, Vol. 48/4, pp. 929-952, http://dx.doi.org/10.1017/S0007123416000326. [33]

Annex 1.A. Measuring and interpreting perceptions and preferences of inequality

The literature, as well as public debate, uses a wide range of measures to study people's views on inequality. They may be classified as belong to three broad dimensions:

- Domain. Inequality of outcomes (e.g. income disparities) or inequality of opportunities (e.g. chances of climbing the social ladder).
- Perspective. Views of the overall distribution of outcomes and opportunities in the population in a given country, or views of the individual's own position in that distribution.
- The state of the world. Surveys may ask people about their perception of the current situation as it is, or what they would like it to be. Alternatively, they might ask them to express their concern about the current state of the world – a reflection of the gap between what they perceive and what they wish. The International Social Survey Programme, for instance, has been asking since 1987 whether respondents agree or not with the statement "Income differences in [your country] are too large". Agreement with the statement measures the tension between what people think existing disparities are and what they think they should be.

A simple conceptualization, summarized in Annex Figure 1.A.1 and inspired by Alesina, Miano and Stantcheva (2020[17]), helps connect the different elements discussed in the report:

- People formulate perceptions about the distribution of outcomes and opportunities in their society, and about their position in this distribution (Hauser and Norton, 2017[22]). The perceptions are shaped by experience – such as personal history of success (Piketty, 1995[23]; Gärtner, Mollerstrom and Seim, 2021[24]), shared historical experience (Corneo and Grüner, 2002[25]), and information acquired from media or other sources (Diermeier et al., 2017[26]; Perez-Truglia, 2019[27]; Phillips et al., 2020[28]). People also hold beliefs about the role of luck, merit or circumstance in explaining income disparities. These beliefs are crucial in explaining different attitudes towards redistribution and are closely tied to perceptions (as such, they are classified along perceptions in Table 1.1). However, they are actually a combination of perceptions and concerns, because they tend to conflate a positive statement (about the actual source of disparities) with a normative one (which relates to people's meritocratic attitudes).
- Individuals have preferences as to what extent of inequality in outcomes and opportunities might be acceptable (Clark and D'Ambrosio, 2015[29]). Preferences might be transmitted through generations (Luttmer and Singhal, 2011[30]) and depend on national history (Corneo and Grüner, 2002[25]; Alesina and Fuchs-Schündeln, 2007[31]). They are also shaped by experience. The evidence shows that people might become more accepting of inequality (or believe in stronger meritocracy) when they live in a more unequal society (Benabou and Tirole, 2006[32]; Trump, 2018[33]; Mijs, 2019[34]). Having experienced hardship, though, seems to make them less willing to accept wider inequality (Giuliano and Spilimbergo, 2013[35]). Perceptions may also influence preferences. First, those who perceive themselves as relatively rich are less likely to be concerned by inequality for motives of self-regard (Hvidberg, Kreiner and Stantcheva, 2020[36]). Second, extensive literature has shown that people are at least partly prepared to accept disparities in income if they believe that equal opportunities are available, or that higher incomes are the result of effort rather than circumstance or sheer luck (Piketty, 1995[23]; Alesina and Giuliano, 2011[37]). It is also possible that preferences and other related subjective factors (e.g. political views) in turn

influence perceptions, shaping the way people interpret and weigh information and experience (Alesina, Miano and Stantcheva, 2020[17]; Phillips et al., 2020[28]).

- People's concern about inequality arises from the distance between their perceptions and their preferences. Their scale of concern may depend on whether they perceive that the current level of inequality is greater than they would prefer it to be.
- Concern about inequality might lead individuals to prefer more redistribution and demand policies designed to reduce disparities. However, preferences for redistribution depend also on their perceptions of policy effectiveness, as well as on their personal gains and costs – i.e. benefits and taxes, or "pocketbook considerations". Perceived gains and costs hinge on individuals' perceived position in the distribution (Cruces, Perez-Truglia and Tetaz, 2013[38]), as well as on expectations of future mobility (Piketty, 1995[23]; Benabou and Ok, 2001[39]).
- Preferences for redistribution and how they relate to perceived and actual inequality also depend on people's views of the role of government in narrowing disparities (Osberg and Bechert, 2016[40]). For instance, perceived inequality might not translate into more support for redistribution if people have limited confidence in the effectiveness of policies.

Annex Figure 1.A.1 assumes that some of these dimensions do not influence each other. In reality, the framework may well be more complicated. For instance, preferences might shape people's experience (by changing their social network) and how they gather information (e.g. by influencing which sources they deem trustworthy). The report does not address these further considerations, as its focus is on how actual income inequality shapes perceptions of inequality, and how those perceptions influence demand for redistribution.

Annex Figure 1.A.1. Perceptions, preferences and concerns about inequality

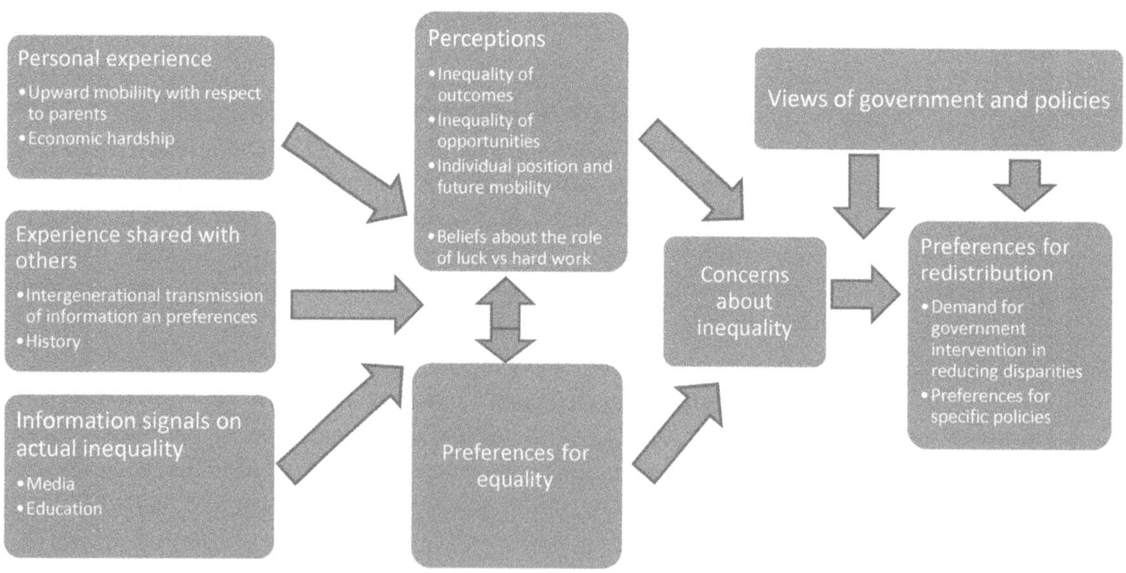

Note: The arrows indicate the direction in which one element influences another. For simplicity's sake, only one arrow per box was included for the first three aspects on the left, even though they all influence both perceptions and preferences.

Notes

[1] As users of CYI are not representative of the population, the figures are estimated using a re-weighting procedure that makes the CYI sample similar to the general population on the basis of age, gender, household size and disposable income (Balestra and Cohen, 2021[42]).

[2] In this report, the term "conventional statistical indicators" indicates the estimates of inequality based on household income data (such as the Gini index derived from the *OECD Income Distribution Database*), in order to distinguish them from people's perceptions, which refer to a subjective factor. It should be noted, however, that inequality indices have a normative interpretation (Atkinson, 1970[41]) and, therefore, also the use of different statistical indices can correspond to different social preferences.

[3] As a result, cross-country differences in average levels of concern do not always align with conventional statistical estimates of inequality: not only might people perceive a level of inequality that differs from the statistical measures, but people's preferred levels of inequality are also likely to differ from one country to another.

2. How do people perceive economic inequalities?

This chapter discusses how perceptions of and concern over income and earnings disparities vary across countries and change over time. It shows that such concern has increased strongly since the early 1990s and correlates with changes in conventional indicators of income inequality. The chapter then disentangles people's perceptions of the current extent of disparities from their preferred level of disparities. It shows that perceived income and earnings disparities are wider in countries where inequality, measured by conventional indicators, is greater; the inference is that people incorporate information about disparities in their perceptions thereof. Perceived earnings disparities have grown considerably over time. However, people have partly adapted their preferences for equality and become more tolerant of inequality. The chapter also discusses how concern over income disparities is influenced by perceptions of the intergenerational persistence of advantages and disadvantages and by belief in the importance of hard work.

2.1. How people's concern over income disparities has evolved

Concern about income disparities is great and growing

Concern over income disparities (Table 1.1 and Annex 1.A) is widespread in OECD countries. According to the latest available data from the International Social Survey Programme (ISSP) and Eurobarometer (Annex 2.A), the vast majority of people agree with the statement that income disparities in their country are too wide. Indeed, in 2017, an average of some 80% of respondents agreed, and almost half agreed strongly (Figure 2.1).

There are sizeable differences between countries, however. Shares of people who strongly believe income disparities are too wide range from 17% in Denmark to 63% in Hungary. Considerable differences are also observed between socio-demographic groups. The elderly, women and people who regard themselves as belonging to lower social strata all show higher levels of concern over income disparities (Ciani et al. (2021[1]) for more details).

Figure 2.1. Most people are concerned about wide income disparities in their countries

Share of respondents by level of agreement with the statement "Differences in income in [your country] are too large", 2017

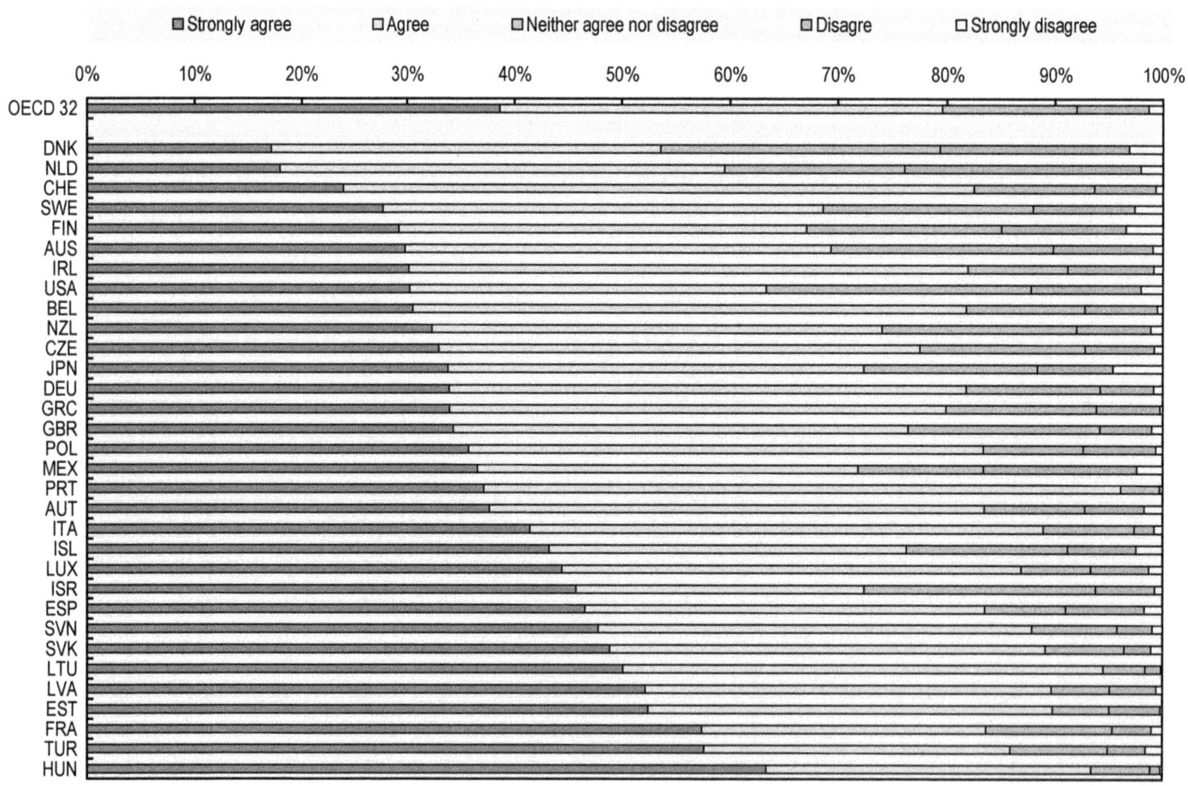

Note: In ISSP, respondents are asked their opinion about the statement "Differences in income in [country] are too large". In Eurobarometer the statement reads: "Nowadays in [country] differences in people's incomes are too great". The scale of answers is identical. The OECD average is the unweighted average across the countries included in the figure. For the United Kingdom, data from ISSP refer to Great Britain only.
Source: OECD calculations on International Social Survey Programme (ISSP) 2017; Eurobarometer 471/2017 for Belgium, Estonia, Greece, Ireland, Italy, Luxembourg, Latvia, Malta, Netherlands, Poland, Portugal and Romania.

StatLink https://stat.link/7m0i5g

People's concern over income disparities has long been growing (Figure 2.2 and Bussolo et al. (2019[2])).[1] Across OECD countries, the share of respondents who strongly agree that income differences are too wide had been on the rise since the early 1990s before reaching its peak at the onset of the global financial crisis. An alternative source, the European and World Values Survey, reveals a similar pattern (Ciani et al., 2021[1]). Data from the latest ISSP waves (2017 and 2019) suggest that concern has slightly decreased, on average, in the decade since the onset of the global financial crisis.[2]

The trend in people's concern mirrors the evolution of income inequality in OECD countries as described by conventional statistical measures. Indeed, the data from the *Income Distribution Database* increased between the mid-1980s and late 2000s and point to a somewhat flatter trend since.

Figure 2.2. Concern about income disparities increased over time before reaching a peak during the global financial crisis

Share of respondents who strongly agree with the statement that income differences in their country are too large, OECD average

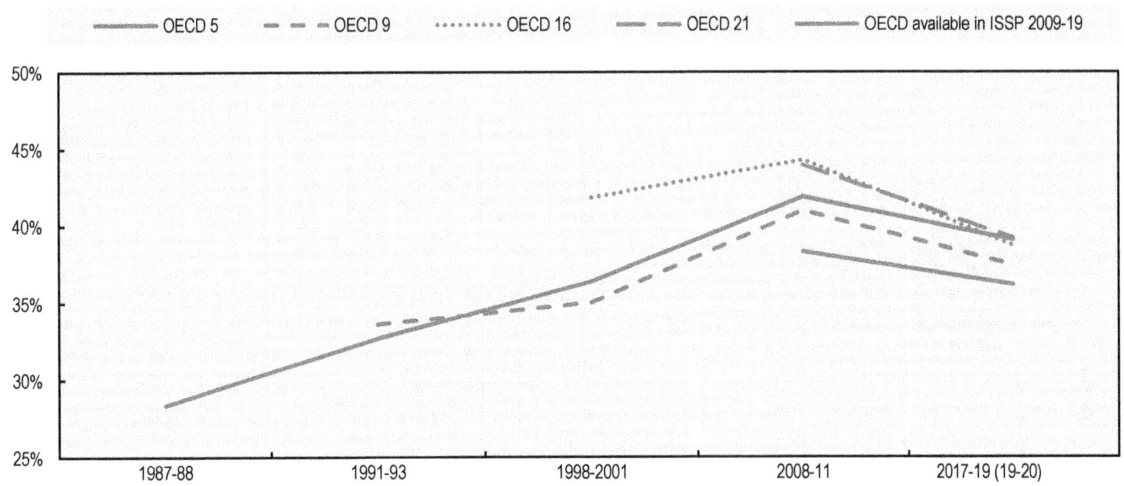

Notes: Unweighted average across countries of the share of respondents who strongly agree that income differences (in their country) are too great. See Ciani et al. (2021[1]) for trends in alternative summary measures. Blue lines – the most recent data point is from ISSP 2017 (conducted out in 2017-19). Red line – most recent data point is from ISSP 2019 (conducted in 2019-20).
OECD 5 – Austria, Australia, United Kingdom, Hungary, United States. OECD 9 – plus Germany, New Zealand, Slovenia, Sweden. OECD 16 – plus Czech Republic, Denmark, Spain, France, Israel, Japan, Slovak Republic. OECD 21 – plus Switzerland, Finland, Iceland, Lithuania, Turkey. OECD available in ISSP 2009-19 denotes the countries in both ISSP 2009 and 2019, for which the trends are more fully comparable – Australia, Switzerland, Chile, Czech Republic, Germany, Denmark, Finland, United Kingdom, Italy, Japan, New Zealand, Norway, Slovenia.
Source: OECD calculations from ISSP 1987, 1992, 1999, 2009, 2017 and 2019; 2019 also uses the Australian Survey of Social Attitudes 2019; Norwegian part of ISSP 2019; British Social Attitudes 2019, which are the national components of ISSP.

StatLink https://stat.link/3a82o5

The swell of concern in the two decades before the global financial crisis (for which data are most fully and widely comparable) spared only Norway and New Zealand (Figure 2.3).[3] And the increase was steep in Australia, Switzerland and the United States, although it started from very low levels in those countries. In Italy, too, however, the share or people who felt strongly that income differences were too wide rose from a much higher 40% in 1988 to 70% in 2011. The increase was sharpest in Hungary, which was going through economic and political transition. Concern also rose in Poland with the political transition, albeit to a lesser extent.

Concern has abated a little in the last decade on average. Although in half of the countries with long-term observations it has actually grown or remained stable, it has dropped significantly in others. In Italy, concern dropped to its 1987 levels, after having reached a climax during the global financial crisis, which coincided with the sovereign debt crisis that hit the country in 2011 (the year in which ISSP 2009 was fielded in Italy). Similarly, in Austria and Poland, the latest available data suggest lower levels of concern than in the late 1980s. However, the trend is subject to caution as the data are from the ISSP 2017 wave and Eurobarometer 471/2017, respectively, which are not fully comparable with other waves.

Figure 2.3. In the two decades up to the global financial crisis, concern over income disparities increased in most countries

Share of respondents who strongly agree that income differences are too large

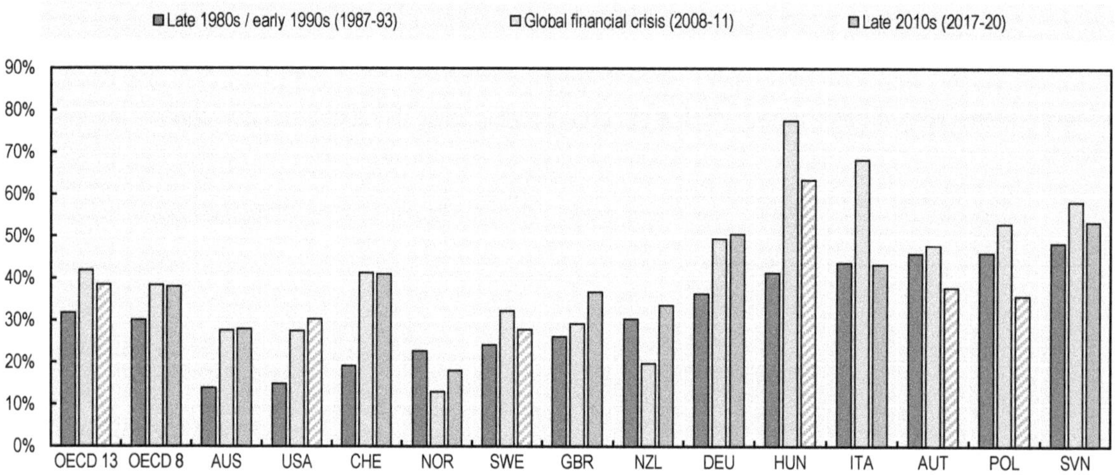

Note: The columns with a different pattern relating to the late 2010s are from not fully comparable waves. For each country, the figure shows concern in the first observed wave (either ISSP 1987 or ISSP 1992), during the global financial crisis (ISSP 2009) and in the latest available wave (ISSP 2017 or 2019; Eurobarometer 2017 for Poland). The OECD average is a simple average of the first observed wave for the OECD countries included in the figure. OECD 8 refers only to the countries fully comparable in the latest wave (ISSP 2019). The first wave is ISSP 1987 for all countries apart from Germany, Norway, New Zealand, Slovenia and Sweden (ISSP 1992). The latest wave is ISSP 2019 apart from Austria, Hungary, United Kingdom, United States, Sweden (ISSP 2017) and Poland (Eurobarometer 471/2017). For Australia, Norway and the United Kingdom the data come from the national ISSP components (Australian Survey of Social Attitudes 2019; Norwegian part of ISSP 2019; British Social Attitudes 2019). For the United Kingdom, data refer to Great Britain only.

Source: OECD calculations from ISSP 1987, 1992, 2009, 2017 and 2019; Eurobarometer 471/2017; Australian Survey of Social Attitudes 2019; Norwegian part of ISSP 2019; British Social Attitudes 2019.

StatLink https://stat.link/9sy1t3

Changes in concern are related to changes in observed inequality

At any moment in time, cross-country differences in concern over income disparities do not match differences in the magnitude of inequality estimated with conventional statistical measures (Figure 2.4 and Gimpelson and Treisman (2018[3])). In some countries, nevertheless, levels of concern over income disparities are similar to the extent of inequality measured by conventional indicators. Nordic countries, for instance, exhibit both lower Gini indices and lower concern, while Turkey display high levels of inequality and concern, as do other Eastern and Southern European countries and Israel. The "low-Gini-high-concern" group includes some European countries that transitioned to a market economy, as well as France. By contrast, most English-speaking countries belong to the "high-Gini-low-concern" group, although their average levels of concern are quite close to the median and to levels observed in Japan and some Central and Southern European countries, such as Germany and Greece.

Figure 2.4. Concern over income disparities only weakly correlates with conventional measures of income inequality

Levels of concern about income disparities and Gini coefficients, 2017

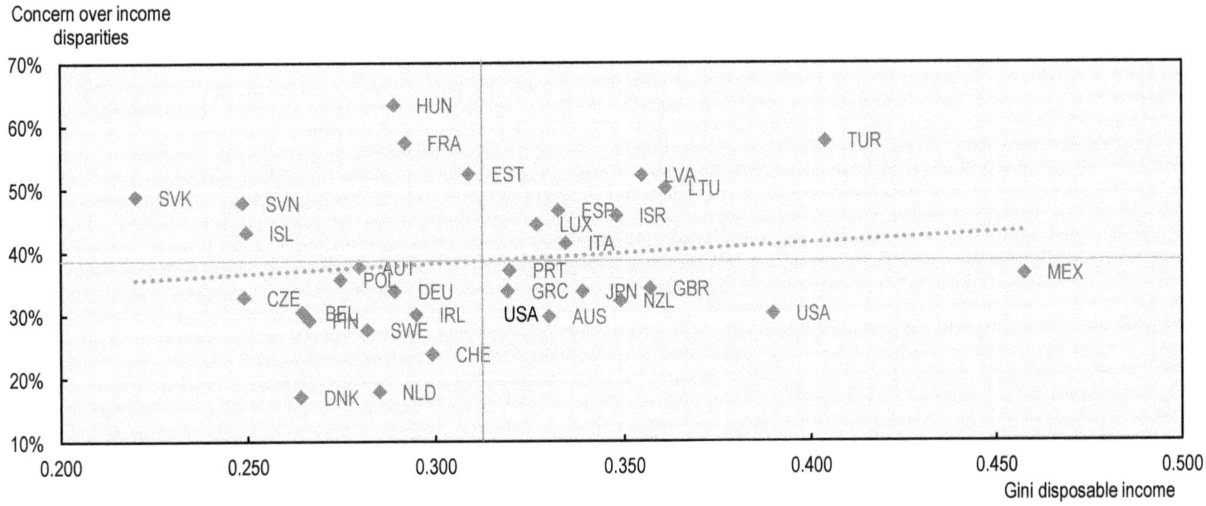

Note: The horizontal and vertical lines denote median values. Concern about income disparities (y axis, percentages) is measured by the share of respondents who strongly agree that income differences are too large in their country. The Gini coefficient (for the total population) measures inequality in incomes after taxes and transfers (x axis) and refers to the year of interview (2017 for most countries, 2018 for Austria, Germany, Iceland, Israel, Lithuania, Mexico, Slovenia, United States, 2019 for Turkey), or to the calendar year preceding the interview. The dotted blue line is the linear relation between the two variables. For the United Kingdom, data on concerns about income disparities refer to Great Britain only, while the Gini coefficient refers to the United Kingdom.

Source: OECD calculations from ISSP 2017 and Eurobarometer 2017 for concern about income disparities (see Figure 2.1); *OECD Income Distribution Database* for the Gini index (data available at the time of writing the report: update December 2020).

StatLink https://stat.link/mvxade

By contrast, changes in concern over income disparities correlate positively with changes in conventional inequality indicators (Figure 2.5).[4] In those countries where the Gini coefficient rose the most, concern over income disparities also increased more steeply, from which it may be inferred that people's concern reflects the changes in income disparities that have occurred in their country over the years. The inference is in line with a body of literature that has highlighted how within-country differences in perceptions and concerns, either over time or across regions, tend to correlate with statistical estimates of inequality (Kerr, 2014[4]; McCall et al., 2017[5]; Bussolo et al., 2019[2]; Kuhn, 2019[6]; Colagrossi, Karagiannis and Raab, 2019[7]; Giger and Lascombes, 2019[8]; Xu and Garand, 2010[9]; Newman, Shah and Lauterbach, 2018[10]; Franko, 2017[11]).

Figure 2.5. People's concern reflects changes in inequality over time

Deviations from the country average, net of time components common to all countries

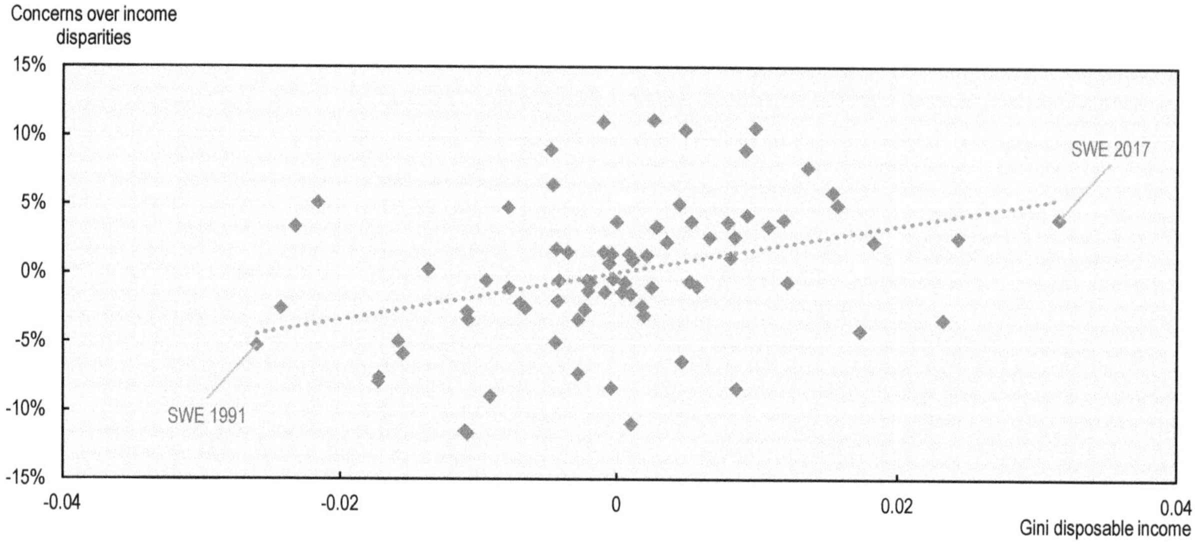

Note: The dotted line is the linear fit line. Each point refers to a country in a single year and represents the deviation from the average for that country across all available years. Taking Sweden as an example, the first to the right along the linear fit represents Sweden in 2017, when both concern over income disparities and the Gini coefficient were higher than the average values for Sweden throughout the period of observation, once time trends common to all countries are taken into account. The opposite holds for Sweden in 1991, which is the first point to the left along the linear fit. These deviations also account for time changes common to all countries (period effects).
Source: OECD calculations from ISSP 1987, 1992, 1999, 2009, 2017 and Eurobarometer 2017 for concern over income disparities (see Figure 2.1 for the list of countries for which Eurobarometer is used); *OECD Income Distribution Database* for the Gini index.

StatLink https://stat.link/3xoldi

At country level, changes in levels of concern over income disparities are more closely related to changes in inequality measured in disposable rather than market income (Table 2.1, Columns 1-3). The inference is that people's perceptions take into account the redistribution operated through income taxes and cash transfers. Thus, if market income inequality increases, but is offset by effective redistribution, then concerns will not change significantly. Similarly, if market inequality does not change, but redistribution weakens, then concern over inequality tends to rise.[5]

Changes in concern over income disparities do not seem closely related to macro-economic conditions. For example, higher employment rates and GDP per capita reduce concern, while lower unemployment seems actually to increase it, though not by much in either case (Table 2.1, Column 4).

The average respondent also seems to be concerned chiefly about income differences between the top and the middle of the distribution (Table 2.1, Column 5), while the gap between the median and the bottom of the distribution has no significant effect on the average level of concern. The inference is that the income growth dynamics of the middle class relative to the top is particularly important in explaining concern over income disparities in the country as a whole. The finding is also in line with the conclusions of Lupu and Pontusson (2011[12]), who argue that the structure of inequality – as captured by the distance between the 90th percentile and the median income – is a key driver of actual redistributive policies. Fisman et al. (2020[13]) also provide evidence that the relative standing of high-income individuals is a particularly salient determinant of individuals' concern about income distribution. Their results show, moreover, that people keep an eye on the incomes of individuals just above them in the distribution.

Column 6 in Table 2.1 estimates whether alternative estimates of fiscal income inequality from the *World Inequality Database* yield results consistent with those of conventional indicators. The *World Inequality Database* relies on tax data and better captures the top of the distribution. Results suggest that the most powerful driver of concern is the share of income owned by the richest 10%, while the share owned by the richest 1% does not, per se, exert a significant effect.

Results are similar at the individual level, after controlling for a broad set of characteristics that influence concern. At the individual level, it is also possible to look at the impact on the entire range of possible responses to the ISSP question. When inequality rises in their countries, respondents are more likely to agree strongly that income disparities are too great and less likely to answer anything else (Figure 2.6).

Table 2.1. Changes in concern over income disparities correlate with changes in inequality within countries after tax and transfers

Percentage point increase in the share of respondents who strongly agree that income disparities are too large, associated with 1 percentage point increases in different variables

	(1)	(2)	(3)	(4)	(5)	(6)
Gini market income (before taxes and transfers)	0.66*		0.29	0.10		
	(0.35)		(0.36)	(0.56)		
Gini disposable income (post taxes and transfers)		1.71**	1.55**	1.69**		
		(0.67)	(0.71)	(0.73)		
Unemployment rate				-0.01*		0.00
				(0.00)		(0.01)
Employment rate				-0.15		0.29
				(0.57)		(0.32)
GDP per head (logarithm)				-0.17		-0.15
				(0.25)		(0.10)
90th percentile vs median income ratio					0.29**	
					(0.12)	
median income vs 10th percentile ratio					-0.03	
					(0.08)	
Top 10% share (WID)						2.54**
						(1.20)
Top 1% share (WID)						-1.68
						(1.24)
Observations	78	78	78	78	78	84
Countries	29	29	29	29	29	28
Country fixed effects	Included	Included	Included	Included	Included	Included
Period fixed effects	Included	Included	Included	Included	Included	Included

Note: * denotes statistically significant at the 10% level, ** at 5%, *** at 1%. All coefficients can be read as percentage point changes, e.g. in column (1) a 1 percentage point increase in the Gini coefficient of market income is associated, on average, with a 0.78 percentage point increase in the share of respondents who strongly agree that income differences are too large. Standard errors clustered by country in parentheses. Results are from fixed (country) effects regressions, including period fixed effects. GDP per head is in logarithms, but the original values are expressed in constant prices and PPP (2015 USD PPP).

Source: OECD calculations from ISSP 1987, 1992, 1999, 2009, 2017 and Eurobarometer 2017 for concern over income disparities (see Figure 2.1 for the list of countries for which Eurobarometer is used); *OECD Income Distribution Database* for the Gini coefficient; *World Inequality Database (WID)* for the income share of the richest 10% and 1% (pre-tax national income, adults, including elderly (20+), household income of couples attributed to each individual assuming equal-split).

StatLink https://stat.link/d95w4p

Figure 2.6. When income inequality rises respondents become more likely to strongly agree that income disparities are too large

Percentage point increase in the probability that respondents express different levels of agreement with the statement "income differences are too large", associated with a 1 percentage point increase in disposable income inequality

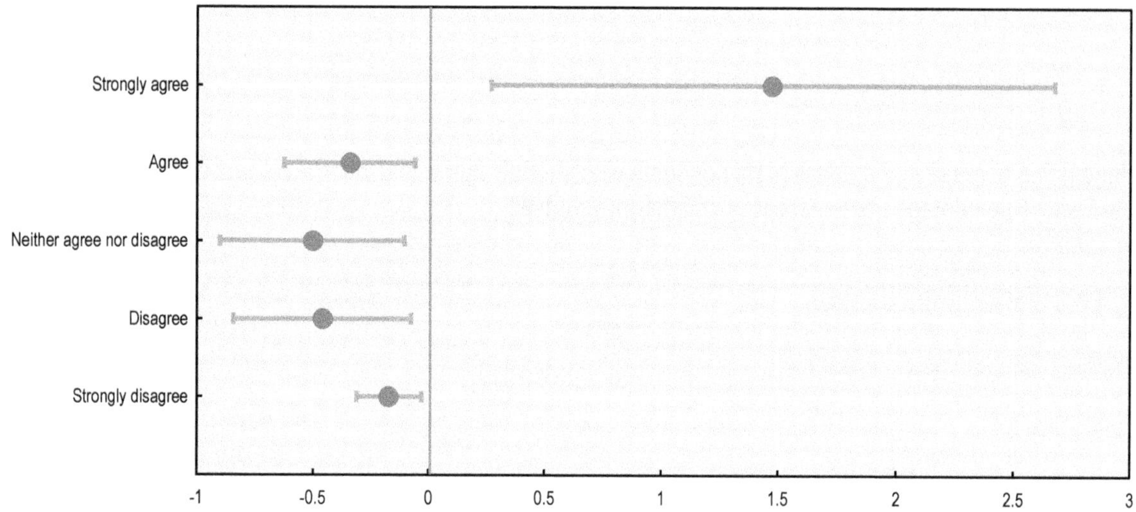

Note: Dots represent the percentage point changes in the share of respondents (for each response category) associated with a 1 percentage point increase in the Gini coefficient of disposable income, keeping constant the respondents' socio-demographic characteristics. For instance, the red dot in the top of the Figure means that a 1 percentage point increase in the Gini disposable income is associated with a 1.5 percentage point increase in the share of respondents who strongly agree that income differences are too large (the interval around the dot represents statistical uncertainty around the estimate). The results are displayed as average marginal effects from an ordered probit regression at the individual level, controlling for age, gender, household size, employment status (employed, unemployed and reference category "inactive"), educational level (less than secondary, secondary and reference category "tertiary") and the log of relative income (with respect to the country average in that point in time). All regressions include country and period (wave) dummies.
Source: OECD calculations from ISSP 1987, 1992, 1999, 2009, 2017 for concern over income disparities and individual covariates; *OECD Income Distribution Database* for the Gini indices.

StatLink https://stat.link/tpcmdf

People's concern over income disparities is shaped by their perceptions and preferences

In order to understand how and why concern over income disparities has changed with time in response to income inequality, it is crucial to recall that it combines two elements:

- individuals' perceptions of the extent of income inequality, i.e. what they think it is;
- individuals' preferences for income equality, i.e. what they think it should be.

An increase in inequality might therefore influence concern over income disparities in two ways:

- People may incorporate information about rising inequality in their perceptions (perceptions adjust to reality), which could heighten their concern about inequality.
- People's preferences adapt to high inequality as they grow gradually more tolerant of inequality, so that they eventually prefer higher levels of inequality (Trump, 2018[14]).

Perceptions and preferences may combine differently in response to increases in inequality. Thus, when inequality grows, so might concern if people's perceptions of inequality diverge from their preferences. Concern may not change if people overlook the signs, or if the changes in perception and preference balance each other out. And it may even fall, if people adapt to greater inequality.

Evidence as to how people's concern over inequality evolves in the long run (Figure 2.3) and how it relates to inequality indicators (Table 2.1) suggests that adjusting perceptions to reality generally prevails over people adapting their preferences.

A crucial determinant of people's concern about inequality is their own income – indeed, those at the bottom of the income distribution are more concerned about inequality than those at the top (Rueda and Stegmueller, 2020[15]). When inequality increases, the average level of concern may rise, too, but not only because people become more concerned about the overall level of inequality (Alesina and Giuliano, 2011[16]). Concern also grows because more people's incomes fall below average and they perceive that their relative position in the distribution has worsened. This is the mechanism behind the standard Meltzer-Richard model (Meltzer and Richard, 1981[17]), whereby demand for redistribution rises as inequality grows, because the median voter becomes poorer than the average. The inference is that:

- perceptions of both the overall level of inequality and the individual's own position in the distribution are crucial;
- the impact of inequality on concern about inequality and preferences for redistribution likely depends on relative income.

Chapter 3 discusses in detail the role of people's own income – both real and perceived – in shaping perceptions of and concerns over inequality, which it relates to preferences for redistribution.

Concern over income disparities also depends on beliefs about the sources of such disparities. People who believe that hard work is a more important determinant of economic success than other factors are more inclined to accept that some individuals earn more than others as a consequence of their efforts (Fong, 2001[18]; Alesina and Giuliano, 2011[16]; Karayel, 2015[19]; Clark and D'Ambrosio, 2015[20]; Daniels and Wang, 2019[21]; Mijs, 2019[22]; Almås, Cappelen and Tungodden, 2020[23]). Conversely, those who believe that luck and sheer circumstance drive economic success are more concerned about inequality (Figure 2.7). And in countries where more people believe that parental wealth matters little for getting ahead in life and that hard work matters there is less concern over income disparities. Countries where there is a strong belief in equal opportunities include some Nordic countries – Iceland, Sweden and Norway, but not Denmark and Finland – and most English-speaking countries (see also the related evidence by Benson (2021[24]) on the importance given by respondents from the United Kingdom to meritocracy). While the United States is usually described as a country of social mobility, it is in fact at the median when it comes to the perceived importance of parental wealth. However, it is also the country that believes most strongly in the importance of hard work. Patterns in other countries are less cut and dried. Post-transition and Southern European countries tend to harbour the perception that parental wealth matters, although in some of them the average respondent believes that hard work pays. Although its level of concern over equality is almost the same as the average English-speaking country, Japan accords less importance to both parental wealth and to the virtue of hard work. Korea, by contrast, is at the opposite end of the spectrum, deeming parental wealth very important and having great faith in hard work.

The next two sections seek to further disentangle people's perceptions of and preferences for inequality and how they evolve over time. Section 2.2 considers perceptions and 2.3 preferences. The discussion necessarily entails addressing people's views of equality of opportunities and the virtue of hard work.

Figure 2.7. There is less concern over income disparity in countries where people believe that hard work, not parental wealth, is what matters for getting ahead in life

The bubbles denote countries and the larger they are the higher the share of respondents who strongly agree with the statement that income disparities are too large, 2009

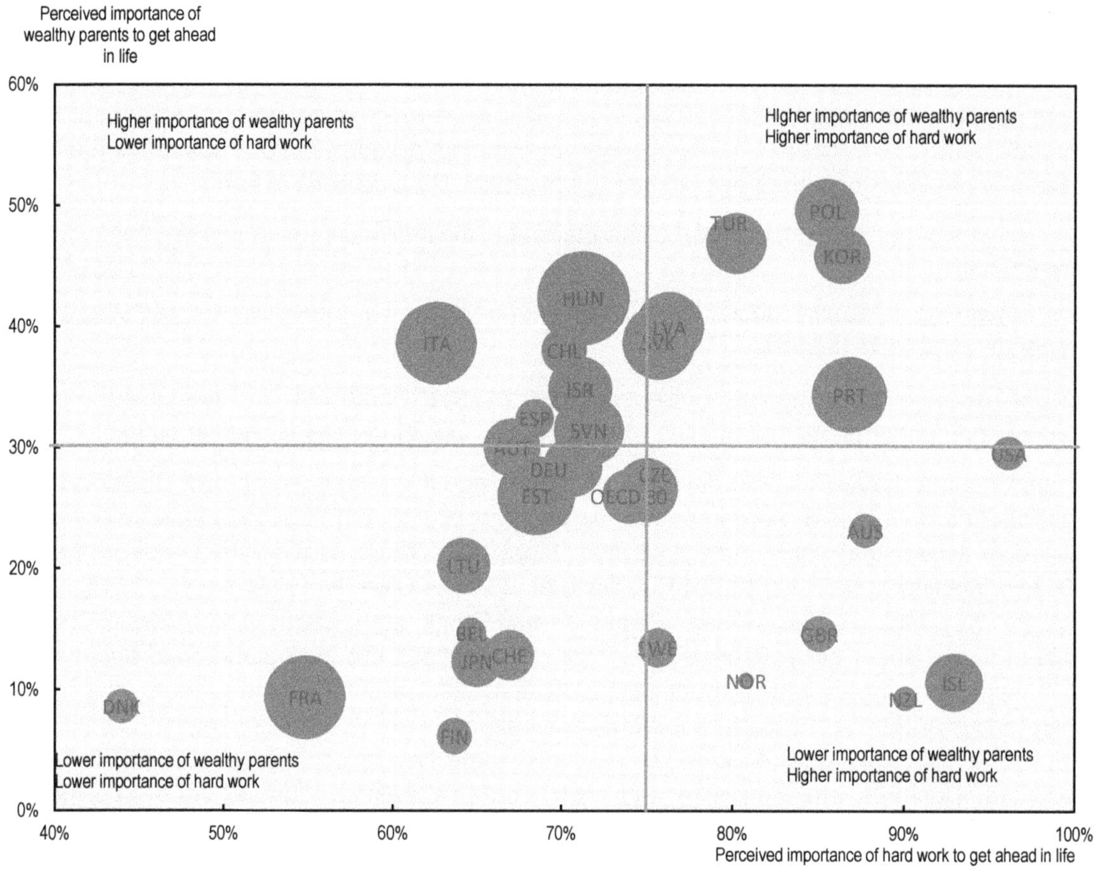

Note: The area of each bubble is larger where is a higher share of respondents strongly agree with the statement that income disparities are too large. The importance of hard work is measured as the share of respondents who believe that hard work is very important or essential for getting ahead in life. The importance of having wealthy parents is measured as the share of respondents who believe that coming from a wealthy family is very important or essential for getting ahead in life. The horizontal and vertical lines refer to the median values of the two variables.
Source: OECD calculations from ISSP 2009.

StatLink https://stat.link/jrco62

2.2. Behind concern over income disparities lie people's perceptions of income and earnings disparities

Perceived income and earnings disparities are wide

One way to unbundle the different drivers of people's concerns about income inequality is to ask them what they think the current level of economic inequality is (their perceptions), and what they would like it to be (their preferences).

Surveys which collect information on people's perceived economic disparities focus on different outcomes. The OECD Risks that Matter survey asks about household income, while ISSP asks respondents about earnings disparities.[6] Despite their differences, looking at perceptions of disparities in either economic outcomes is useful for two reasons. First, a single survey covering perceptions of both earnings and income inequality is not available. Moreover, data on both perceptions are not always available for all OECD countries and for all the relevant periods. In fact, the analysis of changes is possible only on ISSP for perceived earnings disparities. Secondly, one needs to take into account that perceptions of and preferences for earnings disparities might differ from those for income disparities. For example, people might be more tolerant of earnings disparities, because these can be attenuated by welfare transfers to households with low-earners. In fact, earnings are only one component of income and, therefore, concern over earnings disparities can be considered as one of the determinants of the overall concern over income disparities.

Most people perceive high levels of both income and earnings inequality. According to the results of the 2020 OECD Risks that Matter survey, average respondents believe that the share of their country's total income that goes to the richest 10% of households is extremely large (Figure 2.8). In all 25 countries surveyed, the average perception is that the richest 10%'s share of national income is 42% – ranging from 38% in Denmark to 67% in Turkey. To put perceptions in perspective, the latest average estimate from the *OECD Income Distribution Database* is that the richest 10%'s share of disposable income is actually 25% in the countries which Risks that Matter surveyed.

ISSP 2009, which covers a wide set of countries, considered perceptions of earnings disparities. It found, on average, that median respondents believed that highly skilled earners (doctors and CEOs) earned around 9 times more than an unskilled factory worker. Yet there is substantial variation in countries' perceived top-bottom earnings ratio, which ranges from 3 in Sweden to 26 in Korea.

Figure 2.8. Perceptions are that there is great income and earnings inequality

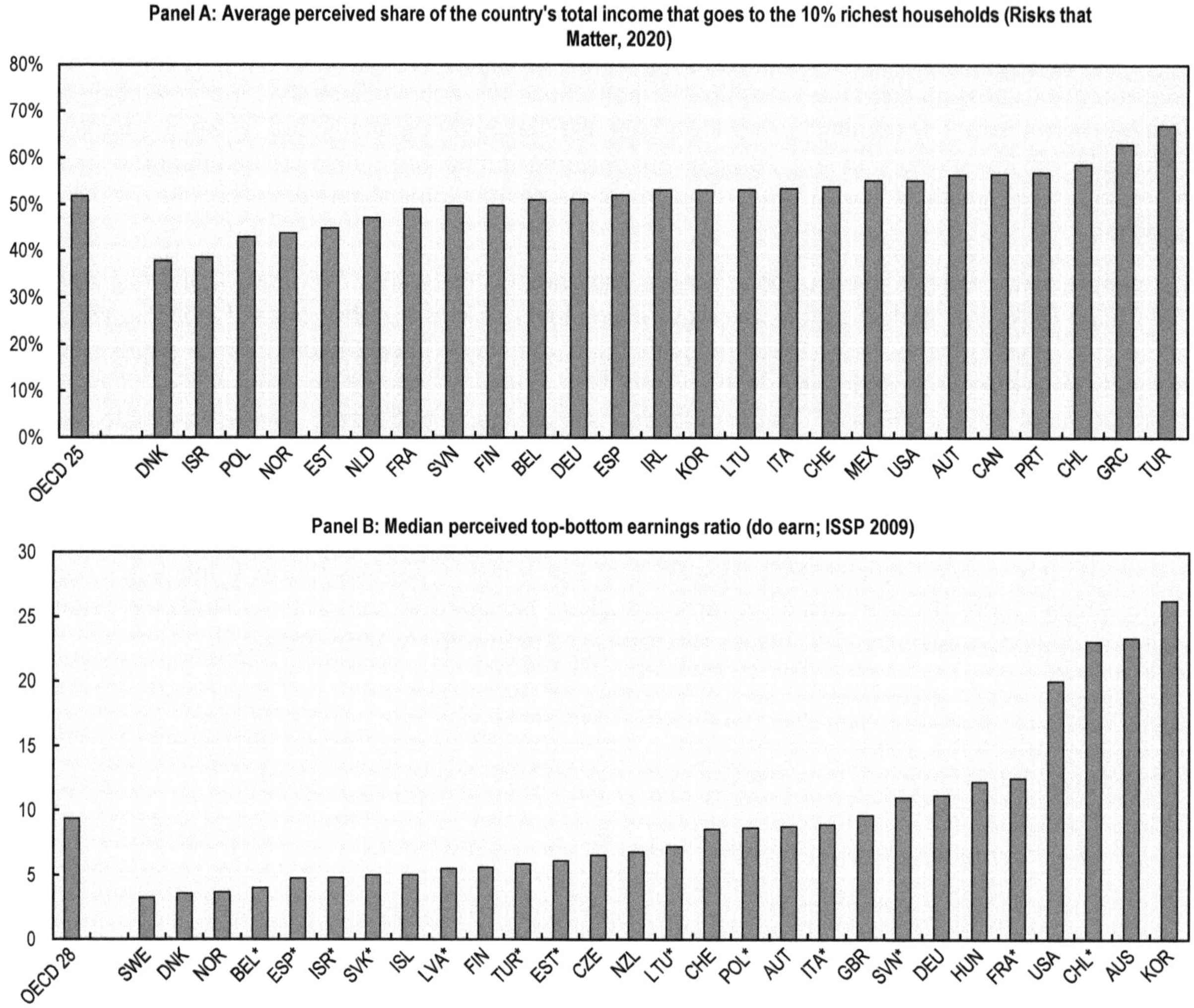

Note: Panel A reports the average answer to the question "According to you, how much of your country's total income goes to the richest 10%? Please enter a number between 0 and 100 to indicate the percent of your country's total income that goes to the richest households." In the Panel B, top earnings are the average between earnings of doctors in general practice and chairmen of large national companies and bottom earnings are those of unskilled workers in a factory. The perceived ratios are calculated at the individual level and the figure plots the median value for each country. In countries marked by * questions refer to net earnings, while in the others the question refers to gross earnings. More details on the calculation of the ratio and the correction for underreporting can be found in Ciani et al. (2021[1]).The Risks that Matter sample consists only of working age respondents (18-64), while ISSP surveys the entire adult population (with few exceptions).
Source: OECD calculations from Risks that Matter 2020 (Panel A); ISSP 2009 (Panel B).

StatLink https://stat.link/28qki1

In most countries, the prevailing perception is that income inequality has increased in the last decade (Figure 2.9).[7] A retrospective question is usually more likely to prompt the answer that inequality has been on the rise. Evidence from other surveys, like the French *Baromètre d'opinion,* the recent Ipsos MORI survey conducted in the United Kingdom for the Deaton review (Garret and Day, 2021[25]) and the American Election Studies (Macdonald, 2019[26]), report similar findings, with most respondents asserting that inequality has been on the rise in recent years.

Figure 2.9. Most people perceive that income inequality has increased in the recent decade

Share of respondents by type of answer

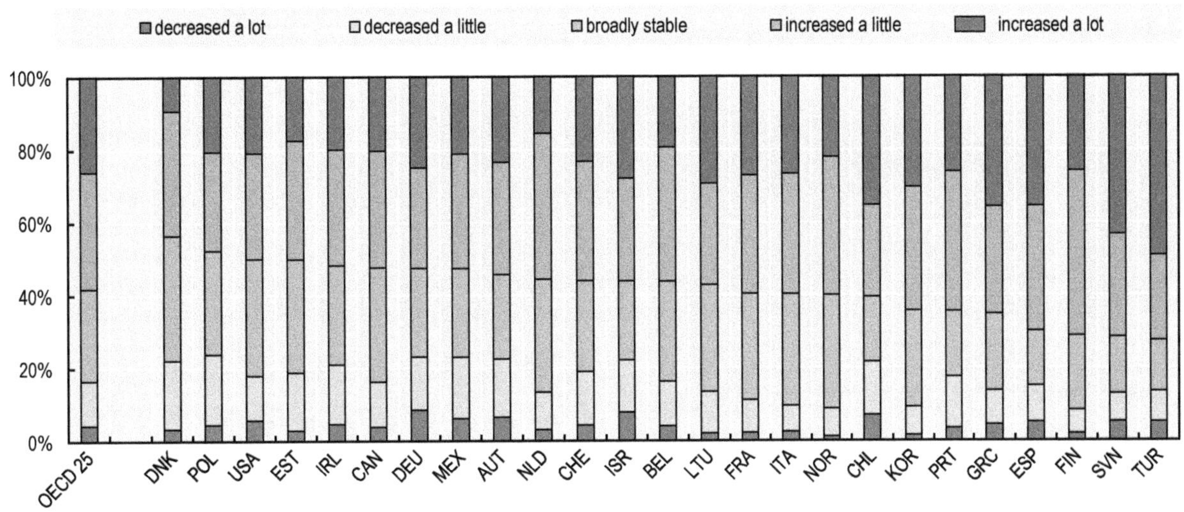

Note: Coloured segments in the bars denote the shares of answers to the question "Thinking now more generally about the evolution of income inequality in your country over the last decade, do you think that it has decreased, remained stable, or increased?"
Source: OECD calculations from Risks that Matter 2020.

StatLink https://stat.link/2coj5i

Most people believe that intergenerational income persistence is high and related to inequality of outcomes

As documented by the extensive literature (Alesina and Giuliano, 2011[16]), people's opinions of intergenerational mobility play a crucial role in shaping their concern over current inequality of outcomes (either earnings or income). This crucial role is consistent with the interpretation of Benabou and Ok's Prospect of Upward Mobility hypothesis (POUM) in an intergenerational perspective (Benabou and Ok, 2001[27]). POUM advances that people might be less concerned by their current situation if they believe that their offspring have good chances of climbing the income ladder. Furthermore, research has shown that income inequality and social mobility are negatively related, both across countries (OECD, 2018[28]) and within them, as the chances of scaling the income ladder are lower in areas with wider income disparities (Chetty et al., 2014[29]). Whether people's perceptions are aligned with this finding – so that perceived intergenerational mobility is lower where perceived income or earnings inequality is greater – is less well known (see Alesina, Stantcheva and Teso (2018[30]) for evidence relative to different areas in the United States).

The latest Risks that Matter survey finds that, in OECD countries, people believe that a child from a household in the bottom 10% of the income distribution is highly likely still to be in there when s/he grows up (Figure 2.10, Panel A). The average share of respondents who hold that belief is 55%, ranging from 47% in Norway, Poland and Denmark to 64% in Austria. Women perceive intergenerational persistence as more prevalent than men, but do not believe the richest 10%'s share of income is as high as men do (Ciani et al., 2021[11]).

Figure 2.10. The poor are seen to have little chance of climbing the social ladder

Panel A: Average perceived probability that children coming from the poorest 10% of households in terms of income will remain in a poor household (the poorest 10%) once they become adults; Risks that Matters, 2020

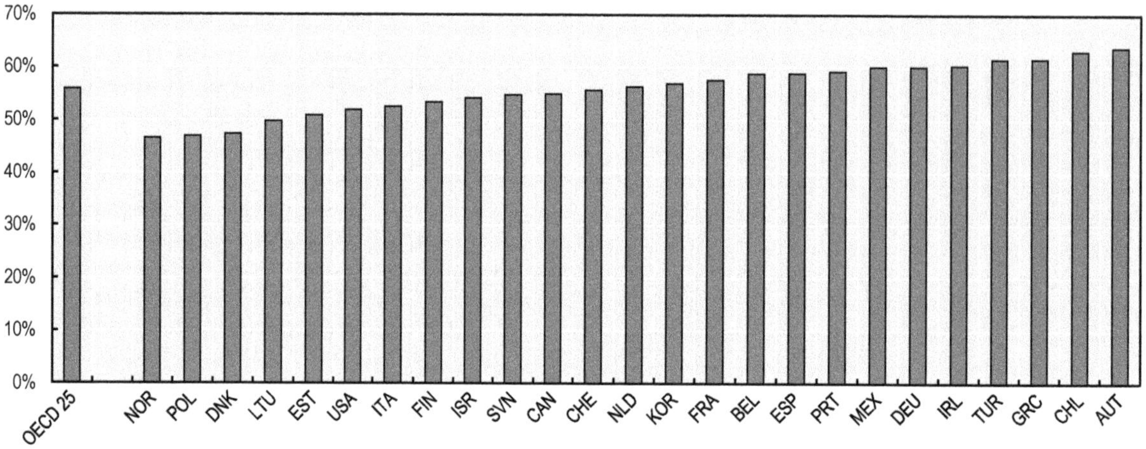

Panel B: Share that believe that coming from a wealthy family or having well-educated parents is very important to get ahead in life (percent), and index of perceived intergenerational persistence (values); ISSP, 2009

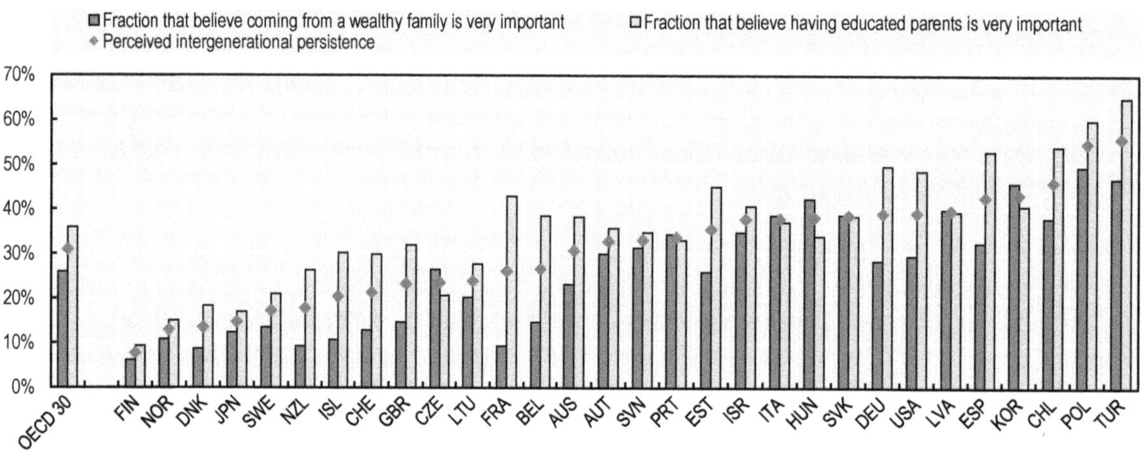

Note: Panel A shows average answers to the question "In your country, out of 100 children coming from the poorest 10% of households in terms of income, how many do you think will still be living in a poor household (the poorest 10%) once they become adults? Please note that we refer to the poorest in terms of post-tax and benefit income." Panel B shows the shares of respondents who believe coming from a wealthy family or having educated parents is very important or essential for getting ahead in life. The perceived intergenerational persistence (denoted by a diamond) is the average of the two shares.
Source: OECD calculations from Risks that Matter 2020 (Panel A) and ISSP 2009 (Panel B).

StatLink https://stat.link/4yu83m

It is possible to paint a more qualitative picture from ISSP respondents' beliefs about the importance of family background (Brunori, 2017[31]). It considers two types of parental characteristics: family wealth and the parents' education. There are conceptual differences between the two, even though they correlate. Wealthy parents, for example, might finance their offspring's education or entrepreneurial activities. Similarly, highly educated parents might influence offspring's success independently of family wealth – by transmitting different knowledge, for instance. Indeed, in France, Belgium, Spain and Chile, a much higher share of respondents agree that having well educated parents is more important for getting ahead in life than having wealthy ones (Figure 2.10, Panel B).

A perceived intergenerational persistence index, built by averaging the perceived importance of parents' education and wealth, points to wide differences between countries (Figure 2.10, Panel B). Perceived intergenerational persistence is strong in Turkey and Poland, but slight in Finland, Norway and Denmark. The United States, often cited as the country where most people are confident of social betterment, ranks in the middle of the distribution.[8]

On average, people's perceptions of intergenerational mobility are in line with the so-called "Great Gatsby Curve", whereby greater inequality spells less next-generation upward mobility. In the Risks that Matter survey, perceptions of intergenerational persistence in the shares of income of the richest and poorest 10% are closely related (Figure 2.11). Similarly, ISSP 2009 finds the perception of very wide top-bottom earnings ratios is associated with the belief that family wealth and parental education are particularly important for success in life.[9] These findings from Risks that Matter and ISSP are in line with experimental evidence suggesting that, when people are provided with pessimistic information about the level of inequality, they also weaken confidence in intergenerational mobility (McCall et al., 2017[5]; Davidai, 2018[32]; Browman, Destin and Miele, 2020[33]) and, similarly, when provided with pessimistic information on low mobility, perceptions of high inequality increase (Shariff, Wiwad D and Aknin, 2016[34]).

Figure 2.11. The perceived Great Gatsby Curve: perceptions of intergenerational persistence and economic disparities are closely related

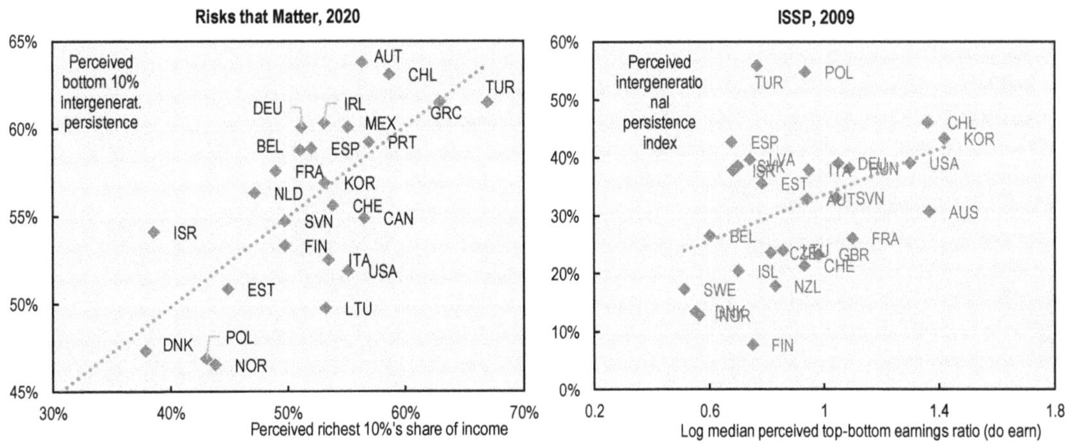

Note: The slope of the linear fit in the left-hand panel is 0.51 (p value 0.00, R2 0.47), implying that a 1 percentage point increase in perceived inequality (top 10% income share) is associated with a 1 percentage point increase in perceived intergenerational persistence among the poorest 10%. The slope of the linear fit in the right-hand panel is 19.7 (p-value 0.06, R2 0.17). As the median perceived top-bottom earnings ratio is in log scale, a 10% increase in the ratio is associated with a doubling of the perceived intergenerational persistence index.
Source: OECD calculations from Risks That Matter 2020 and ISSP 2009.

StatLink https://stat.link/7awfxc

Perceptions are correlated with conventional measures, but do not necessarily align with them

Perceptions across countries significantly correlate with conventional estimates of inequality, with reference to both income and earnings inequality (Figure 2.12). Similarly, where perceived intergenerational persistence is higher, also estimates of father-son elasticity in either earnings or education are higher (higher elasticity means that the son's earnings/education are more strongly related with the father's, indicating higher intergenerational persistence) (OECD, 2018[28]).[10] The inference is that people form their perceptions of income inequalities and social mobility by incorporating at least some information on the real economic outcomes. The inference is also consistent with previous observational evidence from Kuhn (2019[6]), Bussolo et al. (2019[2]), Roth and Wohlfart (2018[35]) and Domènech-Arumí (2021[36]).

Figure 2.12. Perceived inequality and intergenerational persistence are consistently related to conventional indicators of the same phenomena

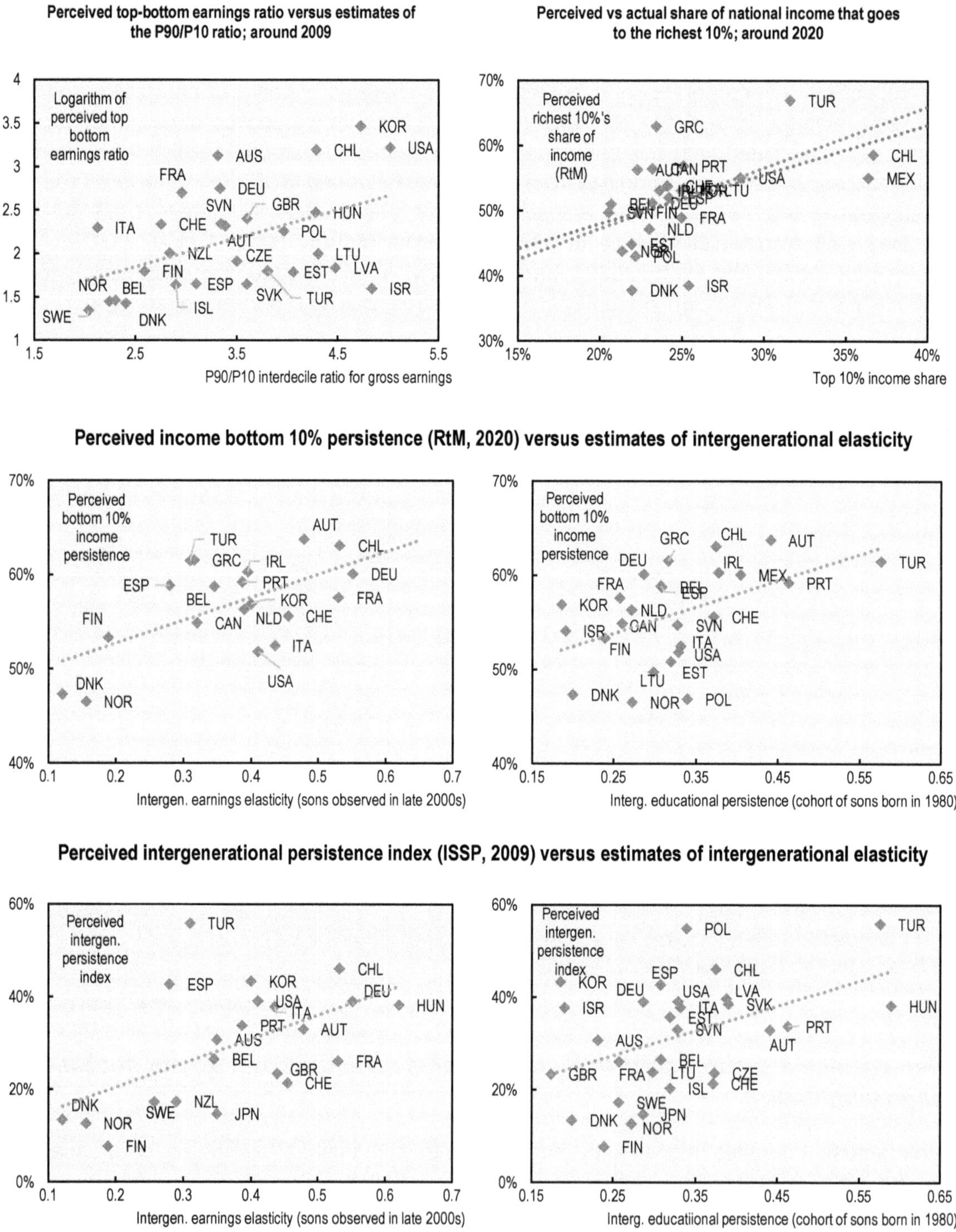

Note: The standardized slopes of the linear fits (which can be read as the standard deviation change in the y axis associated with one standard deviation change in the x axis) are 0.47, 0.49, 0.62, 0.52, 0.53, 0.45 (all statistically significant at the 5% level). The red line in the upper-right panel is calculated without the three outliers (Chile, Mexico and Turkey). The upper-left panel shows the average logarithm of the top-bottom earnings ratio.

Source: OECD calculations from Risks that Matter 2020 and ISSP 2009; *OECD Income Distribution Database* for top income shares, *OECD Earnings database* for interdecile earnings ratio, OECD (2018[28]) for intergenerational earnings elasticity, *World Bank Global Database* on Intergenerational Mobility (GDIM) for intergenerational educational persistence.

StatLink https://stat.link/q6p7d5

A series of in-survey experiments has tested how far people's perceptions take in information about the extent of inequality. To that end, researchers fed to a randomized subset of respondents information on the current magnitude of inequality reported in studies or the media. They then compared the subjects' perceptions with those of a subset of participants who had not been given the information. They found that the individuals that received information about high inequality perceived more inequality in outcomes and opportunities and were more concerned about it (Box 2.1), so corroborating observational evidence (e.g. Figure 2.12).

Box 2.1. Evidence from in-survey experiments

The evidence presented in this chapter bears out the hypothesis that, on average, people generally incorporate information about the extent of inequality in their perceptions. However, this evidence is based on observational data, which makes it hard to single out whether perceptions are indeed shaped by inequality. This because differences in perceptions between countries and changes over time might be influenced by other variables. To isolate the impact of new information about inequality on concerns and perceptions thereof, a growing body of literature has built upon survey experiments.

In these experiments, a randomly selected proportion of respondents is provided with information on the distribution of outcomes and opportunities in the population (or about their own position in the income distribution). Usually this information points to a large degree of inequality. Therefore, the hypothesis is that, if people incorporate such information, they should increase their perceptions of and concern over inequality. As the provision of the information takes place at random, comparing the answers of the group with information and the group without makes it possible to test this hypothesis. Some experiments also examine the role of other factors, such as trust, in explaining results.

Ciani, Fréget and Manfredi (forthcoming[37]) conduct a meta-analysis of the experiments that measure the impact of information on perceptions and concerns about economic inequality. Because the experiments use a heterogeneous range of measures, results are standardized with regard to the standard deviation of each measure in the control group (i.e. in the groups receiving no information). Most estimates of the effect of information on perceptions of and concern about economic disparities are positive, albeit to different extents. The average standardized effect across all studies is 0.17 in the United States, 0.15 in EU countries and 0.16 in other countries. Thus the provision of additional information produces an average increase in perceptions and concerns that is above 0.15 standard deviation, in line with the hypothesis outlined above. Meta-regression analysis shows that that the effect on perceptions is stronger than on concerns, but the latter is still sizeable (between 0.09 and 0.13 standard deviation) and statistically different from zero. This evidence therefore suggests that people interpret information correctly and incorporate it into their outlook.

Some experiments also back up the hypothesis that people partially adapt their preferences upon receipt of signals of increased or high inequality. Trump (2018[14]) finds that informing US and Swedish respondents about the true extent of inequality increases both perceived and preferred levels of earnings disparities. As a result, the effect on concern over income disparities is not statistically different from zero. Hoy and Mager (2020[38]) find that supplying respondents in the United States with the facts about the actual levels of inequality and social mobility lessens how strongly they agree with the statement that income differences are too wide. The change in perception, say the authors, is driven chiefly by respondents who, prior to the experiment, stated that high levels of inequality do not exist. Hoy and Mager (2020[38]) also interpret this as evidence that people increase their preferred level of inequality when they find out its true extent.

Perceptions and conventional indicators of inequality do not fully match. Perceptions of the richest 10%'s share of income and intergenerational income persistence among the bottom 10% exceed conventional measures. For instance, the top 10%'s average perceived share of income across the 25 countries in Risks that Matter is 52%, while the average estimate from the *OECD Income Distribution Database* is 25%. The Compare Your Income tool, which uses a different approach, displays similar findings for the richest 10%'s share of income.

As for statistical measures of how likely the poorest children are to be poor as adults, they are not available for all countries. Those that are reveal once more a divergence between perception and statistics. Respondents to the Risks that Matter survey in Italy and the United States believe that intergenerational persistence will affect respectively 53% and 52% of children in the poorest 10% of households. Statistical estimates find much lower shares –16% in a 1980 cohort for Italy (Acciari, Polo and Violante, 2019[39]) and 20% in 1980-82 cohorts for the United States (Chetty et al., 2014[29]).

These differences between perception and conventional indicators should not necessarily be interpreted as a measure of bias for three main reasons (detailed in Box 2.2):

1. People may think in terms of wealth, rather than income, even though the Risks that Matter questions refer explicitly to income.
2. Conventional estimates reflect methodological choices, while people probably use other, different definitions.
3. Questions are complex for respondents and estimated differences between perceived values and conventional estimates are highly sensitive to how the question is defined and framed.

The answers to the quantitative questions about perceived inequality and social mobility provide valuable and interesting results that go beyond the calculation of a bias. Despite the complexity of definitions and questions, people's average perceptions consistently correlate with conventional estimates across countries, showing that they reflect real disparities. Looking at perceptions – particularly of income inequality, earnings disparities and intergenerational persistence – affords researchers insight into how people process information (Phillips et al., 2020[40]). Furthermore, as Chapter 3 shows, answers to these quantitative questions on perceived inequality and social mobility are powerful predictors of preferences for redistribution, both at the individual and country level. Lastly, they provide descriptions of the distribution (and polarization) of perceptions in the same country (see Chapter 4). Such descriptions are both richer and different from those derived from qualitative questions, where most people tend to respond with the same value, i.e., "agree". Nevertheless, for methodological reasons, it is important to:

- employ a wide array of perception measures, which should include qualitative questions;
- analyse preferred disparities and how they diverge from perception.

Box 2.2. Understanding the differences between average perceptions and conventional estimates

Average perceptions of the magnitude of the richest 10%'s share of income and intergenerational persistence among the bottom 10% (measured by responses in the OECD Risks that Matter survey) tend to be significantly greater than conventional estimates. Such divergence should not necessarily be interpreted as bias for three main reasons.

First, it is likely that people think of a different or broader concept of economic outcomes, even though both questions specify income. The average perception of the level of the richest 10%'s share of income suggests that people might be thinking more of wealth than income (Balestra and Cohen, 2021[41]). Indeed, the average perception is closer to the top 10%'s share of household wealth, which is 53% for the 19 countries for which data are available in the *OECD Wealth Distribution Database*. It also seems to be closer to the top 10%'s share of fiscal income in the World Income Distribution Database, which paints a more accurate picture of top incomes, usually underrepresented in household income surveys. Across the 25 countries covered in Risks that Matter, the latest estimate of the top 10%'s share of fiscal income is 38%.

Second, conventional statistical indicators to measure economic inequality depend on a number of methodological choices that include:

- the definition of income, e.g. which sources to include and exclude;
- the adjustment of income for household size and needs, e.g. equivalence scales;
- the population of reference, e.g. which cohorts to use for measuring intergenerational persistence) and others.

While these choices reflect statistical conventions and consensus between experts, there is no single method. And the sensitivity of numerical estimates to methodological variations makes it hard to find the "perfect" counterpart to each measure of perceptions, as people might unconsciously use other and different definitions.

Third, results are highly dependent on how questions are framed (Jachimowicz et al., 2020[42]). The importance of the question seems particularly relevant when it comes to determining bias with respect to "actual" values. The methodological debate between Eriksson and Simpson (2012[43]) and Ariely and Norton (2013[44]) shows that measuring income disparities as group shares of total income (like the top 10%'s income share in Risks that Matter) or income levels (as in the ISSP questions) might lead to different conclusions about whether respondents under- or overestimate income inequality.

As for intergenerational mobility, Swan et al. (2017[45]) find questions asked with reference to income quintiles or tertiles yield different results as to the "bias" of perceived intergenerational mobility in the United States. In fact, Swan et al. (2017[45]) suggest that measures of perception are better suited to questions that go beyond merely calculating bias and consider how perceptions shape attitudes towards redistribution and vary from group to group. In addition, as the Risks that Matter survey does, dividing the population into 10 income deciles is a complex exercise for respondents, and people may simply refer to "the rich" for the top 10% and "the poor" for the bottom 10%.

Clearly, it is important to use different measures of perceptions and to elicit preferences. To that end, researchers should use different methods to elicit quantitative responses (e.g. asking them as shares of total income – as for the perceived share of income of the top 10% in Risks that Matter – or asking levels for different group – as for example in the perceived earnings of different occupations in ISSP) and support them with qualitative estimates (e.g. the perceived intergenerational persistence in the bottom 10% from Risks that Matter and the "get ahead in life" questions from ISSP).

Numerical questions about perceptions have two main advantages:

- First, it is easier to frame the question in a way that pre-empts any judgement about whether a disparity is "too" large.
- Secondly, they help better reflect the heterogeneity of perceptions among citizens of the same country. Answers to qualitative questions tend to bunch at certain values (e.g. "agree"), so masking a marked underlying heterogeneity across the population. When it comes to concern over income disparities, most people might agree that they are too wide in their country. Yet, in reality, the differences between what people believe the top 10%'s share of income is and what they think it should be vary widely (Chapter 4).

One way to compare countries' perceptions and conventional estimates without looking at the precise definitional difference is to use both as yardsticks to rank the countries according to whether they score high, medium, or low. Table 1.2 ranks countries using the *OECD Income Distribution Database* estimate of the richest 10%'s share of income with the average perceived share from the Risks that Matter survey. As for intergenerational persistence, it compares the country ranking according to estimated earnings elasticity between fathers and sons (available for a wide set of OECD countries) with the perceived intergenerational persistence among the poorest 10%.

The results for income inequality are broadly consistent in the countries ranked top and bottom, with the Nordic countries exhibiting relatively low levels of measured and perceived inequality, and Chile, Mexico and Turkey showing high levels. As for intergenerational persistence, the Nordic countries again score low on both counts, and Austria, Germany and Chile relatively high.

Table 2.2. Most countries rank similarly according to perceptions and conventional indicators of inequality, but for some there are important differences

	Income inequality		Intergenerational persistence	
	Estimated income share that goes to the 10% richest (IDD, latest available year)	Perceived income share that goes to the top 10% richest (RtM 2020)	Estimated intergenerational earnings elasticity (sons observed late 2000s; OECD (2018[28]))	Perceived intergenerational income persistence in the bottom 10% poorest (RtM 2020)
SVN	Low	Low	-	-
BEL	Low	Medium	Medium	Medium
NOR	Low	Low	Low	Low
EST	Low	Low	-	-
DNK	Low	Low	Low	Low
POL	Low	Low	-	-
AUT	Low	High	High	High
FIN	Low	Medium	Low	Low
NLD	Medium	Low	Medium	Medium
CAN	Medium	High	Medium	Low
DEU	Medium	Medium	High	High
GRC	Medium	High	Low	High
IRL	Medium	Medium	Medium	High
CHE	Medium	Medium	High	Medium
ESP	Medium	Medium	Low	Medium
FRA	Medium	Low	High	Medium
KOR	Medium	Medium	Medium	Medium
PRT	High	High	Medium	Medium
ITA	High	Medium	High	Low
ISR	High	Low	-	-
LTU	High	Medium	-	-
USA	High	High	Medium	Low
TUR	High	High	Low	High
MEX	High	High	-	-
CHL	High	High	High	High

Note: The countries observed are ranked low, medium or high depending on the distribution of the indicator among the countries observed; for instance, "High" for estimated top 10% income share refers to the 8 countries with the highest values. The ranking for intergenerational persistence is calculated only for those countries for which the intergenerational earnings elasticity is available in OECD (2018[28]).

Source: OECD calculations from Risks that Matter 2020; OECD IDD for top income shares, OECD (2018[28]) for intergenerational earnings elasticity.

StatLink https://stat.link/xlp07q

Nevertheless, a country's perceived and measured levels of inequality and intergenerational persistence may be very different. Some countries rank lower in perceived than conventionally measured inequality – e.g. Italy, Israel, Lithuania, France and the Netherlands – and some the other way round, such as Austria, Belgium, Canada, Finland and Greece. As for intergenerational persistence among the poorest 10%, perceptions thereof in France and Italy are lower than conventional indicators, as in Canada, Switzerland and the United States. Greece, Ireland and Turkey, however, rank higher in perceived than conventionally estimated intergenerational persistence.

Perceived top-bottom earnings ratios have grown over time

Perceived disparities as captured by the top-to-bottom earnings ratio have long increased significantly. They generally reached a peak during the global financial crisis, then fell the following decade. From the 1980s to the global financial crisis, the median perceived top-bottom earnings ratio grew in all 13 countries for which data are available (Figure 2.13 and Giger and Lascombes (2019[8])). On average, it doubled from 5 to 10 between the first ISSP wave and 2009. In the ensuing decade, though still higher than 30 years before, it fell from 10 to 8 (as ISSP 2019 shows).

Among countries observed in ISSP since 1987, the increase was especially steep in Australia (Leigh, 2013[46]) and the United States, as well as in countries transitioning to a market economy, such as Poland and Hungary. As for countries observed since 1992, the increase was marked in Germany, Italy and Slovenia. The fall since the global financial crisis has been particularly robust in Australia, where the perceived earnings disparities had reached a very high level in 2009. They have remained stable, however, in Germany and New Zealand – a possible explanation being that, in both countries, the latest ISSP survey was carried out in 2020, during the pandemic crisis.

Figure 2.13. The perceived top-bottom earnings ratio has increased over time

Median perceived top-bottom earnings ratio

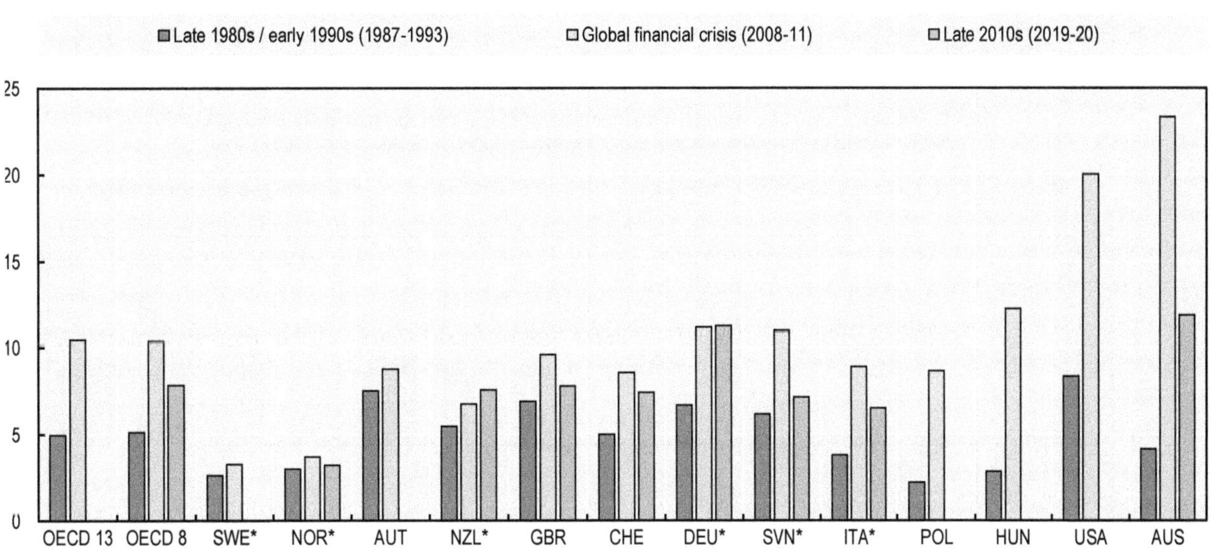

Note: Countries are ranked by the degree of change between the two periods. Only countries observed in ISSP 1987/1992 and 2009 are included, with those observed since 1992 denoted by *. The ISSP survey question refers to gross earnings in all countries, apart from Poland and Slovenia (where it refers to net earnings) and Italy (where the question was framed in gross earnings in 1992 and net earnings in 2009). In Hungary in 1987 the question did not mention gross or net earnings, perhaps because personal income tax was introduced only in 1988.
Source: OECD calculations from ISSP 1987, 1992, 2009 and 2019.

StatLink https://stat.link/aj5egb

During the last 30 years the average perception of intergenerational persistence have only mildly increased, according to the index built from qualitative answers to ISSP about parental characteristics that are important to get ahead in life (Figure 2.14, Panel A). At country level, though, the picture is varied. Between the late 1980s or early 1990s and the global financial crisis, the increase was significant in Australia, Germany, Hungary, Slovenia and the United States on both counts of parental wealth and education (Figure 2.14, Panel B). The change was also sizeable in Poland, where, however, the perceived importance of coming from a wealthy family declined. In New Zealand, Italy, Austria and Sweden, by contrast, respondents to ISSP 2009 reported that persistence was lower than in the late 1980s or early 1990s. In the decade since the global financial crisis, perceived persistence lessened in Australia, Switzerland and, to a lesser extent, in the United Kingdom. It rose in the other countries, however, particularly in New Zealand and Italy, where it more than offset the fall observed in the previous two decades.

Figure 2.14. Changes in perceived intergenerational persistence of inequality were quite heterogeneous across countries

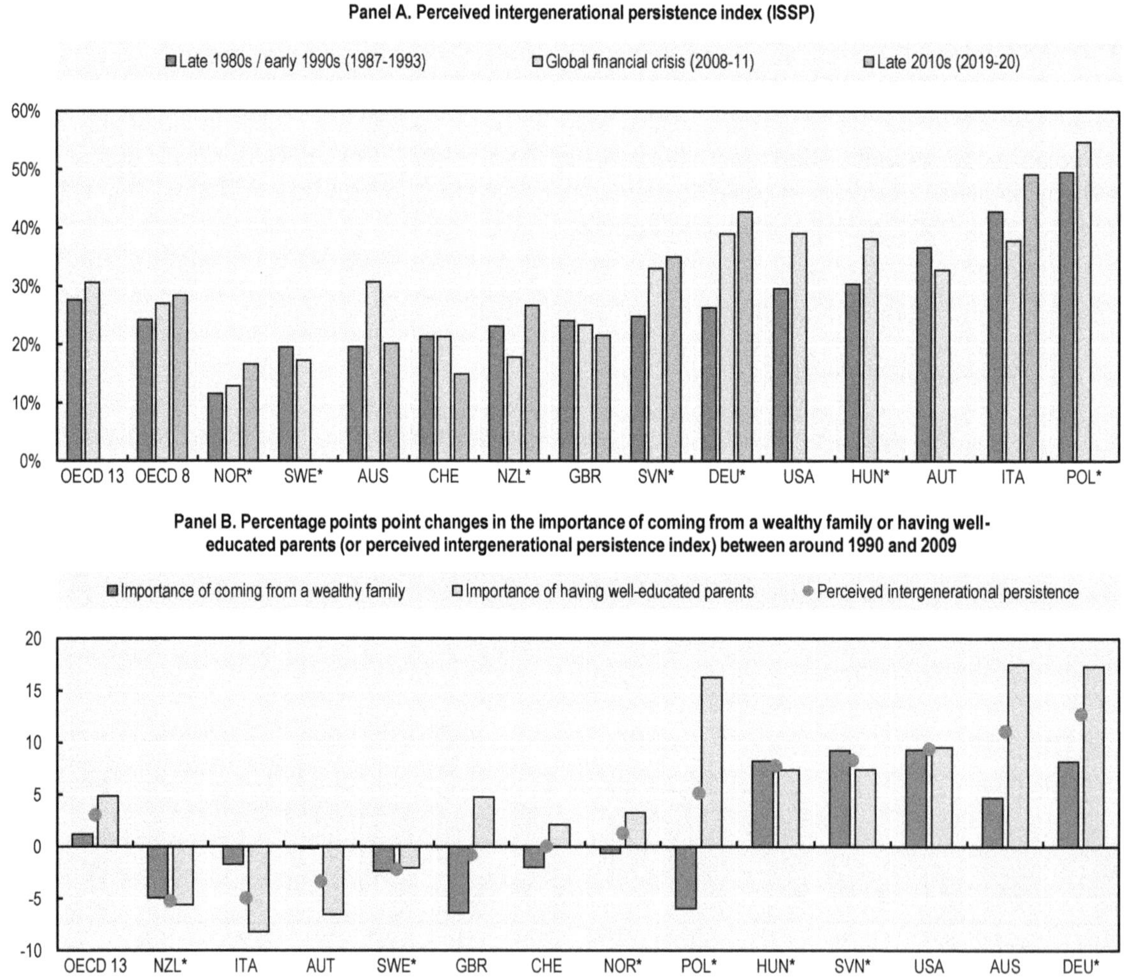

Note: Share of respondents who believe that each dimension is either very important or essential to get ahead in life. Perceived intergenerational persistence is the average of the two dimensions (because of missing values in each dimension, the index might not exactly correspond to the average of the different bars in the figure). Changes are assessed with respect to the early 90s for countries marked with *, and to the late 80s for the other countries. Differently from other figures, for Poland the initial wave is ISSP 1992 (instead of ISSP 1987) because the question on the importance of having educated parents was missing.

Source: OECD calculations on ISSP 1987, 1992, 2009 and 2019.

StatLink https://stat.link/2nzq05

The pandemic has raised awareness of economic disparities

There is evidence that the ongoing pandemic and resulting recession have brought to light pre-existing inequalities (Blundell et al., 2020[47]). People's awareness of income disparities and lack of intergenerational mobility might therefore have risen, too. Indeed, results from the Risks that Matter survey show that people who report having experienced any health or economic hardship during the COVID-19 crisis, either themselves or in their household, perceive greater inequality and intergenerational persistence than others (Table 2.3).[11] (See OECD (2021[48]) for further discussion of household insecurity during the COVID-19 crisis.) The perception is not attributable to differences in respondents' socio-economic status or demographic characteristics. Nor can it be put down to the reported changes in their households' financial situation or their country's macro-economic performance in the previous 12 months. Although people affected by COVID-19 might anyway have perceived higher levels of inequality, the impact of the pandemic and economic inequality may well have compounded those perceptions (Table 2.3).

Table 2.3. Experiencing hardship during the COVID 19 pandemic is associated with perceptions of greater income inequality and intergenerational persistence

Percentage points increase in perceptions of economic inequalities if the living conditions of the respondent or a household member changed with the pandemic

	(1)	(2)	(3)	(4)	(5)	(6)
	Perceived richest 10%'s share of income			Perceived bottom 10% intergenerational persistence		
Experienced health or economic hardship during the pandemic	2.6*** (0.4)	2.2*** (0.4)		3.1*** (0.4)	2.7*** (0.4)	
Experienced physical or mental health problems because of the pandemic			2.5*** (0.4)			2.2*** (0.4)
Experienced job-related disruption during the pandemic			-0.1 (0.4)			0.5 (0.4)
Had difficulties in making end meets during the pandemic			2.6*** (0.5)			1.1** (0.5)
Report that household financial situation worsened during the pandemic	2.2*** (0.4)	1.3*** (0.5)	0.7 (0.5)	2.1*** (0.4)	1.0** (0.5)	1.0* (0.5)
Country fixed effects	included	included	Included	included	included	included
Household and individual characteristics		included	Included		included	included
Observations	25181	24526	24526	25181	24526	24526

Note: * denotes statistically significant at the 10% level, ** at 5%, *** at 1%. Robust standard errors in brackets. The results are based on OLS regressions, including country fixed effects and weighting by sample weights (rescaled so that weights add up to 1 in each country). Household and individual characteristics include age, age2, household size, number of children and dummies for: household disposable income decile, gender, educational level, employment status, marital status, size of town (including an indicator for missing value), housing tenure, perceived changes in national economy and household finance situation with respect to the previous 12 months (on a 5 point Likert scale from much worse to much better; the much better category has been combined with better because of its small size). The regression also includes a dummy for those who opted for "I prefer not to answer" in the question about having experienced physical or mental health problems. Risks that Matter was fielded in September-October 2020.
Source: OECD calculations from Risks that Matter 2020.

StatLink https://stat.link/xqunyk

2.3. To what extent do people tolerate inequality

Preferred economic disparities are lower and more homogeneous across countries

In all countries, what people think economic disparities should be (i.e. "prefer") is considerably lower than what they perceive. In all the OECD and EU countries covered by ISSP 2009, the median preferred top-bottom earnings ratio – what people think earnings should be – is less than half of the ratio they perceive: 4 rather than 9 (Figure 2.15). Similarly, the Compare Your Income web tool shows that, in the OECD countries for which data are available, the preferred income share of the richest 10% is around 20 percentage points lower on average than the perceived level (Balestra and Cohen, 2021[41]).[12]

Figure 2.15. Perceived inequalities in economic outcomes are much greater than preferred ones

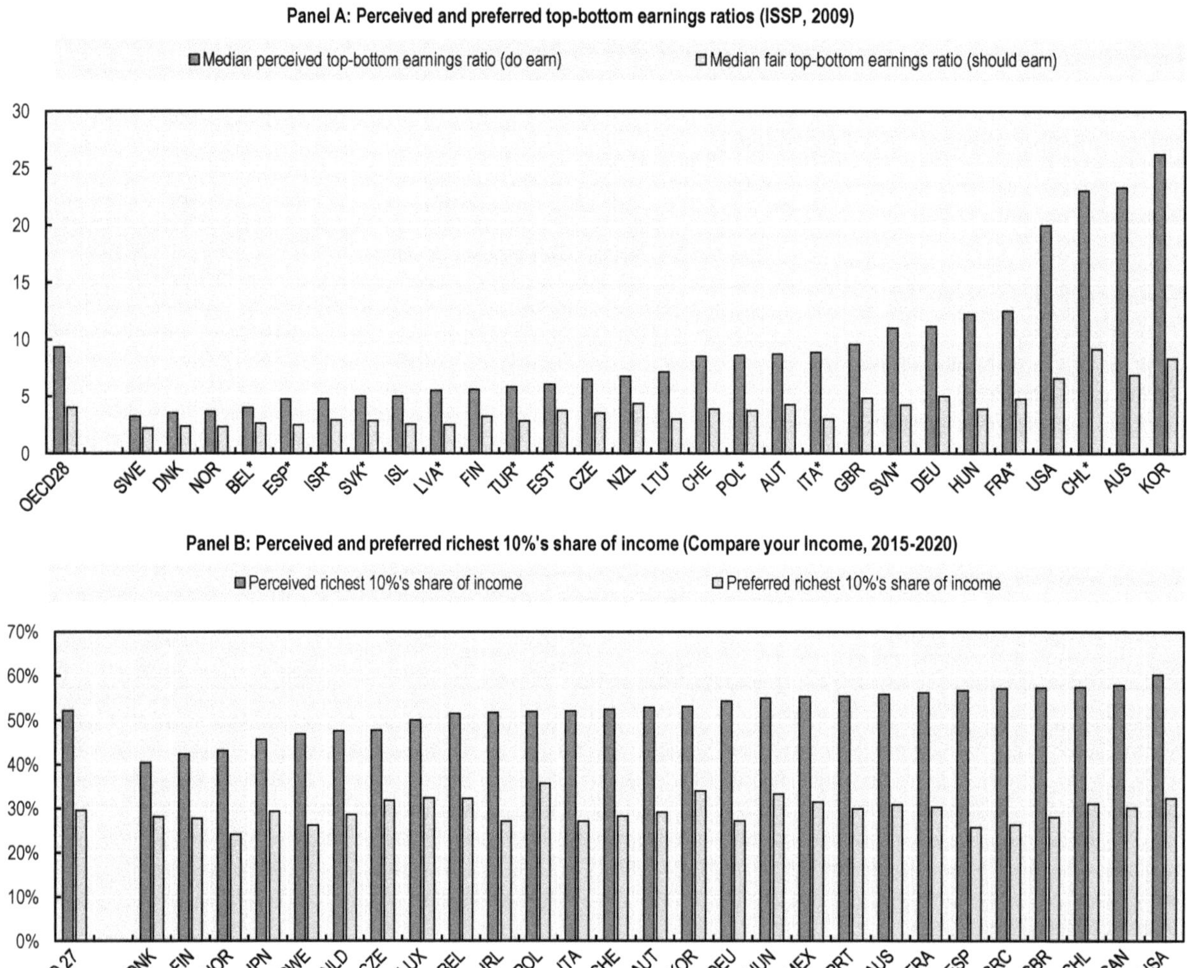

Note: In Panel A, countries denoted by * collect post-tax perceived/preferred earnings data, while others collect before-tax perceived/preferred earnings data.
Source: International Social Survey Programme (ISSP) 2009 (Panel A); Compare Your Income, 2015-2020 (up to May 2020; Panel B).

StatLink https://stat.link/yti0zx

Preferred levels of inequality, in both earnings and income, are also more homogeneous across countries than perceived levels. The preferred top-bottom earnings ratio ranges from 2 in Sweden to 9 in Chile, compared to 3 and 20 respectively in perceived levels. The preferred income share of the richest 10% is lowest in Norway at 24%, and highest in Poland with 36%, while perceived shares vary from 40% to 60%. Most people actually accept some degree of inequality. Indeed, the median "should-be" earnings ratio is always far from 1, and the average preferred income share of the richest 10% is consistently larger than its equality value (i.e. 10%).

Preferred earnings disparities are larger in more unequal countries

A possible explanation for the weak correlation between concern over income disparities and conventional measures thereof (Figure 2.4) is that people in countries with greater inequality tend to be more tolerant of it.[13]

Evidence from preferred top-bottom earnings ratios lends support to this hypothesis (Figure 2.16). In countries where gross earnings disparities are greater, so are preferred disparities (as measured in ISSP surveys). Australia and the United States are cases in point. The median respondents in both countries not only perceive high top-bottom earnings ratios – 23 in Australia and 20 in the United States in ISSP 2009, compared to the OECD average of 9. They also prefer them – with ratios of nearly 7 versus the OECD average of 4.

The hypothesis, by contrast, is not supported by evidence from the Compare Your Income webtool. It finds that the preferred income shares of the richest 10% are no higher in high-inequality countries. One possible explanation of the contrasting evidence for and against the hypothesis is that people are more willing to accept higher earnings disparities (as the ISSP surveys show) rather than household income difference (as in the Compare Your Income data) so they adapt their preferences more easily to actual levels. Indeed, preferences might be more homogeneous with respect to disparities in household income, which takes account of taxes and transfers.

Figure 2.16. Preferred income and earnings disparities are higher in countries that are more unequal when it comes to earnings but not income

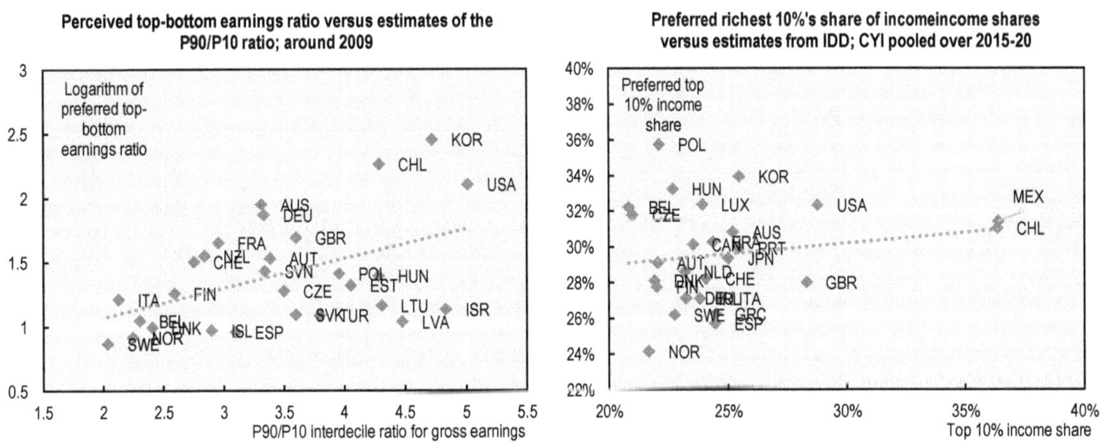

Source: International Social Survey Programme (ISSP) 2009 for preferred top-bottom earnings ratio; Compare Your Income 2015-20 for preferred richest 10%'s share of income; *OECD Earnings Database* for the P90/P10 interdecile ratio for gross earnings; *OECD Income Distribution Database* (averaged across available years from 2015) for the richest 10%'s share of income.

StatLink https://stat.link/nizg6t

Another interpretation is that people build their notion of a preferred top-bottom earnings ratio in relation to what they believe is the current level (Osberg and Smeeding, 2006[49]; Pedersen and Mutz, 2018[50]), as confirmed by the close correlation between the logarithms of perceived and preferred ratios at the individual level (0.69 within the 2009 ISSP wave).[14] The same does not apply to perceived and preferred income shares of the richest 10%, which are almost uncorrelated at the individual level in the Compare Your Income data. Correlation may be so weak because respondents' view the richest 10%'s income share as a more distant concept, since they seldom think of themselves as belonging to the richest 10% (Balestra and Cohen, 2021[41]). Respondents are, therefore, more likely to think about the preferred richest 10%'s share of income from a purely altruistic point of view, even if they are part (or may be part in the future) of that group. As a result, answers are more homogeneous and closer to an "idealistic" setting.

Preferred earnings disparities have increased over time

Between the late 1980s and the global financial crisis preferred disparities increased, but by less than perceived disparities (Figure 2.17), so only partly counteracting them. The gaps between preferred and perceived top-bottom earnings ratios is a measure of concern over earnings disparities, because it captures the tension between what people perceive and what they would be willing to accept. In line with Schneider (2011[51]), this gap is calculated as the logarithmic difference between the two ratios, or as the ratio of ratios. Changes in the gap may be attributed to rises in perceived ratios or to increases in preferred ratios (Figure 2.18, Panel A).

Figure 2.17. The preferred top-bottom earnings ratio has increased over time, though less than the perceived ratio

Changes in the median value of perceived and preferred top-bottom earnings ratios

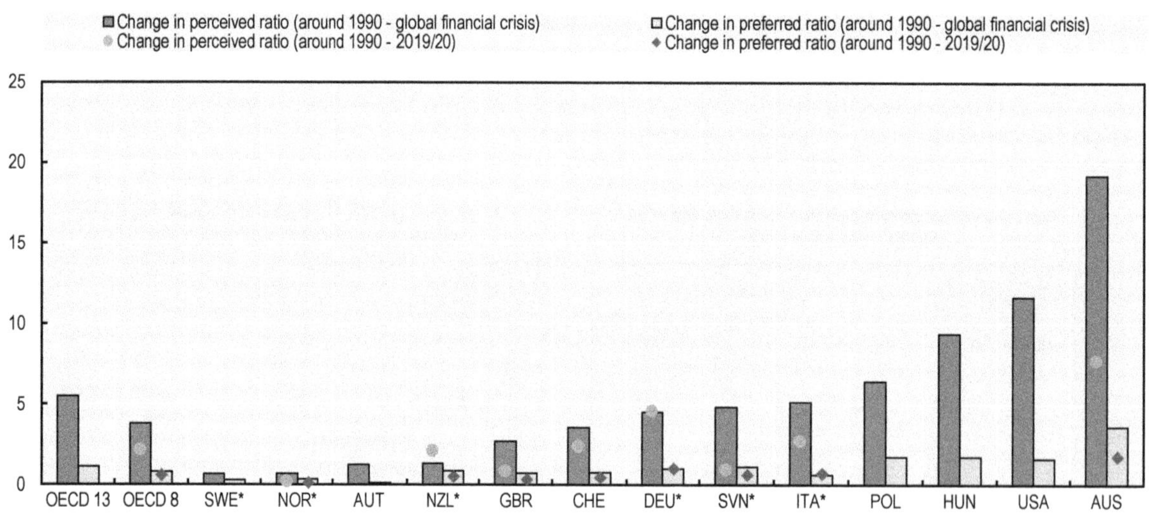

Note: Countries marked denoted by * were surveyed between ISSP 1992 and 2009, and the others between 1987 and 2009.
Source: International Social Survey Programme (ISSP) 1987, 1992, 2009, 2019.

StatLink https://stat.link/2w7pda

Figure 2.18. Over time, the growing preference for higher earnings disparities has only partially offset perceptions of greater disparities

How perceived and preferred earnings ratios contribute individually to overall changes in the gap between them

Panel a. Changes between the Late 1980s / Early 1990s and the global financial crisis

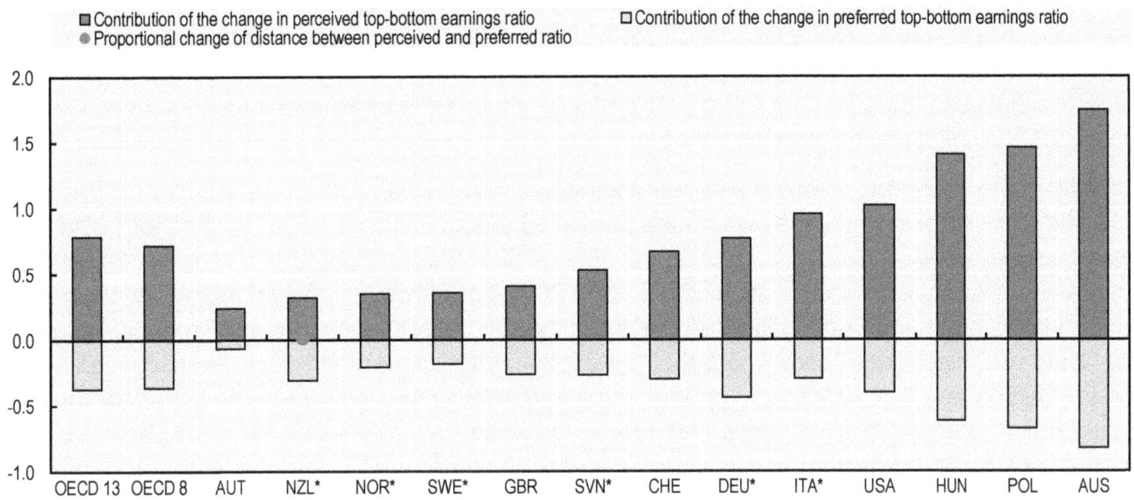

Panel b. Changes between the global financial crisis and 2019/20

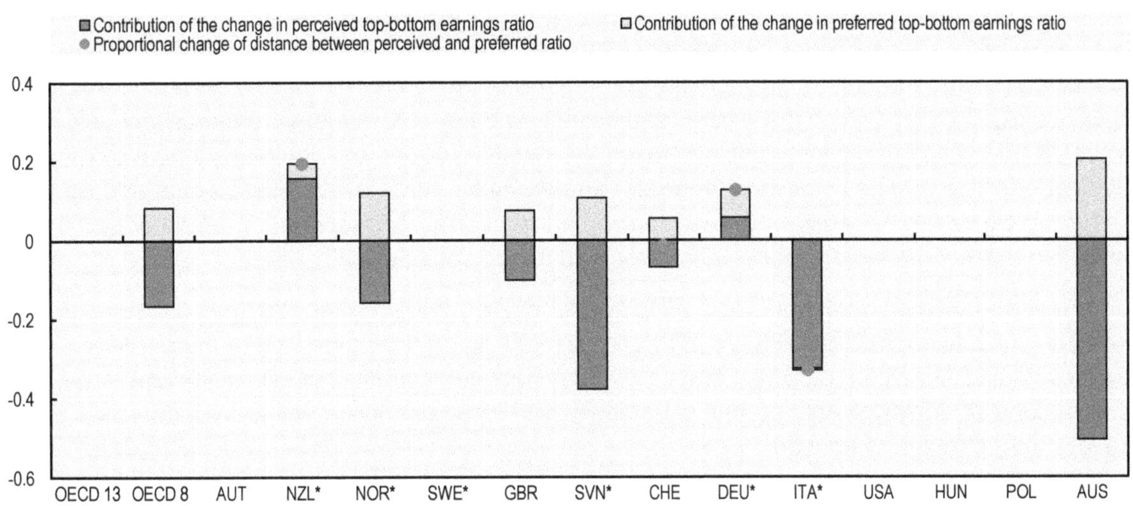

Note: Reading note: between the late 80s and the global financial crisis in Australia the average logarithm of the perceived top-bottom earnings ratio increased by 1.75 (which implies a growth of around 4.7 times of the average perceived ratio), while the average logarithm of the perceived ratio increased by 0.8 (implying 1.3 times for the average perceived ratio); as a result the distance between the perceived and preferred ratios increased by 0.9 in logs (or by 1.5 times in the original scale). These changes correspond only broadly to what is observed in Figure 2.17, as the Figure shows the average logarithms, while Figure 2.17 plots the median of the ratio in its original scale. The logarithmic change is used to approximate the proportional change in the variables and to simplify the decomposition into the two components (beliefs and preferences). Countries marked with * are observed since ISSP 1992, while the others since ISSP 1987.
Source: OECD calculations from ISSP 1987, 1992, 2009 and 2019.

StatLink https://stat.link/2nkux7

Although perceived ratios grew in most countries, so did acceptable levels of disparities. As a result, people's concern over earnings disparities has been weakened by the change in preferences. In fact, if preferred earnings disparities had not increased, the average increase in the gap between perceived and preferred disparities in OECD countries would have been almost twice as large. This offsetting effect has been particularly strong in Australia, but also in Poland and Hungary, countries which started from very low acceptance of wide earnings disparities – in the late 1980s, median ratios were 2/1 and 2/2, respectively (similar to Norway and Sweden in the early 1990s).

In the decade following the global financial crisis there was a slight dip in the preferred top-bottom earnings ratio in most of the countries observed by ISSP up to 2019 (Figure 2.18, Panel B). In Norway, Switzerland and the United Kingdom, the fall compensated for the fall in the perceived ratio and, to a lesser degree in Australia, Italy and Slovenia. However, only in Slovenia did the gap between perceived and preferred earnings disparities fall to the levels of the early 1990s. Finally, in New Zealand and Germany, where the latest ISSP wave was conducted during the COVID-19 pandemic, preferred earnings disparities fell while perceived ones rose, so spelling growing concern.

The increase in the preferred magnitude of earnings disparities between the late 1980s and the global financial crisis was steeper in countries where the perceived extent of disparities grew the most. This trend may reflect "adaptive preferences" – as people become accustomed to living in a less equal society they show increasing tolerance of it (Benabou and Tirole, 2006[52]). However, the change over time in the preferred top-bottom earnings ratio might also be explained by the tendency of respondents to build their notion of "preferred" disparities according to their perceptions of income differences, as discussed above. Although the evidence is not sufficient to choose one explanation over the other, it is important to stress that perceptions of greater earnings disparities tend to be offset by preferences for them, which yields a less pronounced rise in concern over earnings disparities. There is also some evidence from in-survey experiments in Sweden and the United States that people adapt their preferences to information that current levels of inequality are high (Trump, 2018[14]). The evidence to that effect, however, is still limited.[15]

Preferred levels of earnings and income disparities may also have increased because of the spread of the belief that hard work, rather than luck or personal circumstances, is what matters for getting ahead in life (Mijs, 2019[22]). And such beliefs might actually self-reinforce over time. Indeed, Alesina and Angeletos (2005[53]) propose a model in which the widespread belief that hard work matters more than luck might give rise to a society in which both redistribution and taxes are low. Such a society would enshrine the conviction that individual effort determines individual success, and the initial meritocratic belief would end up being proved correct by reality (Piketty, 1995[54]). Initial international differences in meritocratic beliefs, attributable, for instance, to history, could ultimately lead to two societies with different welfare regimes.

Beliefs in the importance of hard work for getting ahead in life grew in most countries between the late 1980s and the global financial crisis (Figure 2.19 and Mijs (2019[22])). However, unlike the prediction of the model by Alesina and Angeletos (2005[53]) that differences between countries would widen over time, there were in fact signs of convergence, as the countries which changed the most were those that initially assigned less importance to hard work.

Between 2010 and 2019, however, the perceived importance of hard work seems to have fallen back, according to country data available in ISSP 2019. Its average level is once again what is was in the late 1980s and early 1990s. This can partially explain the limited extent of the fall in concern over income and earnings disparities since the global financial crisis, even though the perceived top-bottom earnings ratio has shrunk.

Figure 2.19. The belief in hard work for getting ahead in life grew in the two decades up to the global financial crisis

Share of respondents who believe that hard work is very important or essential for getting ahead in life

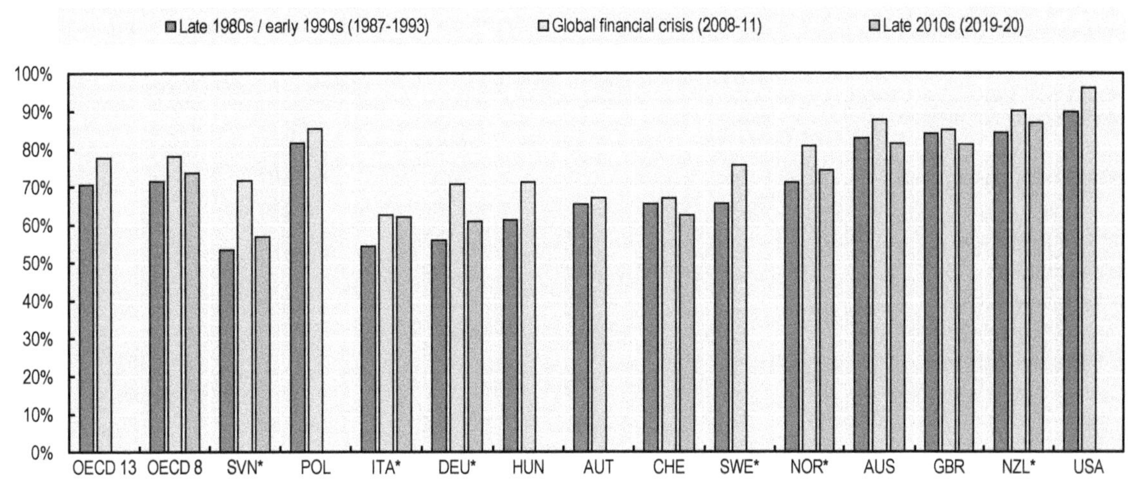

Source: International Social Survey Programme (ISSP) 1987, 1992, 2009 and 2019.

StatLink https://stat.link/j8n065

Round-up: Perceptions of wider disparities explain to a large extent the increase in concern

There are important cross-country differences in both levels of and changes in concern over income disparities. To explain them, it is crucial to disentangle the influence of perceived and preferred disparities in outcomes (such as earnings), perceived intergenerational persistence, and beliefs in the importance of hard work for getting ahead in life.

Columns 1-3 in Table 2.4 show that greater perceived earnings disparities increase concern over income disparities, while greater preferred disparities reduce them. The belief that parental characteristics matter for getting ahead in life increases concern over income disparities, while the importance of hard work has the opposite effect. Importantly, the literature on experimental surveys confirms the role of all those factors. Information-related experiments endorse the importance of perceptions of economic disparities and intergenerational persistence (Box 2.1), while laboratory experiments confirm the importance of belief in hard work (Durante, Putterman and van der Weele, 2014[55]; Almås, Cappelen and Tungodden, 2020[23]).

Table 2.4. Concern over income disparities depends on combinations of both perceptions and preferences

Percentage point increase in the share of respondents who strongly agree that income disparities are too wide, associated with 1% (or 1 percentage point increase) for different factors

	(1)	(2)	(3)	(4)	(5)	(6)
	Cross-country regression, 2009 wave			Country fixed effect regression, 1987-2019		
Perceived top-bottom earnings ratio	0.432**		0.296*	0.382***		0.448***
	(0.173)		(0.164)	(0.0642)		(0.0778)
Preferred top-bottom earnings ratio	-0.594**		-0.428*	-0.465***		-0.534***
	(0.214)		(0.213)	(0.103)		(0.124)
Perceived intergenerational persistence index		0.711***	0.613**			
		(0.202)	(0.236)			
Fraction that believe that hard work matters to get ahead in life		-0.441	-0.441*			
		(0.266)	(0.248)			
Fraction that believe that hard work matters to get ahead in life					0.258	-0.410
					(0.233)	(0.238)
Observations	28	30	28	62	80	62
Countries				21	25	21

Note: *** denotes statistically significant at the 1% level; ** 5%; * 10%. Country level regressions.
Source: OECD calculation from ISSP 1987, 1992, 1999, 2009, 2019.

StatLink https://stat.link/15be6x

The most relevant factor in the rise in concern over income disparities between the late 1980s and the global financial crisis was the growing gap between perceived and preferred earnings disparities. Panel A in Figure 2.20 proposes a simple descriptive assessment of the relative importance of the different factors in explaining changes over time in concern over income disparities:[16]

- the gap between perceived and preferred earnings disparities,
- perceived intergenerational persistence,
- belief in hard work.

The growing gap between perceived and preferred earnings disparities plays a significant role in most countries.[17] By contrast, changing perceptions of intergenerational persistence has little impact in most countries (save for Australia, Germany, Slovenia and the United States). Finally, the rise in the perceived importance of hard work reduced concern in all countries, although only to a limited extent in some.

In the decade from 2010 to 2019 (Panel B), the decline of the perceived importance of hard work in all countries save Italy led to rising concern. The contribution of perceived intergenerational persistence was again heterogeneous and, on average, quite small. In Germany and New Zealand, where the last ISSP wave was fielded during the COVID-19 pandemic, all three factors contributed positively to concern over income disparities.

Figure 2.20. Long run changes in concerns about economic disparities have been mostly influenced by the larger gap between perceived and preferred earnings disparities

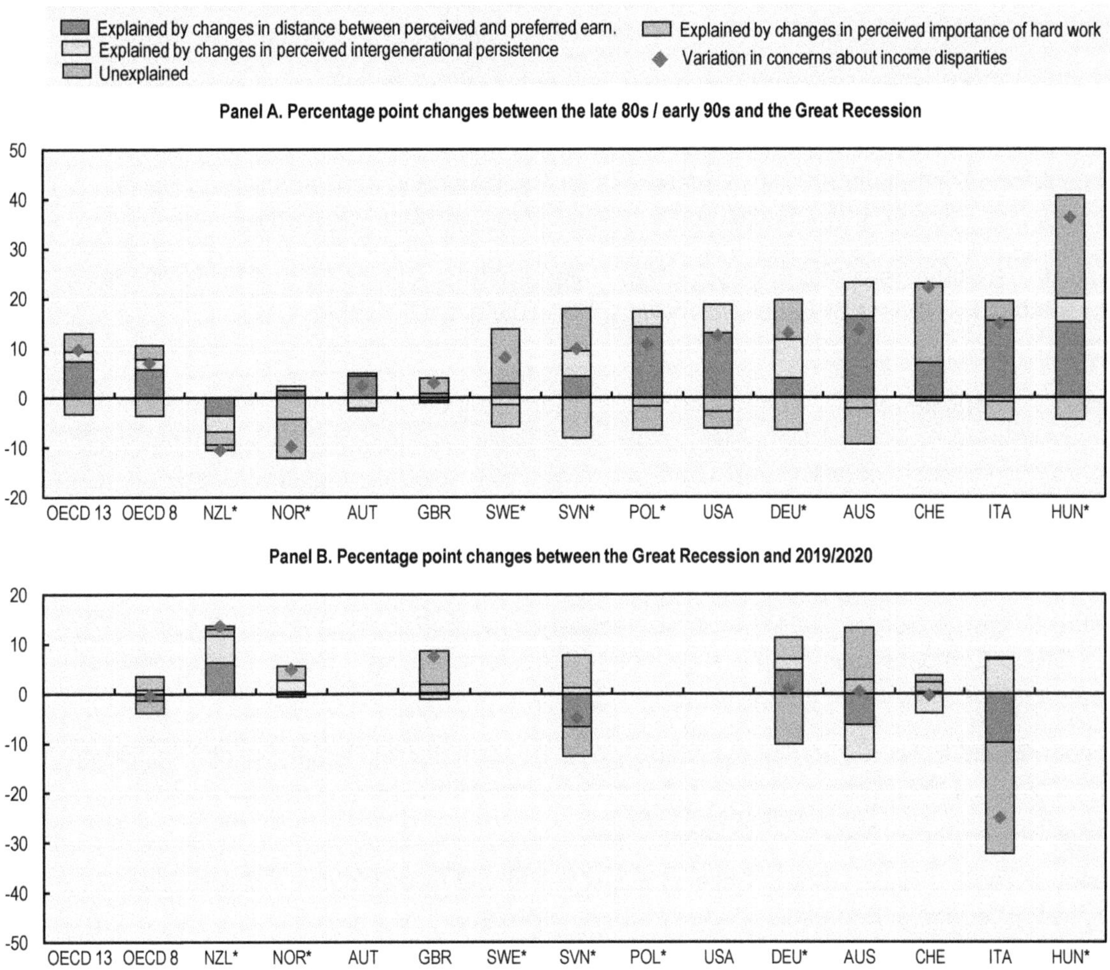

Note: Concerns refer to income disparities, while perceived and preferred refer to earnings disparities. The decomposition is calculated using the coefficients from column (3), Table 2.4. For Poland, all changes refers to the difference between ISSP 1992 and ISSP 2009, while the change in the top-bottom earnings ratio uses ISSP 1987 as initial wave (ISSP 1992 cannot be used because it is the only wave in which it refers to gross earnings). Countries marked with * are observed between 1992 and 2009, while the others between 1987 and 2009
Source: International Social Survey Programme (ISSP) 1987, 1992, 2009 and 2019.

StatLink https://stat.link/ctal4f

References

Acciari, P., A. Polo and G. Violante (2019), *"And Yet It Moves": Intergenerational Mobility in Italy*, National Bureau of Economic Research, Cambridge, MA, http://dx.doi.org/10.3386/w25732. [39]

Alesina, A. and G. Angeletos (2005), "Fairness and Redistribution", *American Economic Review*, Vol. 95/4, pp. 960-980, http://dx.doi.org/10.1257/0002828054825655. [53]

Alesina, A. and P. Giuliano (2011), "Preferences for Redistribution", in *Handbook of Social Economics*, Elsevier, http://dx.doi.org/10.1016/b978-0-444-53187-2.00004-8. [16]

Alesina, A., S. Stantcheva and E. Teso (2018), "Intergenerational Mobility and Preferences for Redistribution", *American Economic Review*, Vol. 108/2, pp. 521-554, http://dx.doi.org/10.1257/aer.20162015. [30]

Almås, I., A. Cappelen and B. Tungodden (2020), "Cutthroat Capitalism versus Cuddly Socialism: Are Americans More Meritocratic and Efficiency-Seeking than Scandinavians?", *Journal of Political Economy*, Vol. 128/5, pp. 1753-1788, http://dx.doi.org/10.1086/705551. [23]

Ariely, D. and M. Norton (2013), "American's desire for less wealth inequality does not depend on how you ask them", *Judgment and Decision Making*, Vol. 8/3, pp. 393-394. [44]

Balestra, C. and G. Cohen (2021), "Income Inequality through People's Lenses: Evidence from the OECD Compare your Income Web-tool, *, Paris, forthcoming.", *OECD Papers on Well-being and Inequalities*, forthcoming. [41]

Benabou, R. and E. Ok (2001), "Social Mobility and the Demand for Redistribution: The Poum Hypothesis", *The Quarterly Journal of Economics*, Vol. 116/2, pp. 447-487, http://dx.doi.org/10.1162/00335530151144078. [27]

Benabou, R. and J. Tirole (2006), "Belief in a Just World and Redistributive Politics", *The Quarterly Journal of Economics*, Vol. 121/2, pp. 699-746, http://dx.doi.org/10.1162/qjec.2006.121.2.699. [52]

Benson, R. et al. (2021), *Attituted to inequalities*, Institute for Fiscal Studies, https://ifs.org.uk/inequality/attitudes-to-inequalities/. [24]

Blundell, R. et al. (2020), "COVID-19 and Inequalities", *Fiscal Studies*, Vol. 41/2, pp. 291-319, http://dx.doi.org/10.1111/1475-5890.12232. [47]

Browman, A., M. Destin and D. Miele (2020), "The Perception of Economic Inequality Weakens Americans' Beliefs in Both Upward and Downward Socioeconomic Mobility", *Mimeo*. [33]

Brunori, P. (2017), "The Perception of Inequality of Opportunity in Europe", *Review of Income and Wealth*, Vol. 63/3, pp. 464-491, http://dx.doi.org/10.1111/roiw.12259. [31]

Bussolo, M. et al. (2019), "I Perceive therefore I Demand: The Formation of Inequality Perceptions and Demand for Redistribution", *Policy Research working paper*, No. WPS 8929, World Bank Group, Washington, D.C. [2]

Campos-Vazquez, R. et al. (2020), "Perception of inequality and social mobility in Mexico", *AFD Research papers*. [62]

Cansunar, A. (2018), "Redistribution by the Rich: Information, Perceptions, and Preferences", *Duke University, PhD Dissertation*. [60]

Chambers, J., L. Swan and M. Heesacker (2015), "Perceptions of U.S. Social Mobility Are Divided (and Distorted) Along Ideological Lines", *Psychological Science*, Vol. 26/4, pp. 413-423, http://dx.doi.org/10.1177/0956797614566657. [59]

Cheng, S. and F. Wen (2019), "Americans overestimate the intergenerational persistence in income ranks", *Proceedings of the National Academy of Sciences*, Vol. 116/28, pp. 13909-13914, http://dx.doi.org/10.1073/pnas.1814688116. [63]

Chetty, R. et al. (2014), "Where is the land of Opportunity? The Geography of Intergenerational Mobility in the United States *", *The Quarterly Journal of Economics*, Vol. 129/4, pp. 1553-1623, http://dx.doi.org/10.1093/qje/qju022. [29]

Ciani, E., L. Fréget and T. Manfredi (forthcoming), "Learning about inequality and preferences for redistribution: A meta-analysis of in-survey informational experiments". [37]

Ciani, E. et al. (2021), "Perceptions of inequality across OECD and EU countries: Long term trends and recent evidence", *OECD WISE Working Paper series* No. 2. [1]

Clark, A. and C. D'Ambrosio (2015), "Attitudes to Income Inequality", in *Handbook of Income Distribution*, Elsevier, http://dx.doi.org/10.1016/b978-0-444-59428-0.00014-x. [20]

Colagrossi, M., S. Karagiannis and R. Raab (2019), "The Median Voter Takes it All: Preferences for Redistribution and Income Inequality in the EU-28", *Publications Office of the European Union*, No. 2019/6, http://dx.doi.org/doi:10.2760/797251. [7]

Daniels, J. and M. Wang (2019), "What do you think? Success: is it luck or is it hard work?", *Applied Economics Letters*, Vol. 26/21, pp. 1734-1738, http://dx.doi.org/10.1080/13504851.2019.1593930. [21]

Davidai, S. (2018), "Why do Americans believe in economic mobility? Economic inequality, external attributions of wealth and poverty, and the belief in economic mobility", *Journal of Experimental Social Psychology*, Vol. 79, pp. 138-148, http://dx.doi.org/10.1016/j.jesp.2018.07.012. [32]

Davidai, S. and T. Gilovich (2015), "Building a More Mobile America—One Income Quintile at a Time", *Perspectives on Psychological Science*, Vol. 10/1, pp. 60-71, http://dx.doi.org/10.1177/1745691614562005. [58]

Domènech-Arumí, G. (2021), "Neighborhoods, Perceived Inequality, and Preferences for Redistribution: Evidence from Barcelona", *mimeo*, https://sites.google.com/site/domenechweb/jmp. [36]

Durante, R., L. Putterman and J. van der Weele (2014), "Preferences for Redistribution and Perception of Fairness: An Experimental Study", *Journal of the European Economic Association*, Vol. 12/4, pp. 1059-1086, http://dx.doi.org/10.1111/jeea.12082. [55]

Eriksson, K. and B. Simpson (2012), "What do Americans know about inequality? It depends on how you ask them", *Judgement and Decision Making*, Vol. 7/6, pp. 741-745. [43]

Fisman, R., I. Kuziemko and S. Vannutelli (2020), “Distributional Preferences in Larger Groups: Keeping up with the Joneses and Keeping Track of the Tails”, *Journal of the European Economic Association*, http://dx.doi.org/10.1093/jeea/jvaa033. [13]

Fong, C. (2001), *Social preferences, self-interest, and the demand for redistribution*, http://www.elsevier.nl/locate/econbase. [18]

Franko, W. (2017), “Understanding Public Perceptions of Growing Economic Inequality”, *State Politics & Policy Quarterly*, Vol. 17/3, pp. 319-348, http://dx.doi.org/10.1177/1532440017707799. [11]

Garret, C. and H. Day (2021), *Perceptions of Inequality in the UK*, Institute of Fiscal Studies, https://ifs.org.uk/inequality/perceptions-of-inequality-in-the-uk-quantitative-survey-for-the-ifs-deaton-review/. [25]

Giger, N. and D. Lascombes (2019), “Growing income inequality, growing legitimacy: A longitudinal approach to perceptions of inequality”, *Unequal Democracies Working Paper*, No. 11, University of Geneva. [8]

Gimpelson, V. and D. Treisman (2018), “Misperceiving inequality”, *Economics and Politics*, Vol. 30/1, pp. 27-54, http://dx.doi.org/10.1111/ecpo.12103. [3]

Hoy, C. and F. Mager (2020), “American Exceptionalism? Differences in the Elasticity of Preferences for Redistribution between the United States and Western Europe”, *ECINEQ Working Paper*. [38]

Jachimowicz, J. et al. (2020), *Inequality in Researchers’ Minds: Four Guiding Questions for Studying Subjective Perceptions of Economic Inequality*, Center for Open Science, http://dx.doi.org/10.31234/osf.io/gn2z5. [42]

Karayel, A. (2015), “Income Inequality Tolerance and Preferences for Redistribution in Turkey”, *European Journal of Economics and Business Studies*, Vol. 1/3, pp. 98-105, http://journals.euser.org/index.php/ejes/article/view/492 (accessed on 7 February 2021). [19]

Kenworthy, L. and L. Mccall (2008), “Inequality, public opinion and redistribution”, *Socio-Economic Review*, Vol. 6/1, pp. 35-68, http://dx.doi.org/10.1093/ser/mwm006. [61]

Kerr, W. (2014), “Income inequality and social preferences for redistribution and compensation differentials”, *Journal of Monetary Economics*, Vol. 66, pp. 62-78, http://dx.doi.org/10.1016/j.jmoneco.2014.03.002. [4]

Kuhn, A. (2019), “The individual (mis-)perception of wage inequality: measurement, correlates and implications”, *Empirical Economics*, http://dx.doi.org/10.1007/s00181-019-01722-4. [6]

Leigh, A. (2013), *Battlers and Billionaires: The Story of Inequality in Australia*, Black Inc. [46]

Lupu, N. and J. Pontusson (2011), “The Structure of Inequality and the Politics of Redistribution”, *American Political Science Review*, Vol. 105/2, pp. 316-336, http://dx.doi.org/10.1017/s0003055411000128. [12]

Macdonald, D. (2019), “Trust in Government and the American Public’s Responsiveness to Rising Inequality”, *Political Research Quarterly*, Vol. 73/4, pp. 790-804, http://dx.doi.org/10.1177/1065912919856110. [26]

McCall, L. et al. (2017), "Exposure to rising inequality shapes Americans' opportunity beliefs and policy support", *Proceedings of the National Academy of Sciences*, Vol. 114/36, pp. 9593-9598, http://dx.doi.org/10.1073/pnas.1706253114. [5]

Meltzer, A. and S. Richard (1981), "A Rational Theory of the Size of Government", *Journal of Political Economy*, Vol. 89/5, http://dx.doi.org/10.1086/261013. [17]

Mijs, J. (2019), "The paradox of inequality: income inequality and belief in meritocracy go hand in hand", *Socio-Economic Review*, http://dx.doi.org/10.1093/ser/mwy051. [22]

Newman, B., S. Shah and E. Lauterbach (2018), "Who sees an hourglass? Assessing citizens' perception of local economic inequality", *Research & Politics*, Vol. 5/3, p. 205316801879397, http://dx.doi.org/10.1177/2053168018793974. [10]

Norton, M. and D. Ariely (2011), "Building a Better America—One Wealth Quintile at a Time", *Perspectives on Psychological Science*, Vol. 6/1, pp. 9-12, http://dx.doi.org/10.1177/1745691610393524. [57]

OECD (2021), *Main Findings from the 2020 Risks that Matter Survey*, OECD publishing, https://doi.org/10.1787/b9e85cf5-en. [48]

OECD (2021), *The impact of shifting demographic and family structures on inequality and its policy implications.* [56]

OECD (2018), *A Broken Social Elevator? How to Promote Social Mobility*, OECD Publishing, Paris, https://dx.doi.org/10.1787/9789264301085-en. [28]

Osberg, L. and T. Smeeding (2006), ""Fair" Inequality? Attitudes toward Pay Differentials: The United States in Comparative Perspective", *American Sociological Review*, Vol. 71/3, pp. 450-473, http://dx.doi.org/10.1177/000312240607100305. [49]

Pedersen, R. and D. Mutz (2018), "Attitudes Toward Economic Inequality: The Illusory Agreement", *Political Science Research and Methods*, Vol. 7/04, pp. 835-851, http://dx.doi.org/10.1017/psrm.2018.18. [50]

Phillips, L. et al. (2020), *Inequality in People's Minds*, Center for Open Science, http://dx.doi.org/10.31234/osf.io/vawh9. [40]

Piketty, T. (1995), "Social Mobility and Redistributive Politics", *The Quarterly Journal of Economics*, Vol. 110/3, pp. 551-584, http://dx.doi.org/10.2307/2946692. [54]

Roth, C. and J. Wohlfart (2018), "Experienced inequality and preferences for redistribution", *Journal of Public Economics*, Vol. 167, pp. 251-262, http://dx.doi.org/10.1016/j.jpubeco.2018.09.012. [35]

Rueda, D. and D. Stegmueller (2020), "Preferences that Matter: Inequality, Redistribution and Voting", *mimeo*. [15]

Schneider, S. (2011), "Income Inequality and its Consequences for Life Satisfaction: What Role do Social Cognitions Play?", *Social Indicators Research*, Vol. 106/3, pp. 419-438, http://dx.doi.org/10.1007/s11205-011-9816-7. [51]

Shariff, A., Wiwad D and L. Aknin (2016), "Income Mobility Breeds Tolerance for Income Inequality: Cross-National and Experimental Evidence", *Perspectives on Psychological Science*, Vol. 11/3, pp. 373-380. [34]

Swan, L. et al. (2017), "How should we measure Americans' perceptions of socio-economic mobility?", *Judgment and Decision Making*, Vol. 12/5. [45]

Trump, K. (2018), "Income Inequality Influences Perceptions of Legitimate Income Differences", *British Journal of Political Science*, Vol. 48/4, pp. 929-952, http://dx.doi.org/10.1017/S0007123416000326. [14]

Xu, P. and J. Garand (2010), "Economic Context and Americans' Perceptions of Income Inequality*", *Social Science Quarterly*, Vol. 91/5, pp. 1220-1241, http://dx.doi.org/10.1111/j.1540-6237.2010.00729.x. [9]

Annex 2.A. Data sources

International Social Survey Programme

The ISSP is a long-standing survey that focuses on social topics. It collects the perceptions and opinions of a representative sample of respondents in a wide set of countries. Each year it addresses a specific subject. The Social Inequality module has been conducted in waves in 1987, 1992, 1999 and 2009. It is fielded by local ISSP committees on a representative sample of a country's population. The year of the survey varies from country to country, but is usually within 2 years of the "module year" – e.g. 2008-11 for the 2009 module. The 2017 module, which addressed social networks, also included questions on income disparities and preferences for redistribution, but not all the other variables appear in this report. The main variables which do appear are consistent throughout the different years and across different countries. There are some exceptions, such as perceived and preferred earnings for different professions, discussed in the relevant sections of this report.

Eurobarometer 471/2017

The Eurobarometer is a survey carried out on an annual basis to monitor public opinion in European member and candidate countries. It comprises a standard part and a special-issue part. The special Eurobarometer 471/2017 focused on "Fairness, inequality and intergenerational mobility". It surveyed the population aged 15 or older in the 28 member states, with a sample of around 1 000 respondents per country.

Risks that Matter

The OECD Risks that Matter (RtM) survey is a cross-national survey that examines people's perceptions of social and economic risks and how well they think government addresses those risks. The survey was conducted for the first time in two waves in the spring and autumn of 2018. The 2020 survey, conducted in September-October 2020, draws on a representative sample of over 25 000 people aged 18-64 years old in 25 OECD countries.

Consistent with other surveys, RtM is implemented online by Respondi Limited using samples recruited online and over the phone. Respondents are paid a nominal sum (around EUR 1 or EUR 2 per survey). Sampling is based on a modified form of quota sampling with sex, age group, education level, income level, and employment status (in the last quarter of 2019) used as the sampling criteria. Survey weights are used to correct for any under- or over-representation based on the five criteria. The target and weighted sample is 1 000 respondents per country.

Compare Your Income

Compare your income (CYI, www.compareyourincome.org) is a webtool developed by the OECD to give users in OECD countries the opportunity to compare their perceptions of income inequality with statistics on the subject from the *Income Distribution Database*. To start, people are asked to provide some basic socio-demographic information on their gender, country of residence, age, household size and household net income. Then, they are asked where they think they fit in their country's income distribution and what minimum income they would need in order to not be considered "poor". There is also a question on how they think their country's population is distributed according to income level and how they would like it to look if it was up to them. In addition to these questions, following a modular approach, short ad hoc modules focusing on specific inequality-related issues were added to the survey over the course of the years.

To mitigate the non-representativeness of the CYI samples and achieve more accurate estimates, a weighting scheme was developed. This allowed to balance out and compensate for over- and under-representation of some population groups, in the sample and between countries (for more details, see Balestra and Cohen (2021[41])). After data cleaning, only those country samples with at least 1 500 observations were retained for analysis.

Annex Table 2.A.1. Number of valid interviews and item-non response (percent) for the question on concerns about income disparities, by country and wave

	1987		1992		1999		2009		2017	
AUS	1 663	5.7	2 203	5.4	1 672	3.6	1 525	5.5	1 317	6.1
AUT	953	2.2	1 027	2.8	1 016	3.0	1 019	3.6	1 200	1.1
BEL							1 115	3.2	1 001	0.4
CAN			1 002	2.4	974	2.8				
CHE	987	3.9					1 229	0.5	1 066	1.5
CHL					1 503	2.2	1 505	0.9		
CZE					1 834	0.7	1 205	0.5	1 405	0.5
DEU			3 391	4.6	1 432	3.6	1 395	2.5	1 701	1.9
DNK					1 823	2.8	1 518	3.6	1 079	4.4
ESP					1 211	1.2	1 215	1.6	1 733	4.0
EST							1 005	0.1	1 005	2.2
FIN							880	3.6	1 074	6.1
FRA					1 889	1.0	2 817	1.6	1 489	3.0
GBR	1 212	2.9	1 066	2.5	804	3.6	958	2.7	1 595	5.2
GRC									1 010	0.1
HUN	2 606	4.1	1 250	1.8	1 208	0.7	1 010	0.2	1 007	0.1
IRL									1 004	3.4
ISL							947	0.3	1 450	2.5
ISR					1 208	0.6	1 193	1.2	1 267	2.4
ITA	1 027	1.0	996	0.3			1 084	2.8	1 029	0.7
JPN					1 325	7.8	1 296	5.4	1 609	7.3
KOR							1 599	0.6		
LTU							1 023	2.2	1 052	0.3
LUX									504	4.2
LVA					1 100	0.7	1 069	0.7	1 000	1.1
MEX									1 002	1.8
NLD									1 040	1.1
NOR			1 538	1.7	1 268	1.4	1 246	4.5		
NZL			1 239	3.8	1 108	3.5	935	3.1	1 357	2.7
POL	3 937	52.8	1 636	5.9	1 135	6.3	1 263	0.9	997	1.1
PRT					1 144	1.0	1 000	0.5	1 089	0.2
SVK					1 082	0.6	1 159	0.5	1 404	0.1
SVN			1 049	1.7	1 006	1.8	1 065	1.3	1 047	1.8
SWE			749	3.1	1 150	1.6	1 137	2.7	1 125	3.5
TUR							1 569	2.8	1 521	0.4
USA	1 564	4.7	1 273	2.3	1 272	6.6	1 581	4.4	1 173	2.6

Source: Yellow shaded cells refer to data from Eurobarometer; in Poland, 1987, half (50.1%) of the sample was not asked the question.

Annex Table 2.A.2. Composition of the main sample in Table 2.1

	Observed in period:					Total
	1987-88	1991-93	1998-2001	2008-11	2017-18	
AUS	0	0	1	1	1	3
AUT	0	0	0	1	1	2
BEL	0	0	0	1	1	2
CAN	0	1	1	0	0	2
CHE	0	0	0	1	1	2
CHL	0	0	1	1	0	2
CZE	0	0	1	1	1	3
DEU	0	1	1	1	1	4
DNK	0	0	1	1	1	3
ESP	0	0	0	1	1	2
EST	0	0	0	1	1	2
FIN	0	0	0	1	1	2
FRA	0	0	1	1	1	3
GBR	1	1	1	1	1	5
HUN	0	0	0	1	1	2
ISL	0	0	0	1	1	2
ISR	0	0	1	1	1	3
ITA	1	1	0	1	1	4
JPN	0	0	1	1	1	3
LTU	0	0	0	1	1	2
LVA	0	0	0	1	1	2
NOR	0	1	1	1	0	3
NZL	0	1	1	1	0	3
POL	0	0	0	1	1	2
PRT	0	0	0	1	1	2
SVK	0	0	0	1	1	2
SVN	0	0	0	1	1	2
SWE	0	1	1	1	1	4
USA	1	1	1	1	1	5
Total	3	8	14	28	25	78

Notes

[1] Unless explicitly stated, here and in the rest of the report the focus is only on the share of respondents who **strongly** agree with the statement "Differences in income in [country] are too large". We do so for two main reasons: (i) a large majority of respondents agree with the statement; (ii) the strongest variation over time is observed in the share of people who strongly agree. Ciani et al. (2021[1]) provide a more extensive discussion and comparison with alternative measures.

[2] It should be noted that the 2017 ISSP questionnaire shows some important differences from the 1987, 1992, 1999 and 2009 waves, as it specifically focuses on social inequalities and does not collect the full set of variables used below to investigate and explain the evolution of concerns. In detail, the ISSP 2017 module focuses on social networks. The question about income disparities is designed as the one in ISSP 1987, 1992, 1999 and 2009. However, 1987, 1992, 1999 and 2009 asked the questions about income disparities after asking the respondent to assess earnings in a wide range of occupations and to state what should be a "fair" level of earnings. This might influence answers to the subsequent, more general question about income disparities. The 2019 wave, though, is fully comparable with the previous waves, but has

been released only for a limited set of countries and is still being carried out in others. Nevertheless, comparing the data from either wave to ISSP 2009 confirms a slightly downward trend.

[3] Only a small share of these changes in concerns about income disparities is explained by socio-demographic compositional changes (see Ciani et al. (2021[1])).

[4] Figure 2.5 and Table 2.1 use only data up to 2017 for two reasons: (i) some of the ISSP 2019 countries are observed in a year for which there are not yet any inequality indicators; (ii) it enable a wider coverage of countries within a single wave, rather than combining data from multiple waves.

[5] These results are robust to a range of sensitivity checks such as removing period dummies, controlling for year of interview (rather than period dummies), using a first difference estimator, using only series with the old income definition from IDD, excluding data from Eurobarometer (or including a dummy for related data points). Adding data points from the Luxembourg Income Study (LIS) leads to similar estimates for both column (3) and (4), although the estimates for column (4) become statistically insignificant; this might be due to the additional measurement error induced in LIS by merging different sources of data. The results are not influenced by a single country. See Ciani et al. (2021[1]) for the full tables of results.

[6] Inequality in earnings and income might differ substantially for different reasons. For example, household income also includes non-employment revenues and earnings refer only to individuals without accounting for her household.

[7] Posing this question is not the same as looking at how individual concern over income inequality has changed over time. In fact, trends in concerns about income disparities (Figure 2.2) actually suggested a *decrease* in concerns during the last decade.

[8] Osberg and Smeeding (2006[49]) also show that, according to these ISSP indicators, the United States is not an exceptional case in terms of perceived intergenerational mobility. Nevertheless, Alesina, Stantcheva and Teso (2018[30]) suggest that residents in the United States overestimate the probability that children from poor families could climb the social ladder. The literature is not unanimous on this (McCall et al., 2017[5]; Cheng and Wen, 2019[63]).

[9] The association in ISSP is weaker than in Risks that Matter. One explanation is that ISSP measures perceived disparities in earnings and intergenerational persistence along with wealth and education, therefore combining different dimensions. Unlike ISSP, both measures in Risks that Matter refer to the income distribution.

[10] While for perceived inequality of outcomes it is possible to compare perceptions and estimates which refer broadly to the same aspect (e.g. top income shares or earnings disparities), for intergenerational persistence it is more difficult to do so. There are two reasons. First, the index built on ISSP is qualitative and captures two dimensions, one of which (intergenerational persistence of wealth) is not covered by internationally measurable statistics. Second, although there is an interest in capturing intergenerational income persistence, estimates are available only for a few countries, as most available conventional estimates are based on earnings and education.

[11] Experiencing any health or economic hardship includes physical or mental health problems linked to the pandemic, job-related disruption during the pandemic, or difficulties in making ends meet during the pandemic.

[12] Results from Compare Your Income regarding the perceived richest 10%'s income share may differ from those of Risks that Matter for multiple reasons, including the period of observation (from May 2015 to

May 2020 for CYI, from September to October 2020 for RtM) and the methodology (online opt-in survey users for CYI, online panel-based survey for the RtM). Nevertheless, for the 20 countries included in both tools, the average perceived income share of the richest 10% is quite similar. The correlation is 0.75 and the average difference is only 2.9 percentage points. Results from the 27 OECD countries analysed by Balestra and Cohen (2021[41]) also confirm that the perceived top 10% is correlated with the *OECD Income Distribution Database (IDD)* values (averaged across available years from 2015). The correlation is 0.5 and the linear fit has a slope of 0.7, statistically significant at the 1% level.

13 For example, Roth and Wohlfart (2018[35]) show that individuals who grew up in periods of high income disparities are more tolerant of current levels, even when their perceptions are in line with reality.

14 This is the anchoring effect discussed by Pedersen and Mutz (2018[50]).

15 The only other experiment available was carried out by Campos-Vazquez et al. (2020[62]), and it does not corroborate Trump's evidence for Mexico. In fact, they find that providing respondents with information on the actual extent of income inequality or level of intergenerational mobility does not affect people's preferred levels of inequality and intergenerational mobility.

16 The main limit of such exercise is that the different variables used in the decompositions are imperfect measures of the underlying concepts (e.g. perceived top-bottom earnings ratio refer to earnings and not income). However, it is still helpful to understand the relevance and direction of the different contributions.

17 The stronger importance of perceived and preferred disparities is highlighted by country fixed-effects regressions (Table 2.3, Columns 4 to 6), which exploit the change over time in the different dimensions. These fixed-effects regressions are, however, based on a small number of countries (21) observed at least twice in all relevant variables (and make it possible to include only the importance of wealthy parents, because the importance of educated parents and hard work are not observed in one of the intermediate waves). Hence the need to treat the results with caution.

3. How does inequality shape the demand for redistribution?

This chapter focuses on how actual and perceived inequality shape preferences for redistribution. It shows that demand for redistribution is closely related to concern over income disparities and what underlies them, i.e. perceptions of and preferences for economic inequality. Changes in actual inequality, as measured by conventional indicators, are associated with changes in demand for redistribution, but only as long as changes in concern evolve in the same direction. The effect of changes in inequality on demand for redistribution reflects both changes in relative income – by making some people poorer and thus more favourable to government intervention – and people's own preferences for the aggregate level of inequality. Despite being related to inequality, demand for redistribution has increased only mildly over time and reacted only to a limited extent to rises in concerns and inequality. The chapter assesses possible explanations, based on observational evidence and a review of survey experiments.

3.1. Perceptions of inequality and the demand for redistribution

Perceptions of and concern over inequality are key drivers of cross-country differences in preferences for redistribution

How do concern over and perceptions of income inequality and intergenerational persistence influence opinions of redistributive policies? In OECD countries, an average share of 70% of respondents in ISSP and Eurobarometer surveys agree that redistribution is the responsibility of the government (Figure 3.1). Confirming a long tradition of studies with a strong transatlantic perspective (see (Kambayashi and Lechevalier[1]) for a recent survey), the share who believe it is the government's duty is lowest in the United States. It is low, too, in Australia, Great Britain and New Zealand. It is highest in European countries, particularly Latvia and Portugal. Within Europe, the share tends to be lower in Nordic countries, where redistribution was extensive until the early 2000s. Countries outside the Europe-Anglosphere ambit are scattered across the distribution. In Japan, a lower-than-average share of people deem that the government should reduce differences in income, while Israel, Mexico and Turkey are located in the middle of the distribution.

Figure 3.1. On average, a large share of people believe it is the responsibility of the government to reduce income differences

Share of respondents who agree or strongly agree, 2017

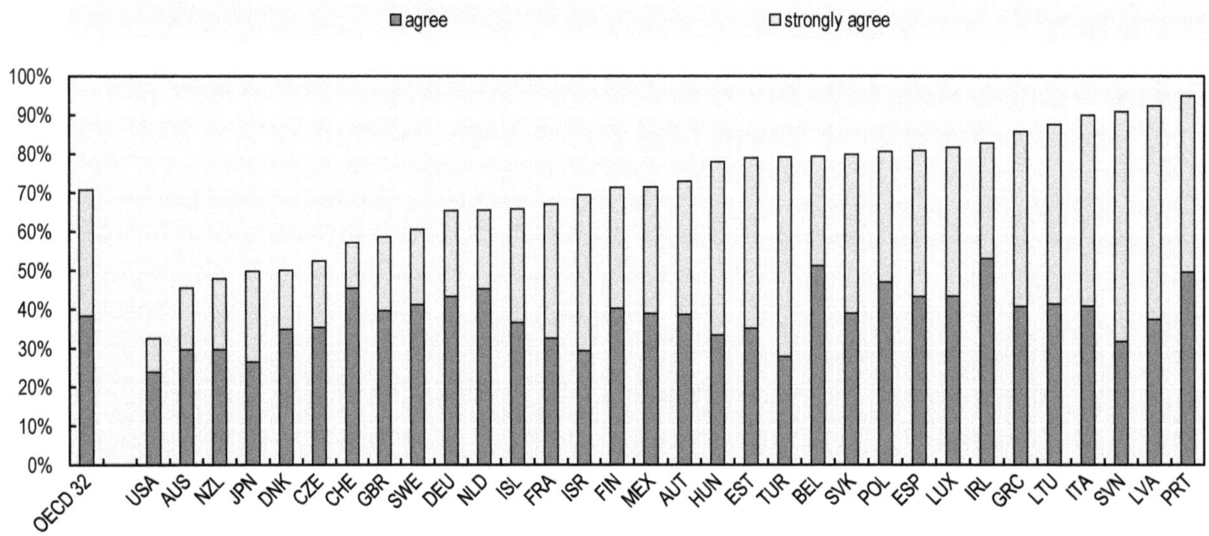

Note: Respondents are asked their opinion about the statement "It is the responsibility of the government to reduce the differences in income between people with high incomes and those with low incomes." In Eurobarometer the statement is slightly different – "The government in (OUR COUNTRY) should take measures to reduce differences in income levels" – while the scale of answers is identical. OECD averages are unweighted averages across the OECD countries included in the figure.
Source: OECD calculations from ISSP 2017, and Eurobarometer 471/2017 for Belgium, Estonia, Greece, Ireland, Italy, Luxembourg, Latvia, Malta, Netherlands, Poland, Portugal and Slovenia.

StatLink https://stat.link/besvj5

Demand for government intervention in tackling inequalities and concern over income disparities are closely related (Figure 3.2). In countries where concern is greatest, respondents are more likely to believe that reducing income differences is the government's duty. The main determinants of international differences in concern about income disparities (see Chapter 2) account for as much as 60% of the cross-country variation in demand for redistribution (Table 3.1). A wider gap between perceived and preferred top-bottom earnings disparities is positively associated with demand for redistribution, which suggests that perceptions and preferences are crucial in shaping support for redistributive policies. Also associated with strong demand for redistribution are perceptions of strong generational persistence. By contrast, where people firmly believe in meritocracy, i.e. the importance of hard work, there is less support for redistribution.

Figure 3.2. Concern over income disparities is closely related with the demand for redistribution

Percentage share of respondents, 2017

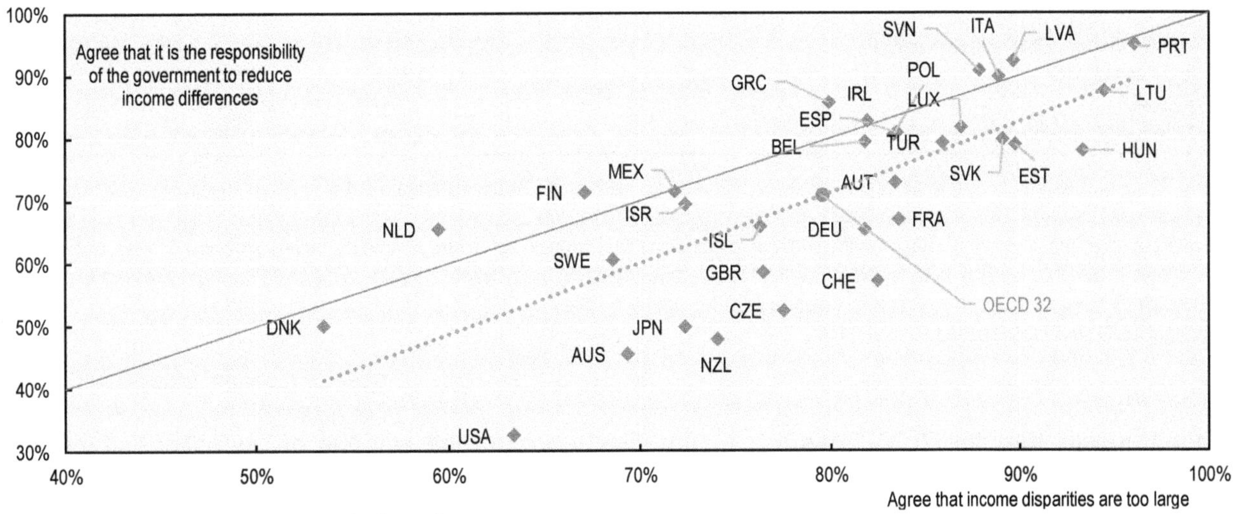

Note: see Figure 3.1. The dotted line is the linear fit.
Source: OECD calculations based on ISSP 2017, and Eurobarometer 471/2017 for Belgium, Estonia, Greece, Ireland, Italy, Luxembourg, Latvia, Malta, Netherlands, Poland, Portugal, Romania and Slovak Republic. For Slovenia, redistributive preferences are from Eurobarometer 471/2017, while concern over income disparities are from ISSP 2017.

StatLink https://stat.link/lb4ygt

Table 3.1. The main determinants of concern over income disparities also drive differences in demand for redistribution in all countries

Percentage point increase in the share of respondents who strongly agree with the statements "Income differences are too large" and "It is the responsibility of the government to reduce income differences", associated with one percent (or one percentage point) increase for various factors

	(1)	(2)
	Income differences are too large	It is the responsibility of the government to reduce income differences
Perceived top-bottom earnings ratio	0.296*	0.253**
	(0.164)	(0.106)
Preferred top-bottom earnings ratio	-0.428*	-0.427***
	(0.213)	(0.145)
Perceived intergenerational persistence index	0.613**	0.513***
	(0.236)	(0.166)
Fraction that believe that hard work matters to get ahead in life	-0.441*	-0.485**
	(0.248)	(0.175)
Countries	28	28
R2 (fraction of variance explained by the variables)	0.45	0.58

Note: *** denotes statistically significant at the 1% level; ** at the 5%; * at the 10%. Robust standard errors in parentheses. The OLS regressions uses as explanatory variable the average logarithm of the perceived/preferred top-bottom earnings ratio; the regression coefficients can therefore be interpreted as the percentage change in the share of respondents who strongly agree that income disparities are too wide, associated with a 1% change in the perceived top-bottom earnings ratio. The average logarithm of top-bottom earnings is calculated using the reweighted sample to account for missing values. The sample includes all OECD countries available in ISSP 2009 for which it was possible to calculate all variables.
Source: OECD calculations based on ISSP 2009.

StatLink https://stat.link/t64w9g

Recent results from the 2020 Risks that Matter survey confirm the key role of perceptions of income inequality and intergenerational persistence in shaping demand for redistribution. The survey asks respondents about their preferences for more redistribution than current levels. Countries where people perceive the richest 10%'s income share to be high express strong demand for greater government intervention to reduce income disparities (Figure 3.3).[1] The same is true of perceptions of wider intergenerational disparities.

Strong perceptions of income inequality and intergenerational persistence are also associated with demand for more progressive taxation – even more closely, in fact, than with support for general government intervention.

Figure 3.3. Demand for redistribution and progressive taxation is higher in countries where people perceive higher inequality and less social mobility

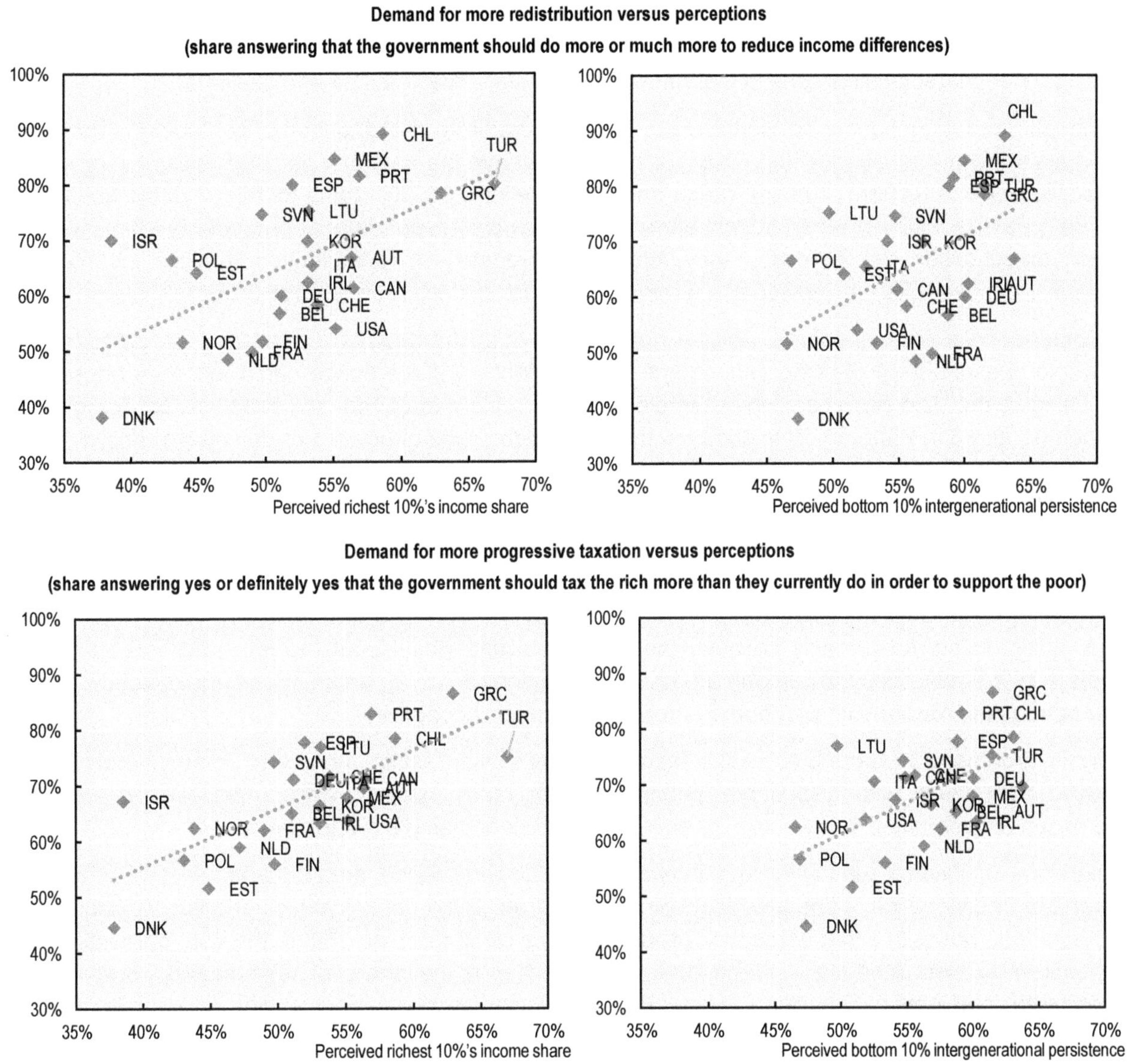

Note: Blue lines are linear fit lines. The top panel shows answers to the question: "Governments can reduce income differences between the rich and the poor by collecting taxes and providing social benefits. In your country, do you think the government should do more or less to reduce income differences?" The bottom panel shows answers to the question: "Should the government tax the rich more than they currently do in order to support the poor?". Individuals answering "Can't choose" are not considered in calculating the shares.

Source: OECD calculations from the 2020 Risks that Matter Survey.

StatLink https://stat.link/76cz4x

Individuals' perceptions of country-wide inequality matter as much as their own income in explaining demand for redistribution

At the individual level, demand for more redistribution and progressive taxation varies from one socio-demographic group to another. These differences, reported in Panel A of Figure 3.4 and estimated by keeping other characteristics constant, confirm previous evidence (Alesina and Giuliano, 2011[2]).

Individuals from high-income households are less favourable to redistribution. The finding is consistent with a standard economic model in which individuals balance the personal gains of redistribution with its costs (Meltzer and Richard, 1981[3]; Rueda and Stegmueller, 2019[4]). Gains for high-income households may be greater equality or other indirect benefits, such as increased national productivity thanks to wider access to education. As for costs, they may be aggregate – if redistribution reduces incentive, for example – or specific to the individual, e.g. higher taxes for the rich (see Section 3.3).

The importance of socio-economic status is not confined to an individual's current situation, but extends to the whole household's well-being and income. Respondents who are concerned about their household's well-being in the next few years, for example, are more likely to call for redistribution and progressive taxation (Figure 3.4, Panel B). This confirms that future prospects of upward or downward mobility are an important determinant of people's preferences for redistribution (Benabou and Ok, 2001[5]). This also because people are, at least to some degree, risk averse, and higher risk aversion is associated with more demand for redistribution as insurance against future shocks (Gärtner, Mollerstrom and Seim, 2017[6]).

For their part, university graduates are less inclined to demand more redistribution, possibly because of their upbringing or their expectations of high earnings later in life. The unemployed and tenants demand more redistribution, presumably because they are more uncertain about the future. Women and older people, too, are more likely to demand greater redistribution (Box 3.1), although the age effect dwindles in older cohorts (its relationship with demand for redistribution is concave).

Analysis of demand for more progressive taxation yields similar results, albeit with some differences. The negative association with disposable income is even more marked, while there are no significant differences between men and women, or between couples and single respondents.

Perceptions of income inequality and intergenerational persistence are important factors in shaping demand for redistribution, even after controlling for different socio-demographic variables. An increase of 40 percentage points in either perception (equivalent to a climb from the 25th to the 75th percentile of the distribution) is associated with a 5-percentage point rise in the share of respondents wanting more government intervention (Figure 3.4, Panel B). This finding is similar to the difference in demand for redistribution between people at the top and bottom of the income distribution. Perceptions of increases in inequality during the previous 10 years are even more strongly associated with demand for redistribution. All these findings are consistent with Fong (2001[7]), who shows that people's beliefs about income distribution and reasons for inequality matter as much as personal income in explaining individual preferences for redistribution. Perceived macro-economic trends are also relevant. Pessimistic views of the country's changing economic situation in the previous 12 months strengthen demand for redistribution, much as the worsening of a household's financial situation does.

Figure 3.4. Individual perceptions of inequality matter for demand for redistribution

Percentage point differences across groups in the shares of respondents who demand more redistribution or more progressive taxation (percentage points and 95% confidence intervals)

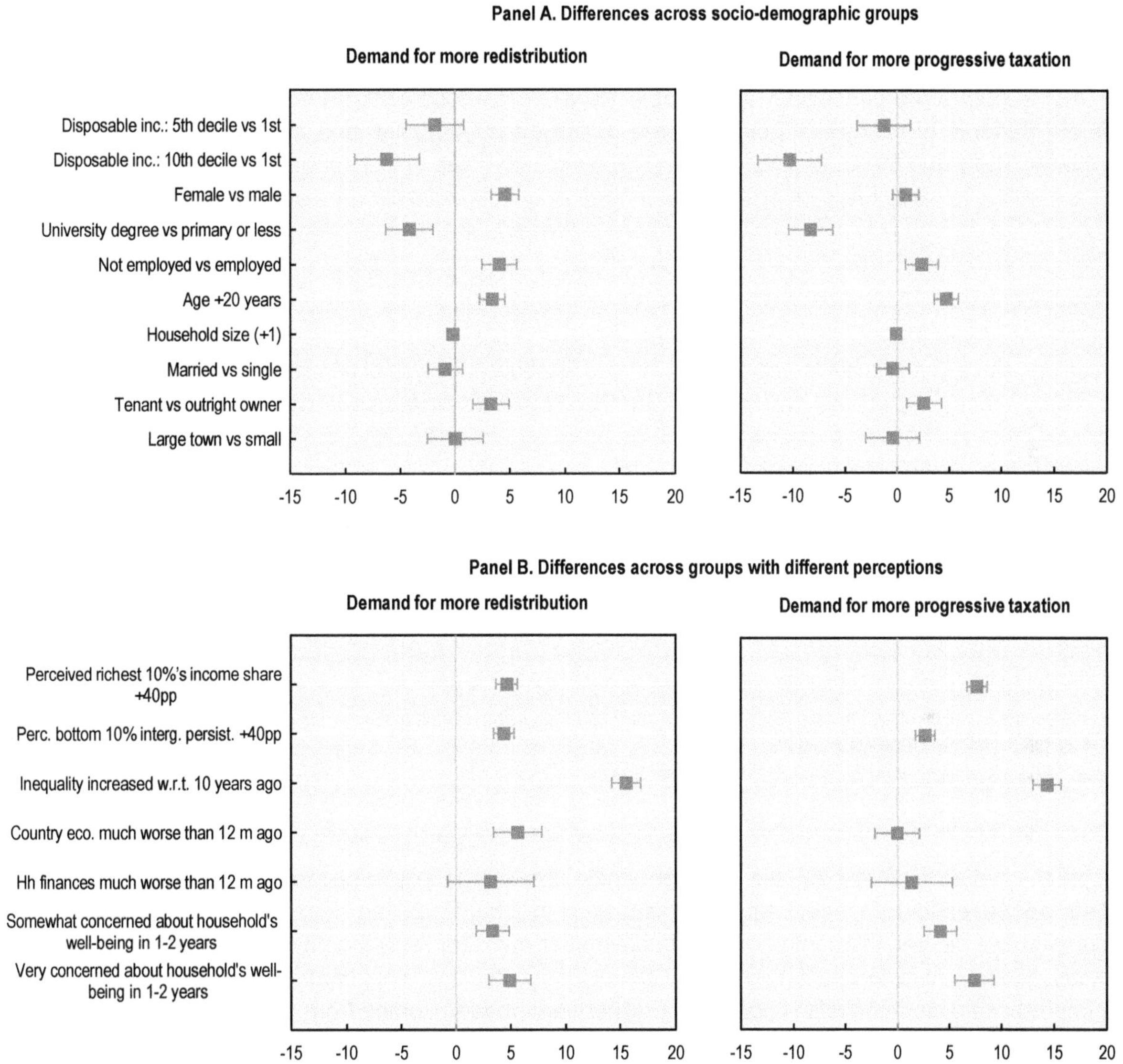

Note: Demand for redistribution refers to respondents who answer "more" or "much more" in response to the question "In your country, do you think the government should do more or less to reduce income differences?", while for tax progressivity it refers to those who answer "yes" or "definitely yes" to the question "Should the government tax the rich more than they currently do in order to support the poor?" The differences associated with different groups, characteristics and perceptions are estimated with other characteristics kept constant, using a multivariate probit model that includes all the characteristics reported in the table (age squared is also included), plus country fixed effects. The reported differences are average marginal effects. Respondents who answer "Can't choose" are not considered.
Source: OECD calculations from the 2020 Risks that Matter Survey.

StatLink https://stat.link/qb9czp

Perceptions of income inequality and intergenerational persistence also shape redistributive preferences, whether or not both or either are perceived to be widespread (Table 3.2). Even when individuals believe that intergenerational persistence is low, their perception that income inequality is high is associated with a stronger demand for redistribution, and vice versa. There is thus no full trade-off between intergenerational persistence and income equality in people's opinions. If equal opportunities at birth made income inequality fully acceptable, then perceived income inequality would not matter when individuals perceive little incidence of intergenerational persistence. The survey experiment conducted by Amiel et al. (2014[8]) supports the conclusion that people have preferences on both counts. Amiel et al. presented different patterns of intergenerational income mobility and inequality to a number of university students from Israel, Italy and the United Kingdom.[2] The conclusion was that respondents value both components and are willing to trade them off against each other only in special circumstances.

Table 3.2. Both perceived income inequality and intergenerational persistence shape demand for redistribution

Percentage share of respondents who demand more redistribution, by type of perceptions

	Perceived richest 10%'s share of income				
Perceived bottom 10% intergenerational persistence	[0,19]	[20,39]	[40,59]	[60,79]	[80,100]
[0,19]	51	54	56	61	68
[20,39]	55	61	62	66	67
[40,59]	54	65	60	66	66
[60,79]	61	68	68	70	73
[80,100]	60	68	71	74	75

Note: Shares have been calculated keeping all other dimensions (socio-demographic characteristics and other perceptions, apart from the beliefs about the evolution of income inequality in the past year) constant, using a probit model as in Figure 3.4, where perceptions have been added as dummies for each category and fully interacted.
Source: OECD calculations from the 2020 Risks that Matter Survey.

StatLink https://stat.link/r2a4lm

People may value income inequality independently from intergenerational mobility because they hold other beliefs about reasons for inequality. As discussed in Chapter 2, the literature examines opinions that circumstances beyond the control of individuals matter more (or less) than hard work for personal success (Piketty, 1995[9]; Alesina and Angeletos, 2005[10]; Fong, 2001[7]). This chapter, too, has already stressed the importance of such beliefs (Table 3.1). Further confirmation comes from the fact that demand for more progressive taxation is lower in countries where a larger share of people believe that the reason why some individuals live in poverty is not social injustice or bad luck, but laziness or lack of willpower (Figure 3.5).

A stream of literature in experimental economics has tried to address the relevance of beliefs about reasons for inequality by putting individuals in laboratory settings where researchers randomly manipulate the sources of income. Durante, Putterman and van der Weele (2014[11]) find that preferences for greater equality are lower when the initial distribution is assigned according to the participants' performance in some task (a quiz or skill game), and higher when they are allotted an income arbitrarily (either randomly or relative to the average income in their place of residence). In a redistributive experiment with representative samples of participants from 60 countries, Almås et al. (2020[12]) asked them to choose whether to change the pay gap between two workers in a real-life situation. The results reveal that, when the pay gap depended on the workers' performance, respondents were more reluctant to narrow the gap.[3]

Figure 3.5. Demand for more progressive taxation is lower where people believe that poverty is due mostly to lack of personal effort

Percentage share of respondents

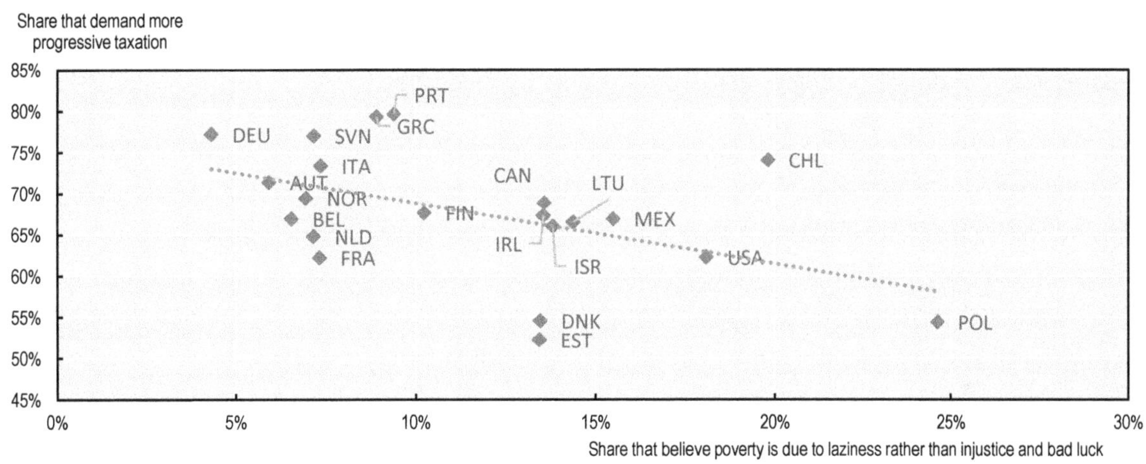

Source: OECD calculations from the 2018 Risks that Matter Survey.

StatLink https://stat.link/4bo6vx

Box 3.1. Gender differences in redistributive preferences

On average, women demand more redistribution than men do in OECD countries (Figure 3.6). The trend is not attributable to socio-demographic differences (e.g. income, employment status), and is consistent with a large body of evidence from other surveys (Alesina and Giuliano, 2011[2]; Goerres and Jæger, 2015[13]; Luttmer and Singhal, 2011[14]), and is found in almost all countries, although not always statistically significant. The female-male ratio of support for redistribution (controlling for differences in other socio-demographic characteristics) is slightly negative, though not statistically significant, only in Mexico, Estonia and the Netherlands, while it is the highest in Israel and Norway.

Women's stronger preference for redistribution is confirmed by laboratory experiments in which researchers manipulate the initial income distribution and sources of disparities among participants, then let them choose whether to alter the levels of inequality. Female participants tend to choose lower levels of inequality (Durante, Putterman and van der Weele, 2014[11]). The main difference appears when the reason for inequality is performance rather than luck or socio-economic background (Buser et al., 2020[15]). Although all participants scale down their redistribution preferences when initial disparities are due to differences in performance on some task, women do so by much less.

Figure 3.6. Women demand more redistribution than men

Female vs. male differences in shares of respondents demanding more redistribution, 2020

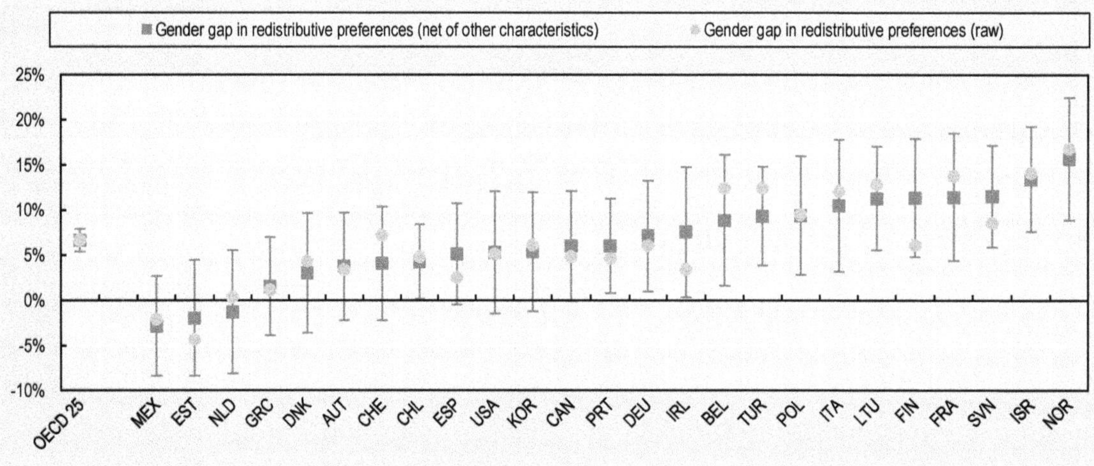

Note: The differences net of other characteristics are estimated using a multivariate probit regression that includes the socio-demographic characteristics as in Figure 3.4.
Source: OECD calculations from the 2020 Risks that Matter Survey.

StatLink https://stat.link/mbx0yl

The gender difference for redistributive preferences is no greater in countries with wide gender wage gaps, which suggests that the difference is not driven simply by the condition of women in the country (Figure 3.7). In Korea and Estonia, which both have wide gender wage gaps, there is no statistically significant difference between men's and women's attitudes to redistribution. In Norway and Slovenia, where the gender wage gap is relatively narrow, women are much more favourably disposed to redistribution than men.

Figure 3.7. The gender difference in demand for greater redistribution is not driven by gender wage gaps

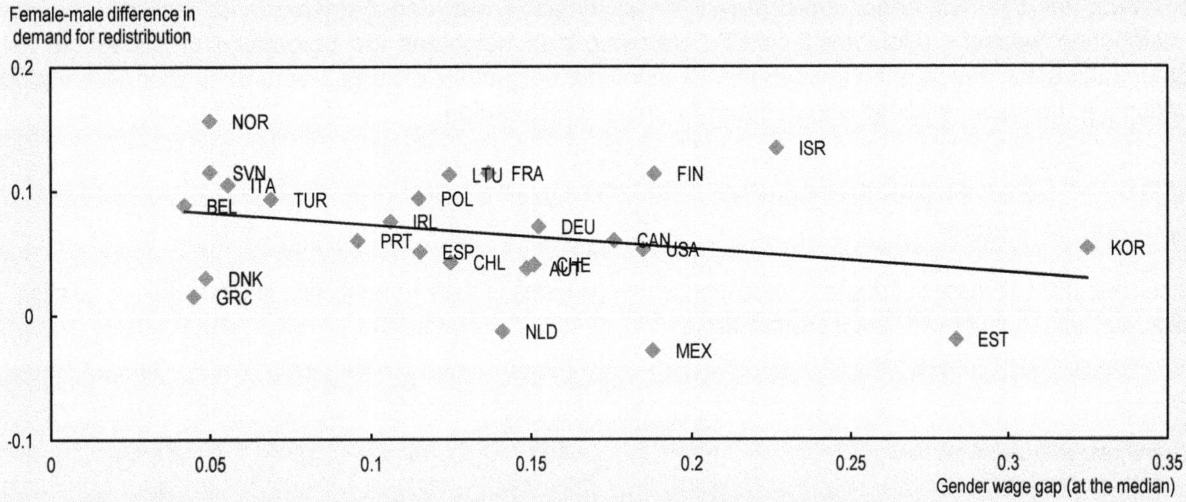

Note: The demand for more redistribution is the share of respondents who answer "more" or "much "more" in response to the question whether the government should do more than it currently does to reduce income differences between the rich and the poor. The gender wage gap is evaluated at the median and refers to the latest available year.
Source: OECD calculations from the 2020 Risks that Matter Survey and *OECD Earnings Database*.

StatLink https://stat.link/mzhn9g

A recent in-survey informational experiment carried out in the United States by Settele (2021[16]) finds that respondents' concern over gender disparities are influenced by information. The author provides randomly selected respondents with two different estimates of the gender wage gap. Those who are shown a wide gender wage gap express greater concern and say the government should do much more to narrow the disparities. However, support for individual policies varies little, apart from a moderate rise in support for stricter equal pay legislation and more robust affirmative action.

One explanation for the limited support for the different policies is that a sizeable share of respondents has little faith in their effectiveness for reducing gender disparities. Another explanation is that, while overall support for some interventions increases, different respondents express different preferences for different policies, so that no individual policy has much support. Both explanations are consistent with results from experiments in which participants are given information on actual inequality (see Section 3.4).

Experiencing hardship during the COVID-19 crisis is associated with greater demand for redistribution

People who experience health problems, economic hardship, or a worsening of household finances during the COVID-19 pandemic tend to call for more redistribution and progressive taxation (Table 3.3, Columns 1 and 4). OECD (2021[17]) further shows that household insecurity during the COVID-19 crisis is associated with higher demand for social protection. In a survey in the United States in October 2020, Klemm and Mauro (2021[18]) also find that people who have lost their job or been seriously ill, or whose loved ones have, are more favourable to progressive taxation. These results are in line with evidence from Alesina and Giuliano (2011[2]) that negative shocks boost preferences for redistribution.

Increases in perceived inequalities and perceived household risk may explain the positive association between exposure to hardship during the COVID-19 crisis and demand for redistribution. The evidence from Risks that Matter shows that both perceived inequalities and risk are factors in explaining the association. Hardship experienced during the COVID-19 crisis heightens perception of inequality. After controlling for the heightened perception, the association between hardship and demand for more redistribution weakens (Columns 2 and 5). Hardship also heightens the perception of household risk. Again, taking the heightened perception of risk into account (Columns 3 and 6) further lessens the relationship between hardship and demand for more redistribution.

Table 3.3. Experiencing hardship during the COVID-19 pandemic is associated with demand for greater redistribution

Percentage point increase in the shares of respondents who demand more redistribution and progressive taxation associated with changes in different characteristics

	(1)	(2)	(3)	(4)	(5)	(6)
	Demand more redistribution			Demand more progressive taxation		
Experienced health or economic hardship during the pandemic (vs not)	1.8**	0.3	-0.0	3.5***	1.8**	1.2*
	(0.7)	(0.7)	(0.7)	(0.7)	(0.7)	(0.7)
Report that household financial situation worsened during the pandemic (vs not)	4.3***	3.9***	3.3***	2.2**	1.7*	0.6
	(0.9)	(0.9.)	(0.9)	(0.9)	(0.9)	(0.9)
Perceived top 10% income share (+40 pp)		4.7***	4.6***		7.8***	7.7***
		(0.5)	(0.5)		(0.5)	(0.5)
Perceived bottom 10% intergenerational persistence (+40 pp)		4.3***	4.4***		2.6***	2.6***
		(0.5)	(0.5)		(0.5)	(0.5)
Believes income inequality increased w.r.t. 10 years ago (vs not)		15.6***	15.4***		14.5***	14.2***
		(0.7)	(0.7)		(0.7)	(0.7)
Somewhat concerned about household well-being in 1-2 years (vs not)			2.9***			3.7***
			(0.8)			(0.8)
Very concerned about household well-being in 1-2 years (vs not)			4.0***			6.8***
			(1.0)			(1.0)
Observations	23506	22770	22645	23628	22801	22683

Note: * denotes statistically significant at the 10% level, ** at 5%, *** at 1%. Robust standard errors in brackets. The results are average marginal effects from probit regressions, including country fixed effects and weighting by sample weights (rescaled so that weights sum up to 1 within each country). Household and individual characteristics are the same as those included in Table 2.2 and Figure 3.4. Experiencing any health or economic hardship includes having experienced physical or mental health problems because of the pandemic, having experienced job-related disruption during the pandemic, or having had difficulties in making ends meet during the pandemic.
Source: OECD calculations from the 2020 Risks that Matter Survey.

StatLink https://stat.link/hw5f97

Unfortunately, it is not possible to test whether respondents who experience hardship also wanted greater redistribution before the crisis, because Risks that Matter does not interview the same individuals over time. However, at the country level, average demand for more progressive taxation in the previous Risks that Matter wave (2018) does not correlate with the share of respondents who experience hardship due to COVID-19 (Figure 3.8). By contrast, there is a positive association between demand for progressive taxation in 2020 and the share of people who experienced hardship.[4] In other words, the change in demand for redistribution is positively associated with the reported impact of the COVID-19 crisis on the respondents and their household members, suggesting that the perceived impact of the crisis might have increased preferences for more progressive taxation. This result is consistent with the findings of Giuliano and Spilimbergo (2013[19]), who show that experiencing a recession – particularly when growing up – leads to higher demand for redistribution. Gualtieri et al. (2019[20]), too, provide evidence that experiencing trauma – e.g. an earthquake – increases demand for redistribution.

Figure 3.8. Demand for more progressive taxation increased the most in countries where more respondents reported hardship during the COVID-19 crisis

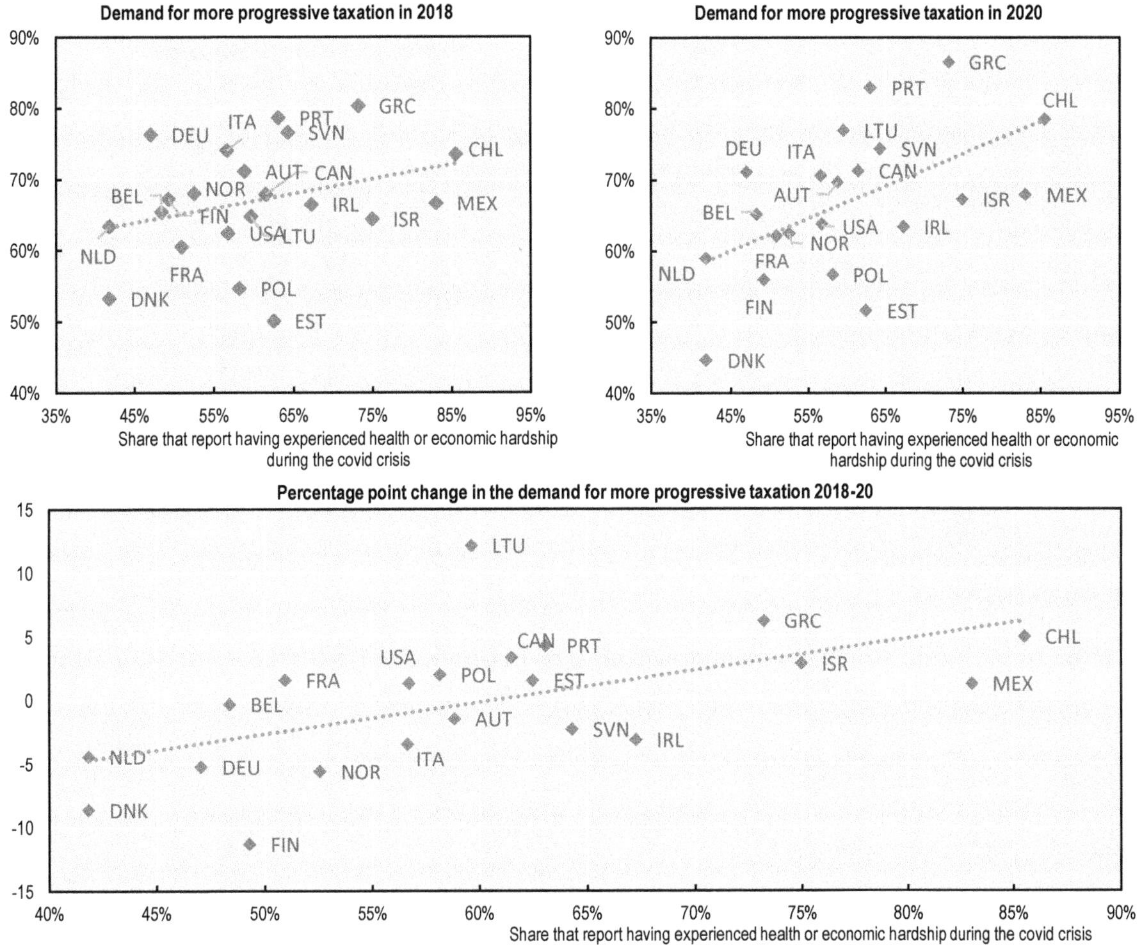

Note: Demand for more progressive taxation is measured as the share that answer "yes" or "definitely yes" to the question "Should the government tax the rich more than they currently do to support the poor?" (excluding respondents who choose "Can't choose"). Experiencing health or economic hardship during the pandemic refers to respondents who report that they themselves or a member of the family experienced physical or health problems because of the pandemic, experienced loss of employment during the pandemic, or had difficulties in making ends meet during the pandemic. For consistency with the 2020 wave, the 2018 values have been calculated only on individuals aged 18-64. Exact differences between the two Risks that Matter waves should be interpreted with some caution due to adjustments in sampling methods and coverage.

Source: OECD calculations from the 2018 and 2020 Risks that Matter Surveys.

StatLink https://stat.link/ave8ln

3.2. Actual inequality and demand for redistribution

Rising income inequality is associated with greater demand for redistribution

When compared at a single point in time, countries which conventional indicators show to have higher levels of inequality (e.g. as measured by the Gini index) do not have higher shares of respondents who agree that it is the government's duty to reduce income differences (Table 3.4, Column 1). Previous studies report zero (Bussolo et al., 2019[21]) or even negative correlations (Kerr, 2014[22]).

Table 3.4. Changes in actual income inequality explain changes in preferences for redistribution, but the association is driven by changes in concern

	(1)	(2)	(3)	(4)	(5)	(6)	(7)
	Cross-country regression	Within-country, over time regression					
Percentage point increase in the share of respondents who **agree** that it is the responsibility of the government to reduce income differences associated with one percentage point increase in….							
…Gini market income (before taxes and transfers)		0.71**		0.57**		0.21	
		(0.26)		(0.26)		(0.27)	
…Gini disposable income (post tax and transfers)	-0.25		0.92*	0.60			0.22
	(0.62)		(0.49)	(0.48)			(0.33)
…Gini market income working age population					0.79**		
					(0.34)		
…Gini disposable income working age population					0.21		
					(0.48)		
…Gini disposable income elderly					-0.00		
					(0.26)		
…distance between the median income of the elderly and working age population					-0.14**		
					(0.05)		
…concern over income disparities						0.68***	0.70***
						(0.10)	(0.09)
Percentage point increase in the share of respondents who **strongly agree** that it is the responsibility of the government to reduce income differences associated with one percentage point increase in….							
…Gini market income (before tax and transfers)		0.58		0.41		0.22	
		(0.43)		(0.45)		(0.45)	
…Gini disposable income (post tax and transfers)	0.02		0.94	0.71			-0.02
	(0.51)		(0.61)	(0.62)			(0.46)
…Gini market income working age population					0.59		
					(0.68)		
…Gini disposable income working age population					0.30		
					(0.69)		
…Gini disposable income of the elderly					-0.16		
					(0.42)		
Distance between the median income of the elderly and working age population					-0.22**		
					(0.10)		
…concern over income disparities						0.54***	0.56***
						(0.09)	(0.09)
Waves	2017	All	All	All	All	All	All
Observations	30	78	78	78	78	78	78
Countries	30	29	29	29	29	29	29
Country fixed effects	No	Included	Included	Included	Included	Included	Included
Period fixed effects	No	Included	Included	Included	Included	Included	Included

Note: *** denotes statistically significant at the 1% level; ** denotes statistically significant at the 5% level; * denotes statistically significant at the 10% level. Standard errors clustered by country in parentheses. Eurobarometer is used for countries not surveyed in ISSP 2017, as in Table 3.1. Data for the Slovak Republic in 2017 are based on Eurobarometer because ISSP 2017 for Slovakia does not include the question on preferences for redistribution. The results are robust to introducing a dummy for the Eurobarometer observations and macro-variables (employment rate, unemployment rate and the logarithm of GDP per head in USD 2015 PPP).

Source: OECD calculations based on ISSP 1987, 1992, 1999, 2009, 2017 and Eurobarometer 2017 for preferences for redistribution; *OECD Income Distribution Database* (https://stats.oecd.org/Index.aspx?DataSetCode=IDD) for inequality and other variables.

StatLink https://stat.link/so6nr0

Nevertheless, changes in inequality indicators correlate positively with changes in demand for redistribution. Where inequality grows the most, so do preferences for redistribution (Columns 2-3). These findings are consistent with several papers, though not all, which look at within-country changes in inequality and preferences for redistribution (Kerr, 2014[22]; Olivera, 2015[23]; Kuhn, 2019[24]).[5] A positive association between inequality and preferences for redistribution also emerges from studies which look at regional variation within countries, such as Rueda and Stegmueller (2019[4]) and Colagrossi, Karagiannis and Raab (2019[25]).

What seems to matter the most in shaping preferences for redistribution is market inequality within the working-age population. Importantly, though, disposable income differences between generations matter as well. In countries where the elderly are relatively better-off, demand for redistribution is lower. For the working age population, the results may be explained by the prospect of upward mobility (POUM) hypothesis (Benabou and Ok, 2001[5]). POUM conjectures that if people expect to climb the income ladder in the future, they will be more reluctant to support redistribution policies. If all inequalities within the working-age population are held equal, differences between the young and the elderly are an indicator of future income prospects.

The association between income inequality and preferences for redistribution is driven by rising concern over income disparities

Changes in concern over income disparities explain the relationship between changes in inequality indicators and preferences for redistribution. Once levels of concern are taken into account, the correlation between the Gini index and demand for redistribution becomes slight (Table 3.4, Columns 6 and 7). The subjective factors embedded in people's concern over income disparities – perceptions of and preferences for inequality – thus appear more relevant than actual inequality for explaining the demand for redistribution, as Gimpelson and Treisman (2018[26]) also argue.

It should not be inferred, however, that preferences for redistribution and actual inequality are disconnected. On the contrary, Chapters 2 and 3 show that when actual inequality (as captured by the Gini index) rises, so does concern about it, and demand for redistribution grows. However, when concern does not change with inequality, neither do redistributive preferences – if perceptions do not fully incorporate the new level of inequality, for example, or a change in other relevant subjective factors (e.g. preferred income disparities or belief in hard work) lessen the impact of inequality. Moreover, increased concern is associated with greater demand for redistribution even when actual inequality remains stable.[6]

There are indications that support for redistribution has increased during the COVID-19 crisis

Recent evidence from the Risks that Matter survey suggests that the cross-country correlation between indicators of inequality and redistributive preferences might have strengthened during the COVID-19 crisis.[7] Indeed, demand for both more redistribution and more progressive taxation is stronger in countries with higher levels of inequality in 2020 (Figure 3.9), unlike Risks that Matter 2018, which observed no association (OECD, 2019[27]).[8]

Figure 3.9. Demand for redistribution is positively associated with income inequality

Share of respondents who answer "more/much more" (or "yes/definitely yes") associated with Gini coefficients of disposable income

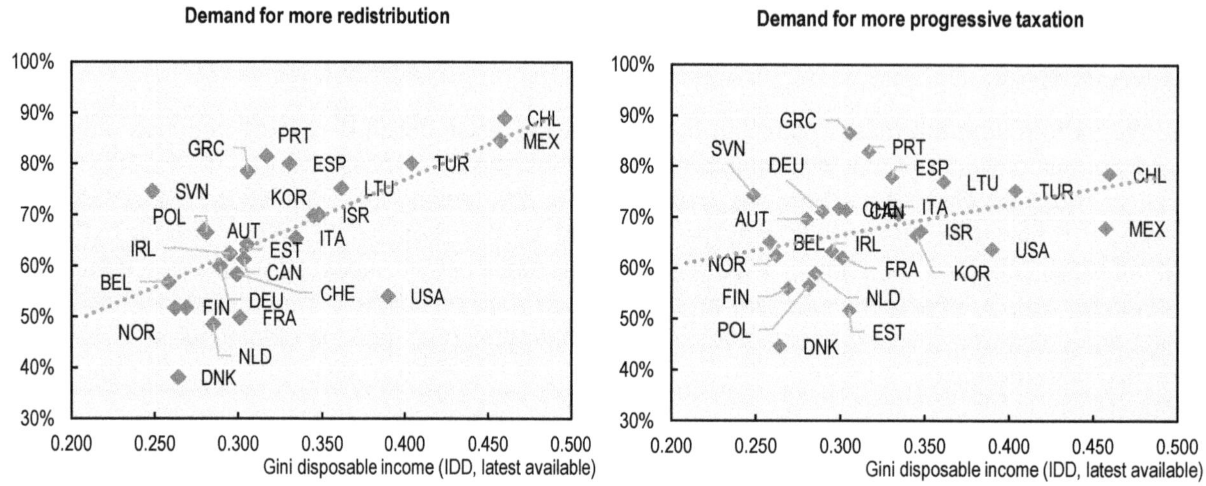

Note: The Gini coefficient for disposable income refers to 2018, apart from 2017 for Chile, Denmark, Germany, Ireland, Italy, Switzerland, the United States, 2016 for Mexico and the Netherlands, and 2015 for Turkey 2015.

Source: OECD calculations from the 2020 Risks that Matter Survey and *OECD Income Distribution Database* (https://stats.oecd.org/Index.aspx?DataSetCode=IDD).

StatLink https://stat.link/lbj35u

Demand for more progressive taxation increased the most between 2018 and 2020 in countries where inequality was already widespread before the pandemic (Figure 3.10). This relation is explained by differences in the share of respondents that reported experiencing hardship during COVID-19. Two mechanisms may explain this trend. The first, discussed above, is that the crisis exposed pre-existing inequalities, therefore raising awareness of inequality in countries where levels were already high. The second is that the experience of hardship has been more widespread in countries that were unequal even before the crisis. The experience of hardship thus likely drives demand for progressive taxation either directly or by exposing pre-existing disparities.

Figure 3.10. Recent changes in the demand for progressive taxation have been greater in countries that are more unequal

Percentage point change 2018-2020 in the shares of respondents who demand more progressive taxation associated with the Gini coefficient for disposable income in 2018 or latest available year

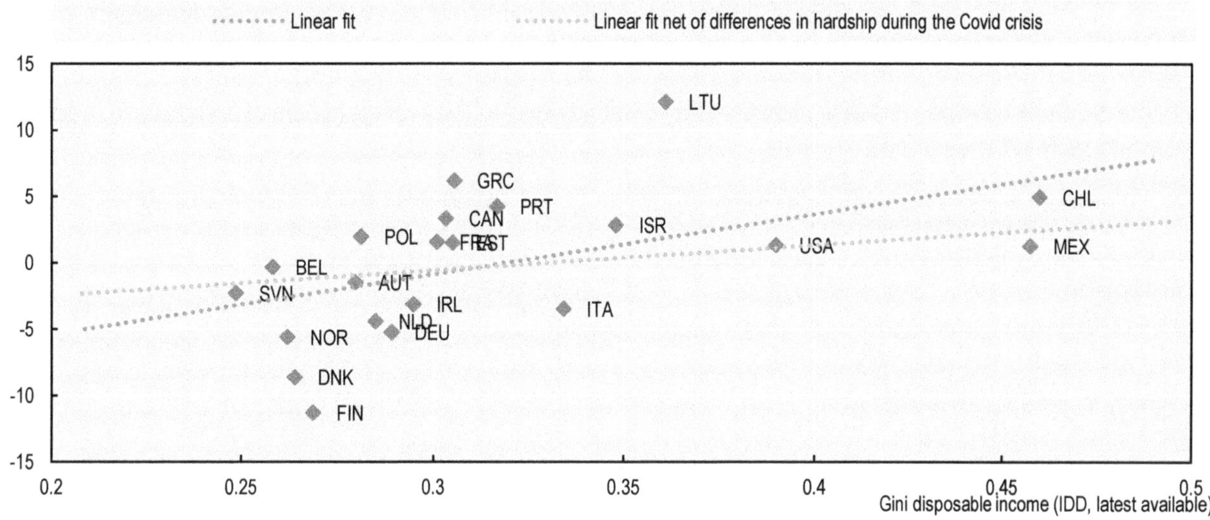

Note: The share of respondents who demand more progressive taxation refers to those who answer "yes/definitely yes" to the question whether the government should increase progressivity to support the poor (excluding those answering "Can't choose"). The linear fit net of differences in hardship during the COVID-19 crisis is obtained by first netting out for the share of respondents who report having experienced health or economic hardship during the COVID-19 crisis. For consistency with the 2020 wave, the 2018 values have been calculated only for individuals aged 18-64. Changes between the two Risks that Matter waves should be interpreted with some caution due to adjustments in sampling methods and coverage.
Source: OECD calculations from the 2018 and 2020 Risks that Matter Surveys, and *OECD Income Distribution Database* (https://stats.oecd.org/Index.aspx?DataSetCode=IDD).

StatLink https://stat.link/d2v1s6

Higher redistribution lowers people's demand for further intervention

People's preferences for redistribution depend on its current level. If taxes and transfers already control income disparities effectively, then people are likely to be less concerned about inequality and do not demand more redistribution. Assessing the relationship between the current level of and demand for redistribution is complicated for one important reason – voters' preferences. They may well determine levels of redistribution, as exemplified by the wide differences in redistribution levels between the United States and Europe.

Risks that Matter partially helps address the relationship between the current level of and demand for redistribution, as it explicitly asks respondents whether they want more (or less) redistribution. It may therefore be expected that, for a given level of market inequality, redistribution that is currently of a high level might reduce demand for more of it.

To help unbundle the association between the current level of and demand for redistribution, it makes sense to measure income inequality and redistribution only within the working-age population for two reasons. First, it appears more salient (Table 3.4) and, second, because assessing redistribution among the elderly is complicated by international differences in pension systems.

The measure of redistribution used is the gap between inequality in market and disposable income, which the literature refers to as the Reynolds-Smolensky (RS) index. The hypothesis is that demand for more redistribution is high in countries where market inequality is also high, and that extensive redistribution reduces demand for further increases. The hypothesis is confirmed by respondents who answer that the government should do much more than it currently does (Figure 3.11, left-hand panel). In the countries where market inequality is greater, so are preferences for redistribution, while more redistribution curbs demand for it. The same is true of demand for more progressive taxation (Figure 3.11, right-hand panel).

Figure 3.11. Demand for more redistribution is lower in countries where the current level of redistribution is higher

The bubbles denote countries and their size the relative (with respect to the average) share of respondents in each country who reply to the questions...

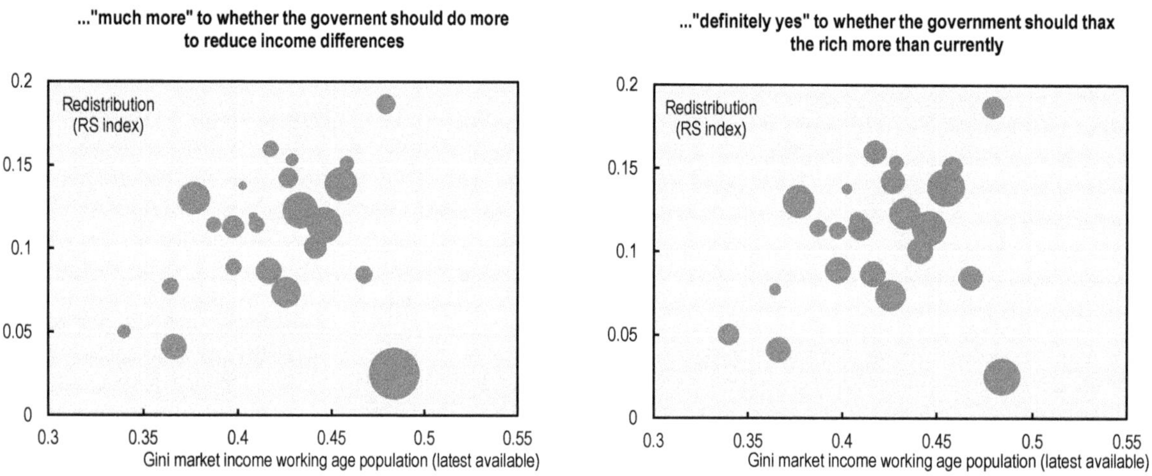

Note: Each bubble refers to a country. The RS index is the difference between the Gini index for market income and the Gini index for disposable income for the working-age population. A higher value indicates that taxes and transfers reduce inequality to a larger extent. Mexico and Turkey are not included because data for these countries exclude taxes paid.
Source: OECD calculations from the 2020 Risks that Matter Survey and *OECD Income Distribution Database* (https://stats.oecd.org/Index.aspx?DataSetCode=IDD) .

StatLink https://stat.link/psjha4

Even when preferences for redistribution are expressed with respect to the current level, other factors that drive actual levels of and demand for redistribution may still influence cross-country comparisons. As Chapter 2 shows, differences between countries in income equality preferences are both wide and persistent.

To account for persistent country differences, Olivera (2015[23]) focuses on changes in redistribution preferences, using a pseudo-panel approach applied to ESS survey data, combined with market income inequality data from the *Standardized World Income Inequality Database* and public social protection expenditure (in % of GDP) from Eurostat. He finds that when market income inequality rises, so do redistribution preferences, while they fall when social protection is strong. Table 3.5 shows similar within-country regressions from the ISSP panel combined with IDD data. The signs of the coefficients in Column 1 confirm that redistributive preferences increase when market income inequality grows, and fall when levels of redistribution and social protection are higher. However, the coefficient on the RS index is not statistically different from zero.[9] There is a more sizeable negative association with the amount of social expenditure per head (Column 3), which is also used in the literature as a proxy for redistribution (Karabarbounis, 2011[28]).

Table 3.5. Changes in redistribution preferences are negatively associated with changes in redistribution, but the link is weak

Percentage point increase in the shares of respondents who agree it is the government's duty to reduce income differences associated with a 1% (percentage point for fractions) increase in...

	(1)	(2)	(3)
...Gini market income (before tax and transfers)	0.87		0.66
	(0.38)		(0.45)
...taxes and transfer redistribution (RS index)	-0.44		
	(0.50)		
...lag of Gini market income (before taxes and transfers)		1.82**	
		(0.84)	
...lag of taxes and transfer redistribution (RS index)		-0.87	
		(0.88)	
...logarithm of total public social expenditure per head			-0.11*
			(0.06)
...logarithm of GDP per capita	-0.10	-0.40**	-0.04
	(0.10)	(0.13)	(0.15)
Observations	80	46	69
Countries	30	15	25
Country fixed effects	Included	Included	Included
Period fixed effects	Included	Included	Included

Note: Standard errors clustered by country in parentheses. The RS index is the distance between the Gini coefficients for market income and for disposable income (the higher the index, the stronger is redistribution). The analysis includes the logarithm of GDP per capita because the amount of redistribution is likely to depend on fiscal constraints. The lag refers to the previous wave year (statutory if the country was not observed or actual if the country was observed, and to 5 years before for wave 1987).
Source: OECD calculations based on ISSP 1987, 1992, 1999, 2009, 2017 and Eurobarometer 2017; *OECD Income Distribution Database* (https://stats.oecd.org/Index.aspx?DataSetCode=IDD) and *OECD Social Expenditure Database* (https://www.oecd.org/social/expenditure.htm).

StatLink https://stat.link/5jd6mv

3.3. Inequality, relative income and preferences for redistribution

High-income individuals demand less redistribution, but not because they perceive smaller disparities

Individuals' relative income is a key driver of preferences for redistribution. People in the upper part of the income distribution have lower redistribution preferences, although even among them a sizeable share of them agree that the government should do more to reduce income disparities.

One interpretation of differences in preferences between high- and low-income individuals – rooted in the Meltzer and Richard (1981[3]) median voter model – is based on personal gains and losses from redistribution. If individuals cared only about their own consumption, those with above-average income would oppose redistribution, and those on below-average income support it.

An alternative interpretation is that poorer individuals overestimate inequality, while those in the upper income tertile underestimate it. However, evidence from the 2020 wave of Risks that Matter survey does not lend support to this hypothesis (Figure 3.12, Panel A). On average, differences in perceptions of income inequality between the lowest, middle and top household-equivalised income tertiles are quite narrow. In some countries, such as Austria, France, Poland, Korea and Turkey, richer respondents even perceive the richest 10%'s share of income to be greater than other groups do. Indeed, if their social network is narrow and their information limited, the better-off may have better knowledge of the income levels of those at the top of the distribution, but know less about those at the bottom (Cruces, Perez-Truglia and Tetaz, 2013[29]).

Despite their similar perceptions of income inequality, people on high incomes favour less redistribution in most countries (Figure 3.12, Panel B). The few exceptions are countries where demand for redistribution is high in all income groups, as in Chile, Spain, Greece, Lithuania, Mexico and Turkey. In the United States, where there is little support for government intervention in narrowing income disparities, demand for more redistribution is low in all income classes. Generally, the middle income tertile in most countries shows redistribution preferences that are closer to people on low incomes than on high ones.

Figure 3.12. Perceptions of income disparities are similar in all income groups, but preferences for redistribution are not

Perceptions and redistributive preferences by tertiles of household-equivalised disposable income, 2020

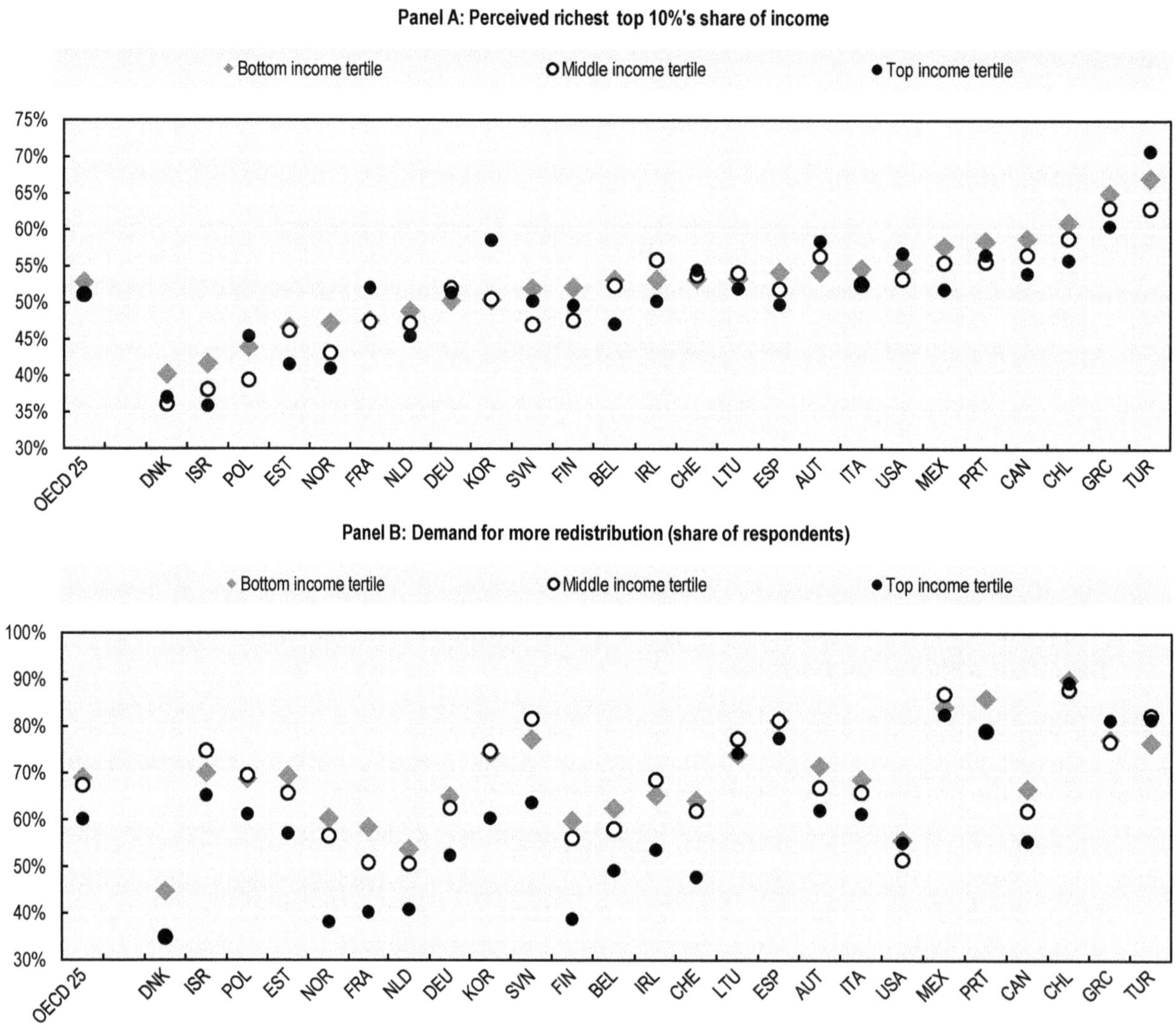

Source: OECD calculations from the 2020 Risks that Matter Survey.

StatLink https://stat.link/nhtie9

As for earnings inequality, high-income individuals again do not always perceive lower disparities. In the OECD countries observed in ISSP 2009, individuals in the top income tertile actually report wider perceived top-bottom earnings disparities than other income groups (Figure 3.13). Their preferred disparities help understand how that finding squares with the lower demand for redistribution observed in the top income tertile. In almost all countries, high-income individuals prefer higher earnings disparities. As a result, in the vast majority of countries, the distance between perceived and preferred disparities is lower in the top-income tertile than in other groups.

Figure 3.13. Both perceived and preferred earnings disparities are wider among high-income individuals

Differences between respondents in different household income tertiles (in log points), OECD average, 2009

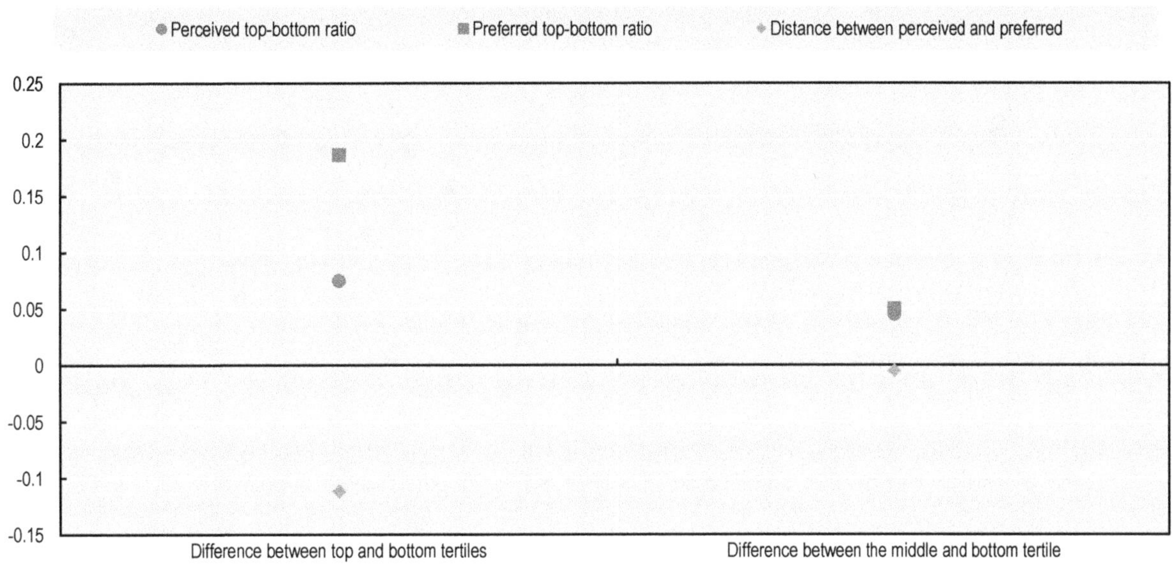

Note: Average across 28 OECD countries (see Figure 2.8, Panel B). Individuals in each country and period are divided into tertiles based on the household income variable (equivalised) available in ISSP. Missing data were imputed following the procedure illustrated in Annex A in Ciani et al. (forthcoming[30]).
Source: OECD calculations from ISSP 2009.

StatLink https://stat.link/7tuzle

A different interpretation of the negative relation between own-income and redistributive preferences is that the better- and worse-off have different beliefs about the reasons for inequality. Piketty (1995[9]) proposes a model in which people draw on their own experience to learn about the actual rate of social mobility in their country. Those who meet with success, and eventually become rich, end up believing that hard work pays and are therefore less favourable to redistribution. Fong (2001[7]) shows that the effect of the belief in hard work on redistributive preferences accounts for a sizeable share of the association between redistributive preferences with income.

It might therefore follow that the rich should take a more optimistic view of the aggregate level of intergenerational upward mobility. However, that is not true of most countries (Figure 3.14). In several, high-income individuals actually believe in weaker intergenerational mobility with respect to what low-income individual believe. Alesina, Stantcheva and Teso (2018[31]), drawing on data for France, Italy, Sweden, the United Kingdom and the United States, suggest that this apparent conundrum is attributable to contradictory views of intergenerational mobility and reasons for personal success. Even if high-income individuals think that most people remain stuck in the same income bracket as their parents, they tend to justify their own position with the belief that, eventually, individual effort pays off. Alesina, Stantcheva and

Teso (2018[31]) also find that individuals at the top of the income distribution are more likely to agree that hard work is the main reason for being rich.

Figure 3.14. Richer people are often less optimistic about intergenerational mobility

Perceptions by income tertile of intergenerational persistence in the poorest 10%

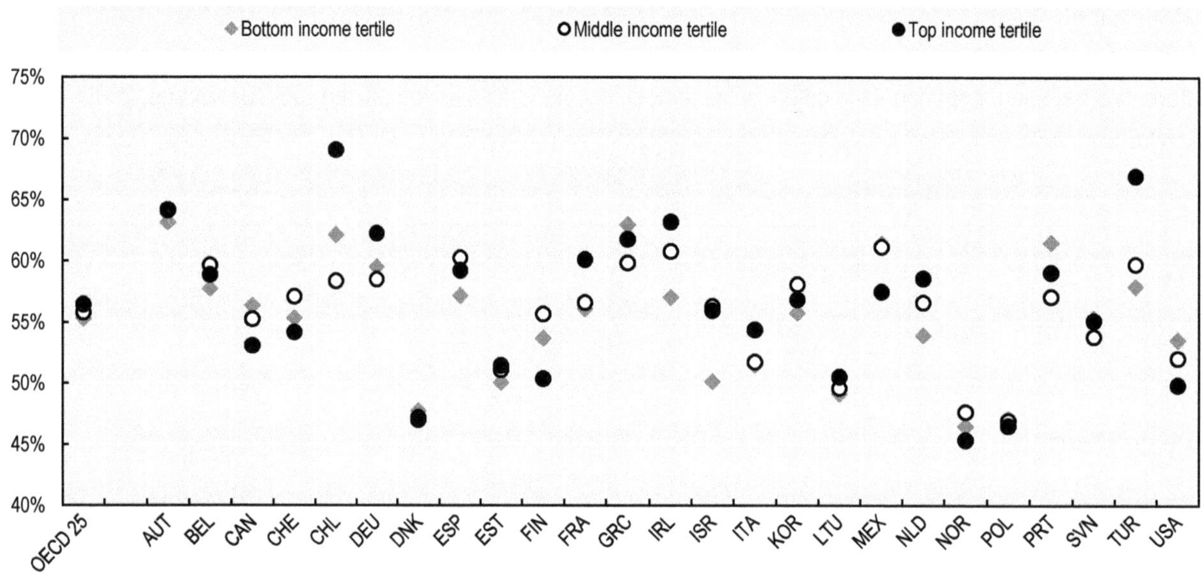

Note: Intergenerational persistence among the poorest 10% refers to the likelihood that a child from a household in the poorest 10% of the income distribution will remain in the same decile upon becoming adult. Income tertiles are calculated on equivalised household disposable income.
Source: OECD calculations from the 2020 Risks that Matter Survey.

StatLink https://stat.link/twgkzu

The fact that better-off people are less in favour of redistribution does not mean that only the poor drive demand for redistribution up or down over time. Indeed, in some countries where preferences for more redistribution have grown over time, that growth was stronger among those in the top income tertile of the distribution (Figure 3.15). Cases in point are the United States, Italy, Slovenia and Switzerland, while in Hungary and Australia the increase was greater in the bottom tertile. Even where average redistribution preferences declined, it was not always attributable to the rich. In the United Kingdom and Austria, the drop was more pronounced among the poor. Furthermore, changes in the preferences of the middle income tertile do not always lie in between the top and bottom tertiles. In Germany and Austria, middle-income demand for redistribution declined less than that of high and low income individuals, while in Australia it rose by a smaller extent than for the other two groups.

Figure 3.15. In some countries, the redistribution preferences of the better-off grew more steeply over time

Percentage point changes in the shares of respondents who agree that it is the responsibility of the government to reduce income disparities, by income tertile, 1990 to 2009

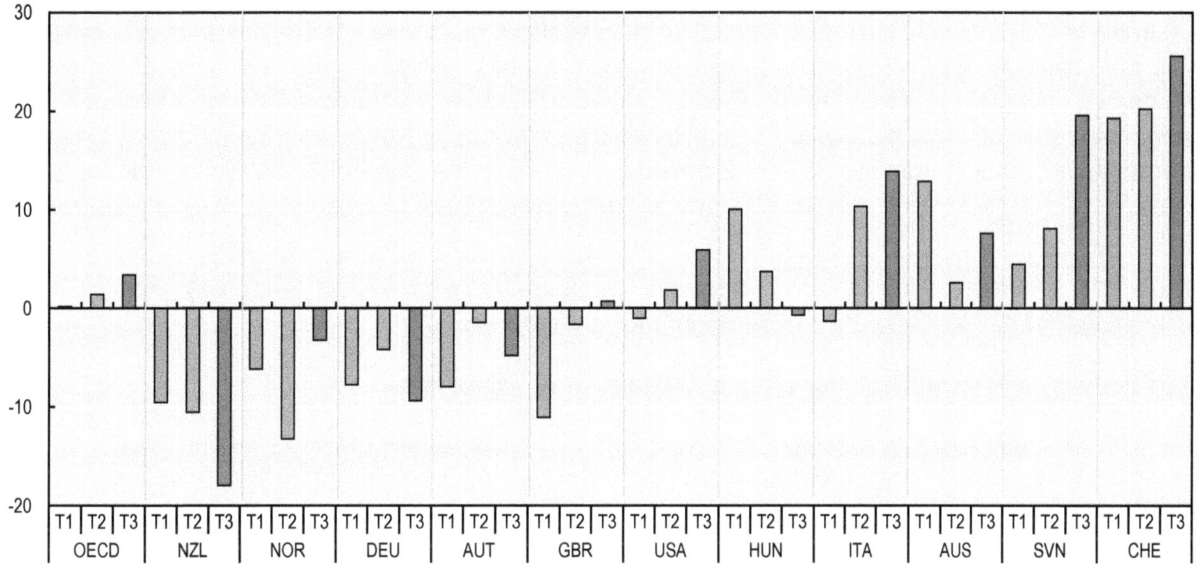

Note: Households are divided into tertiles corresponding to the equivalised income distribution of each of the country in each period (1987-1992 and 2009) according to the household income variable available in ISSP. Missing data were imputed, see Annex A in Ciani et al. (forthcoming[30]) for details and further information on the collection of income data in ISSP.
Source: OECD calculations based on ISSP 1992, 1987, 2009.

StatLink https://stat.link/fd370m

Greater income inequality shapes individual demand for redistribution through both relative income and social preferences

Growth in income inequality may increase demand for redistribution through two channels (Alesina and Giuliano, 2011[2]; Rueda and Stegmueller, 2019[4]):

- The first is through changes in people's relative income. This is the logic behind the Meltzer and Richard (1981[3]) median voter model. When inequality rises, the median voter becomes poorer than the average. Based on models in which voters care only about their individual gains and losses, median voters' relative impoverishment makes them favourable to redistribution. As the income distribution is skewed, the greater the inequality, the higher the share of individuals who demand more redistribution or progressive taxation.
- The second is through people's preferences for equality. Even assuming that only their own consumption matters to people, the macro-level of inequality matters if it affects their consumption – when, for example, greater inequality reduces GDP per capita growth and limits educational investment (Cingano, 2014[32]), or when inequality and poverty increase the fear of crime (Rueda and Stegmueller, 2015[33]). More broadly, people have preferences for macro-levels of inequality (Alesina and Giuliano, 2011[2]; Clark and D'Ambrosio, 2015[34]).

The importance of both channels has been confirmed experimentally, by re-creating in a laboratory setting redistributive situations where the distribution of income is manipulated by the experimenters (Durante, Putterman and van der Weele, 2014[11]). Rueda and Stegmueller (2019[4]) suggest a way to disentangle the effects of the two channels on observational data – by looking at the effects of respondents' income and aggregate inequality and how they interact. Figure 3.16 replicates their results on ISSP microdata by looking at variations of country-wide inequality over time (by including country fixed effects). It shows that the effect of relative income is as predicted by the simplest model in which individuals care only about their personal gains or losses from redistribution: individual with higher income are less concerned over income disparities and demand less government intervention. Therefore, when inequality rises, the income of households at the bottom of the distribution falls further away from the average, and they become more favourable to redistribution. On top of the relative income effect, an increase in the macro-level of inequality shifts the entire curve of preferences for redistribution upward, confirming the relevance of the second channel, i.e. people's preferences for equality. However, macro-level inequality has a stronger effect among the better-off. This finding confirms estimates carried out by Rueda and Stegmueller (2019[4]) on other datasets, ranging from the ESS for European countries to the General Social Survey for the United States.

Figure 3.16. The macro-level effect of inequality on people's concern over inequality and preferences for redistribution is stronger among the better-off

Share of respondents (confidence interval in the shaded area) who agree that...

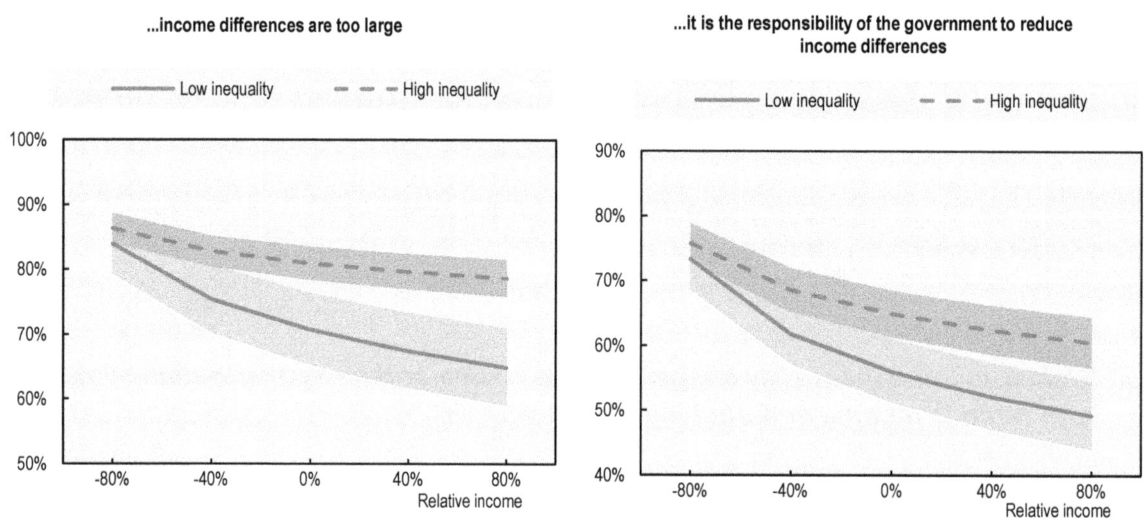

Note: The lines show predicted share of respondents agreeing with the two statements by relative income of respondents and level of income inequality in the country. Low inequality refers to a value of the Gini coefficient for disposable income of 0.26 (the 25th percentile in the sample), while high inequality refers to a Gini coefficient of 0.34 (the 75th percentile). The shaded areas are 95% confidence intervals using standard errors clustered at the level of country (22 countries). Relative income refers to relative family income (equivalised using the square root of household size) compared to the country-wave average (after winsorising to avoid outliers). The estimates are carried out following Rueda and Stegmueller (2019[4]) approach (See Annex 3.A for more details).

Source: OECD calculations from ISSP 1987, 1992, 1999, 2009, 2017, and *OECD Income Distribution Database* (https://stats.oecd.org/Index.aspx?DataSetCode=IDD).

StatLink https://stat.link/hna0lt

There are multiple reasons why the preferences of the better-off should respond strongly to macroeconomic levels of inequality. Rueda and Stegmueller (2015[33]; 2020[35]) argue that the negative impact of redistribution on the consumption of the rich is relatively less relevant than its positive impact on the poor. The rich are likely to accept redistribution's direct impact on higher taxes because they have a social preference for more equality or they care about other indirect effects of inequality on their consumption. Rueda and Stegmueller (2015[33]; 2020[35]) argue that fear of crime also explains why an increase in inequality translates into increased redistribution preferences among the rich.

Another interpretation is that, for the poor, their self-interest is aligned with the thrust of redistribution. And while it might seem puzzling that the rich react more to macro-levels of inequality, it should not be forgotten that the mechanism behind the relative-income channel is still at work – i.e. higher inequality increases the redistribution preferences of low-income individuals by making them even relatively poorer.

Most people believe they belong to the middle class

The impact of the relative-income channel inequality on preferences for redistribution is stronger if people are aware of their position in the income distribution. Often, though, they are not. Evidence from the Compare Your Income webtool shows that most people believe their income is close to the median (Figure 3.17 and Balestra and Cohen (forthcoming[36])). Two opposite forces drive this pattern, which is usually referred to as "middle-income bias" (OECD, 2019[37]; Hoy and Mager, 2021[38]; Cansunar, 2021[39]):[10]

1. People from the bottom of the income distribution tend to overestimate their relative position. In fact, in almost all countries more than 90% of individuals believe that they are located above the 25th percentile of the distribution.
2. High-income individuals tend to underestimate their position, although such misrepresentation varies from country to country. Greater shares of the better-off think they are lower down the distribution in Belgium, Portugal, Greece, Italy and Spain, while in Canada and Australia such underestimation is lower.

The two forces offset each other. Nevertheless, the average respondent in most countries overestimates his/her position.

Figure 3.17. Most people believe their income is close to the median

Distribution of respondents' perceived position in the income distribution: horizontal lines show the distribution of the values (10th, 25th, average, 75th, 90th percentiles) if respondents correctly estimate their relative position

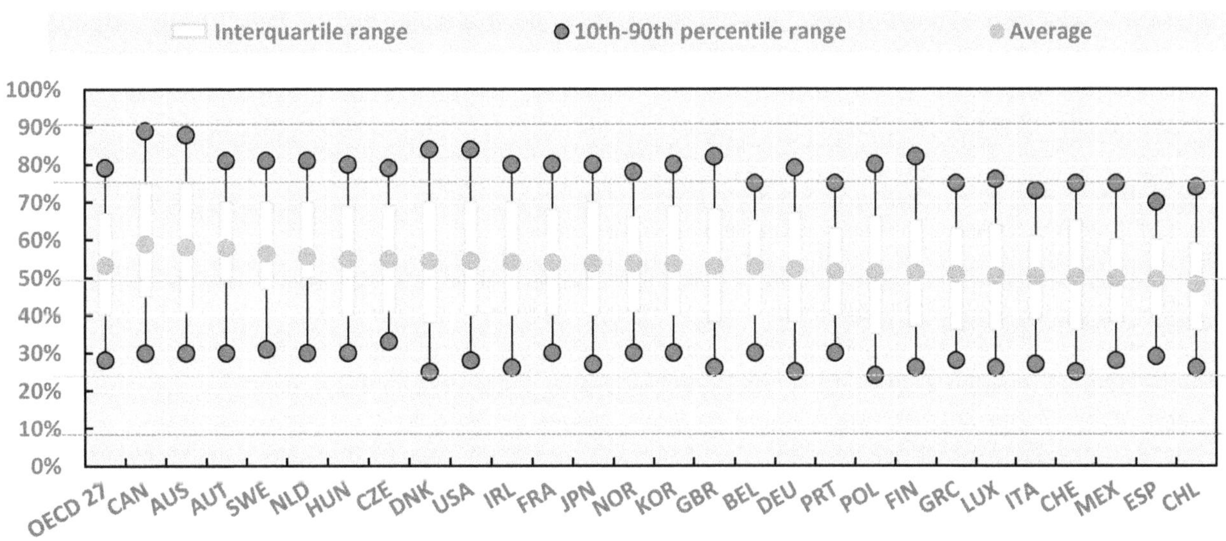

Note: Blue dots are for the 10th and 90th percentiles, the box for the 25th and 75th percentiles, while the grey dot is the average.
Source: Balestra and Cohen (forthcoming[36]) on Compare Your Income 2015-2020.

StatLink https://stat.link/jbx9pq

Evidence from several studies confirms that most people tend to believe their income is close to the median. Cruces et al. (2013[29]) show that in Buenos Aires more than 50% overestimate their relative income position and 30% underestimate it. Karadja et al. (2017[40]) state that most Swedes believe they are poorer than they actually are. Bublitz (2020[41]) provides evidence of differences between perceived and actual relative income position in Brazil, France, Germany, Russia, Spain and the United States. More detailed findings on Denmark from Hvidberg et al. (2020[42]) suggest that the divergence between perceived and actual relative income positions is partly explained by the fact that people are better able to assess their relative position with respect to others in specific reference groups – such as cohorts or co-workers – rather than with reference to the entire population. Nevertheless, they still find that poorer individuals largely overestimate their income position relative to the reference groups that matter the most to them, so limiting their demand for redistribution.

Informing people as to their true income position changes their preferences for redistribution – those who overestimate their income become more favourable to redistributive intervention and those who underestimate it less favourable (Cruces, Perez-Truglia and Tetaz, 2013[29]; Karadja, Mollerstrom and Seim, 2017[40]). However, evidence from available experiments suggests that being informed of the facts generally has – on average – a limited effect on their support for redistribution (Box 3.2).

Box 3.2. Informing people of their true income rank changes their attitudes towards redistribution, though only to a small extent

What would the average level of redistributive preferences be if people were to know their actual position in the income distribution? Answering that hypothesis entails associating true relative income with preferences for redistribution. But that is complicated, mainly because people with a perception of relative income are not selected at random and might differ from others in characteristics that cannot be controlled.

For these reasons, the literature uses in-survey experiments to understand what the consequences would be of informing people of their true position in the income distribution. In such experiments, a randomly selected subset of respondents is given the information before they answer standard questions about preferences for redistribution. Given the random selection, these respondents are no different from those who do not receive the information, so comparing the answers of the two groups measures the effect of the information. In most studies, however, the estimated effect is imprecise, with a large confidence interval. Ciani, Fréget and Manfredi (forthcoming[43]) offer a meta-analysis of the available experiments, which yields a more precise average answer. The average effect across studies is slight, with a narrow confidence interval of around zero.

The small overall effect might just be the result of heterogeneous responses from individuals who overestimate or underestimate their relative income position. If both groups were to revise their expectations, those who overestimate would become more favourable towards redistribution, while those who underestimate would become less favourable. Therefore, two margins would compensate each other. Some studies report heterogeneous results depending on prior perception of income position. Focusing on these studies, the meta-analysis finds results that are consistent with the hypothesis that people who overestimate their position increase their demand for redistribution once they are informed about their actual relative standing, while those who underestimate decrease their support. Cruces et al. (2013[29]), for instance, find that in Buenos Aires the impact of information is statistically different from zero only for those who initially overestimate their position, while Karadja et al. (2017[40]) find the opposite pattern in Sweden. The average effects in each group are, however, slight.

There are two possible explanations for the fact that knowing one's income position has such little effect. The first is that on average the difference between perceived and actual relative position is limited, or alternatively, that the relative income position estimated through national surveys is not necessarily very relevant to gauging people's opinions about the role of government in redistribution. The second explanation is that other beliefs, which may vary widely from country to country, matter more than relative income.[1]

Note

1. For the poor who overestimate their position, Hoy and Mager (2021[38]) suggest that the small effect on redistributive preferences might be driven by respondents who use their income as a "benchmark" to evaluate the condition of other individuals. Before receiveing information, they believe their income is a benchmark for the middle class. After discovering that they are actually poor, they also realise that there are fewer poor people than they expected. In fact, Hoy and Mager (2021[38]) find that in most of the countries of their study, poor people who overestimate their position in the income distribution reduce their concerns with inequality when they are provided with information.

3.4. What shapes the association between income inequality and preferences for redistribution?

Concern over income inequality does not fully translate into higher demand for redistribution

Although concern over income disparities influences preferences for redistribution, it does not translate in the same proportions into higher demand for government intervention. According to the latest available data from the ISSP and Eurobarometer, an average of around 80% of the population in OECD countries agrees that income disparities are too wide. However, the share that thinks the government should act to reduce inequality is less than 80% in most countries (Figure 3.18). The widest gaps are observed in English-speaking countries (apart from Ireland; see Benson et al. (2021[44]) for related evidence for the United Kingdom), Switzerland, the Czech Republic and Japan (Kambayashi and Lechevalier, 2021[1]). The gap is especially wide in the United States, which suggests that the key transatlantic divide with respect to European countries in attitudes towards redistribution stems from the different views of the role of government, rather from concern over income disparities (Osberg and Bechert, 2016[45]). The discrepancy between high levels of concern over income disparities and little call for redistributive action is also significant in some European countries (Austria, France, Germany), despite their strong welfare states, as well as in some post-transition countries (the Czech Republic, Hungary, Estonia and the Slovak Republic).

Figure 3.18. People's demand for redistribution is lower than their concern over income disparities

Differences between the share of people who agree that it is the responsibility of the government to reduce income differences and those who agree that income differences are too large, 2017

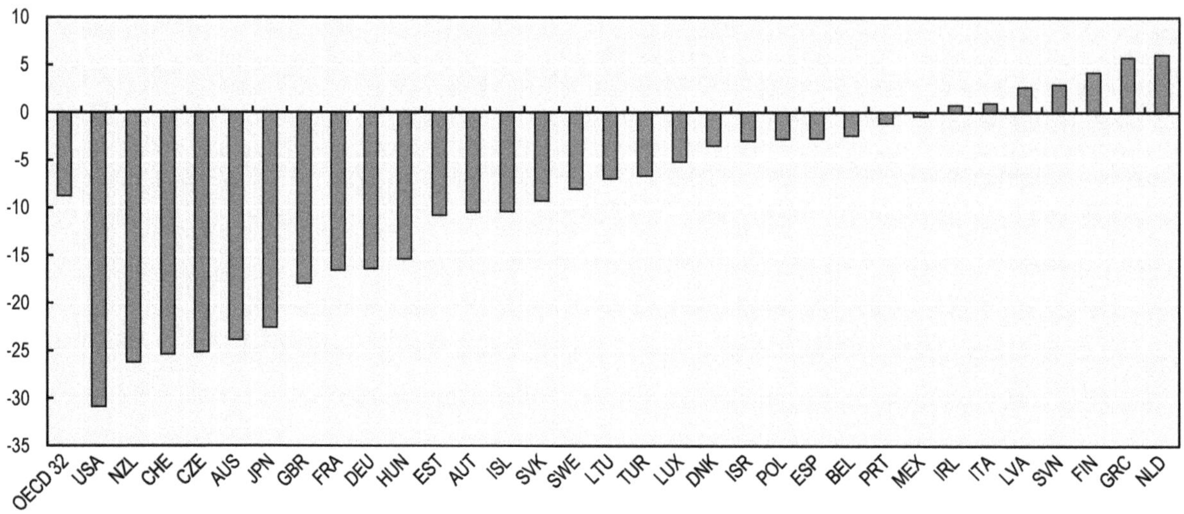

Note: Respondents are asked their opinion about the statements "Differences in income in [country] are too large" and "It is the responsibility of the government to reduce the differences in income between people with high incomes and those with low income". In Eurobarometer the statements are slightly different: "Nowadays in [our country] differences in people's incomes are too great" and "The government in [our country] should take measures to reduce differences in income levels", but the response scale is identical. Data from ISSP are used where available.
Source: OECD calculations from ISSP 2017; from Eurobarometer 471/2017 for Belgium, Estonia, Greece, Ireland, Italy, Luxembourg, Latvia, Netherlands, Poland, Portugal whose data are; for Slovenia, concern are from ISSP and preferences for redistribution from Eurobarometer.

StatLink https://stat.link/imqs5z

The mismatch between concern about income disparities and preferences for redistribution is manifest in aggregate trends. Over the last three decades, redistribution preferences have increased, but by less than concern over income disparities (Figure 3.19). The average increase on both counts was steepest between the late-1980s/early-1990s and the onset of the Great Recession, though the increase in the demand for redistribution was only half that of concern about inequalities.[11]

Focusing on countries observed between (approximately) these two points in time and on the share that strongly agree with the statements, only two demonstrate both decreased concern over income disparities and reduced preference for redistribution – New Zealand and Norway (Figure 3.20, upper panel). In all other countries, concern over inequality has grown over time, while changes in preferences for redistribution have been smaller or even negative. Only in Italy and Australia have they increased at a similar pace.

Figure 3.19. Preferences for redistribution have increased by less than concern about income disparities

Average across countries in the share who strongly agree that…

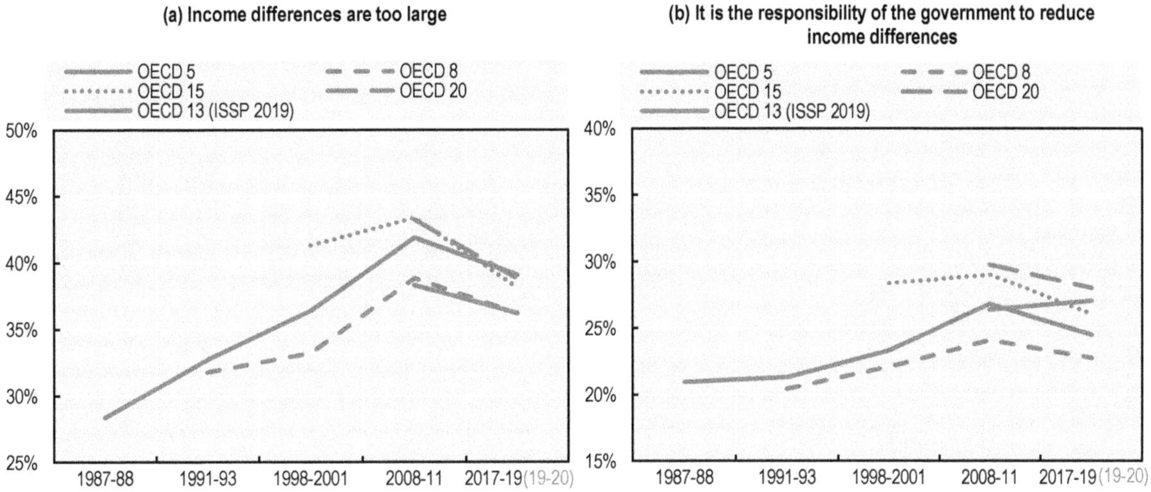

Note: Unweighted average across countries of the share of people who strongly agree that income disparities (in their country) are too large. Despite the availability of data, the figure does not include Germany in 1987 (only West Germany was surveyed). Nor does it include the Czech Republic and the Slovak Republic in 1992, which still made up Czechoslovakia; although separate samples are available. In 1992, the question referred to the whole of Czechoslovakia. As the aim is tracking the evolution over time, countries that have gaps (Italy and Switzerland) or do not appear in ISSP 2017 are not included. Unlike Figure 2.2, Slovenia is not included because the question on government intervention was not asked in ISSP.

OECD 5: Australia, Austria, Great Britain, Hungary, United States; OECD 8: + Germany, New Zealand, Sweden; OECD 15: + Czech Republic, Denmark, Spain, France, Israel, Japan, Slovak Republic; OECD 20: + Switzerland, Finland, Iceland, Lithuania, Turkey; OECD 13: Australia, Switzerland, Chile, Czech Republic, Germany, Denmark, Finland, United Kingdom, Italy, Japan, New Zealand, Norway, Slovenia.

Source: OECD calculations based on ISSP 1987, 1992, 1999, 2009, 2017, 2019.

StatLink https://stat.link/p2swfe

In the decade from 2009 to 2019, concern fell slightly, while average demand for redistribution actually grew a little. In New Zealand and the United Kingdom, concern over income disparities grew more than demand for redistribution, while concern contracted sizeably in Italy and Slovenia, as did redistribution preferences, albeit by less. Norway, Germany, Australia and Switzerland actually showed a greater rise in demand for redistribution than in concern, so narrowing the gap between the two.

The evolution from the late 1980s to 2019 is similar if we look at the shares of people who agreed or agreed strongly (Annex Figure 3.A.1). The increase in the preference for greater redistribution during the last decade has, however, been stronger if measured with this share, and brings it more into overall line with the rise of concern, so highlighting the fact that differences lie chiefly in the strength of people's agreement.

Figure 3.20. Changes in concern about income disparities and preferences for redistribution in selected countries

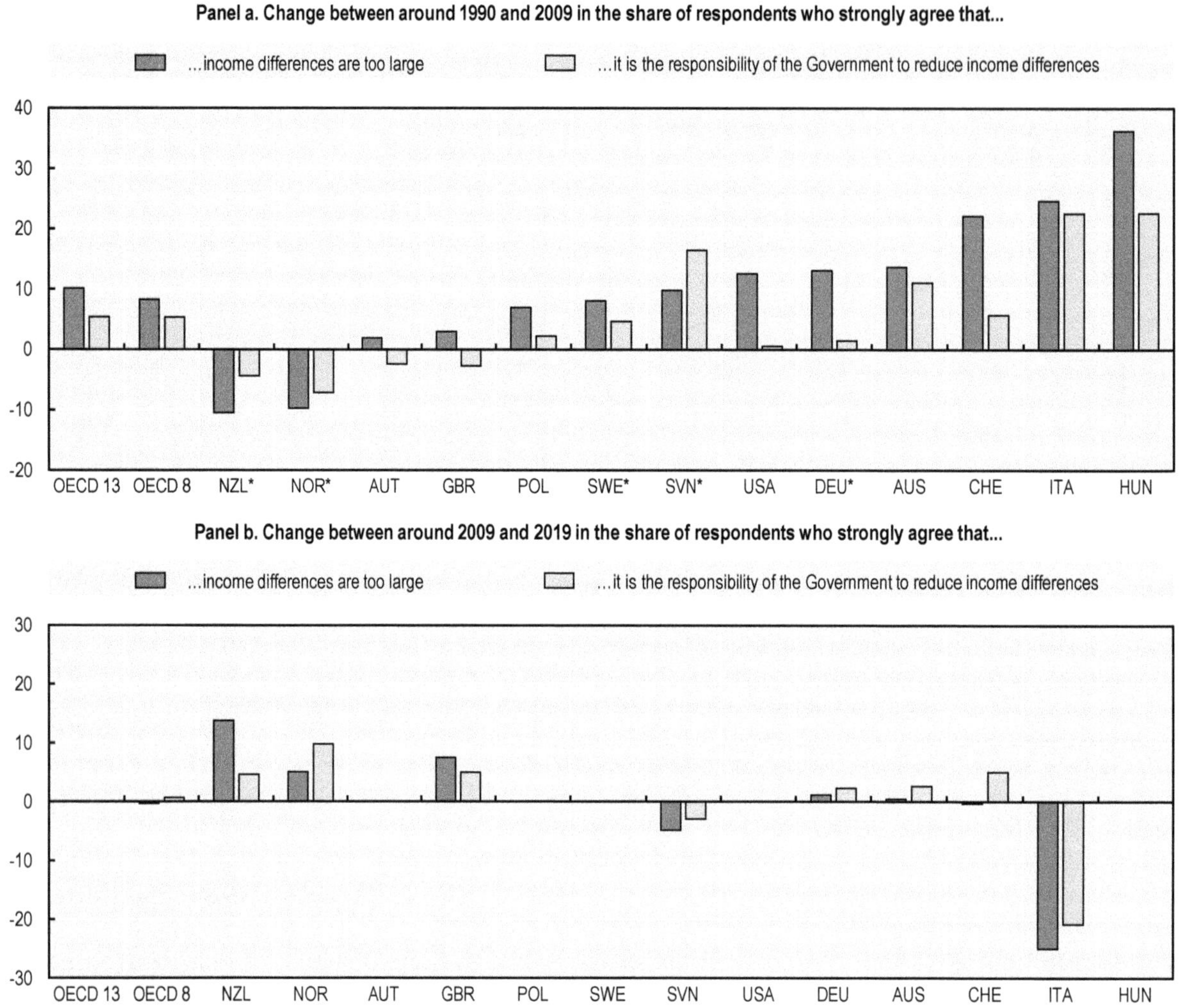

Note: The initial year depends on when countries are observed. For countries denoted by * it is 1992-93, for the others 1987-88.
Source: OECD calculations based on ISSP 1987, 1992, 2009, 2019.

StatLink https://stat.link/vpmljd

The association between changes in income inequality and changes in redistribution preferences is weaker than between changes in income inequalities and people's concern about them (Table 3.6). The difference is driven mostly by the weaker association between the shares of respondents who strongly believe that income inequality is too great and the share that strongly believes it is state's duty to reduce it. A 1 percentage point increase in the disposable income Gini coefficient is associated with an increase of 1.7 percentage points in concern and only 0.9 in the demand for redistribution.

Table 3.6. Rising inequality increases people's concern over inequality but has a weaker effect on their preferences for redistribution

Percentage point increase (or score increase for average answer) associated with a 1 percentage point increase in...

	(1)	(2)	(3)	(4)
	Income differences are too large		Government should reduce the income differences between the poor and the rich	
	Share that strongly agree	Share that agree or strongly agree	Share that strongly agree	Share that agree or strongly agree
		Panel A		
...Gini market income	0.66*	0.74***	0.58	0.71**
	(0.35)	(0.24)	(0.94)	(0.26)
		Panel B		
...Gini disposable income	1.71**	0.98**	0.94	0.92*
	(0.67)	(0.41)	(0.61)	(0.49)
Observations	78	78	78	78
Countries	29	29	29	29
Country fixed effects	included	included	Included	included
Period fixed effects	included	included	Included	included

Note: * denotes statistically significant at the 10% level, ** at 5%, *** at 1%. All coefficients can be read as percentage point changes.
Source: OECD calculations from ISSP 1987, 1992, 1999, 2009, 2017 and Eurobarometer 2017 for concern over income disparities; *OECD Income Distribution Database* (https://stats.oecd.org/Index.aspx?DataSetCode=IDD) for the Gini coefficient.

StatLink https://stat.link/icu14w

The weaker effect of inequality on redistribution preferences is confirmed by the meta-analysis of in-survey experiments proposed by Ciani, Frẽget and Manfredi (forthcoming[43]). Learning the true extent of inequality increases redistribution preferences, but only a little. The effects are generally positive but slight, and weaker than the impact on perceptions of and concern over inequality. In 36 experiments that examined the effect of learning the true magnitude of inequality on people's perceptions and concern and their redistribution preferences, one standard deviation increase in perceptions/concern is associated with an increase in redistribution preferences of less than 1/5. These results confirm that the increased perceptions and concern over inequality translate only partially into higher preferences for redistribution.

One reason why demand for redistribution responds only partially to growing inequality is that people's tolerance of it also grows. Trump (2018[46]) finds that showing people that income inequality is higher than they thought increases the level of disparities deemed fair. In a similar experiment in Mexico, Campos-Vazquez et al., (2020[47]) find, however, that informing respondents as to the true extent of income inequality, or the true level of intergenerational mobility, does not affect what they think levels of inequality and intergenerational mobility should be – i.e. their preferred levels. The effect of information about inequality on preferred level of inequality is still a largely unexplored issue as few experimental studies examine and collect preferred levels of inequality. Nevertheless, it is important to mention that rising tolerance of income disparities may explain the limited rise in demand for redistribution when actual inequality grows, but not why concern over income disparities does not.

The perceived effectiveness of redistribution policies influences public support

Different factors may weaken the impact of perceived and actual inequality on the demand for redistribution. To begin with, different individuals may hold very different views about the "feasible and legitimate role of government" (Bechert and Osberg, 2016, p. 1[48]). Some may believe that state redistribution is ineffective in addressing inequality, or that the efficiency costs of redistributive policies (such as a lower labour supply) outweigh their benefits.

Findings from Risks that Matter 2020 show that people's views of the effectiveness of policies and the potential waste of public resources are associated with demand for redistribution. Accounting for other characteristics, those who claim that many people receive public benefits without deserving them are less likely to support redistribution or progressive taxation (Figure 3.21). This perception may offset increases in preferences for redistribution prompted by perceptions of greater inequality or intergenerational persistence. The belief that benefits are granted undeservedly may be seen both as an indictment of how government policy targets benefits and as an expression of the belief that social benefits claimants cheat. Drawing on data from the European Social Survey, Algan, Cahuc and Sangnier (2016[49]) find that people who think many welfare claimants are not entitled to the benefits which they receive are less supportive of the welfare state.

Figure 3.21. People who believe that public benefits are mistargeted demand less redistribution

Differences across groups in shares of respondents who demand more redistribution or more progressive taxation, net of differences attributable to other characteristics (percentage points and 95% confidence intervals)

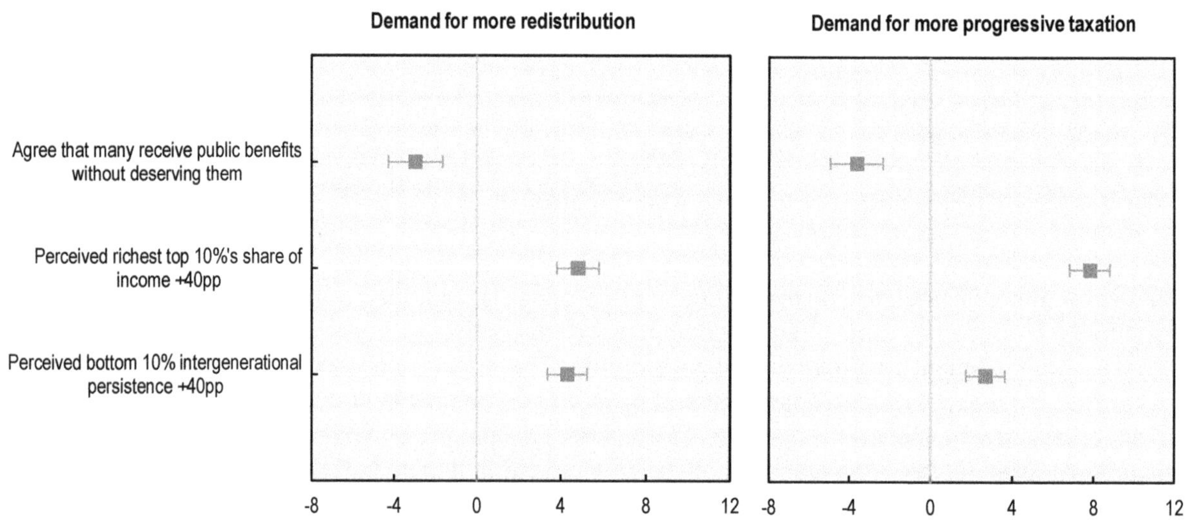

Note: Demand for redistribution refers to respondents who answer "more" or "much more" to the question whether the government should do more than it currently does to reduce income differences between the poor and the rich. Support for progressive taxation refers to respondents who answer "yes" or "definitely yes" to the question whether the government should tax the rich more than they currently do to support the poor. The differences associated with different groups/characteristics/perceptions are estimated using a multivariate probit model including all the characteristics in this figure and in Figure 3.4.
Source: OECD calculations from the 2020 Risks that Matter Survey.

StatLink https://stat.link/c34nuf

The importance of people's perceptions of policy effectiveness is confirmed by observational and experimental evidence. When asked about specific policies, respondents often fail to recognize their redistributive effect. Bartels (2005[50]), studying the wide support for the tax cuts enacted in the early 2000s in the United States, argues that individuals struggle to evaluate the redistributive effects of tax reforms. Accordingly, Kuziemko et al. (2015[51]) show that informing people how poor families benefit from different government programmes boosts the effect of information about inequality on redistribution preferences. Stantcheva (2020[52]) collects people's views of tax policies' consequences for redistribution and finds that they shape support for redistribution. Indeed, in her experiment, raising respondents' awareness of the implications of progressive taxation for redistribution increases support for such policy.

On the other hand, people may doubt the ability of policies to reduce inequality, even if they are aware of their implications. Lergetporer, Werner and Woessmann (2020[53]) show that providing scientifically based information about the effectiveness of equality-enhancing educational policies increases respondents' support for them. Similarly, Pellicer, Piraino and Wegner (2019[54]) find that supplying South African respondents with evidence that income inequality is lower in similar countries challenges their belief that inequality is inevitable and increases their preferences for redistribution. Settele (2021[16]) shows that giving people the facts about the wide gender wage gap has only a limited impact on demand for policies to reduce that gap, because a sizeable share of respondents believe that such policies are ineffective (see Box 3.1).

The perceived efficiency costs of redistributive policies – that they reduce the labour supply, for example – may also shape redistribution preferences. Hayes and Guay (2020[55]) supply respondents with information about the possible efficiency costs of inequality-reducing policies. They find that doing so reduces support for them, while telling the truth about benefits has no effect. Mishagina and Montmarquette (2018[56]) also find that informing respondents about the employment and price costs of a minimum wage policy reduces support for it. However, Stantcheva (2020[52]) shows that getting respondents to consider the efficiency of progressive taxation – e.g. labour supply responses and reduced aggregate revenue – affects their redistribution preferences only slightly.

Evidence from laboratory experiments supports the conclusion that efficiency considerations do affect people's redistributive preferences, but that the effect is slight. Durante, Putterman and van der Weele (2014[11]) – using large group laboratory experiments where researchers manipulate initial income distribution and the efficiency cost of redistribution – find that imposing a large efficiency cost of redistribution prompts participants to lower their demand for redistribution.

Moreover, efficiency costs are less important than social preferences for greater equality and the self-motivated preferences of lower-income groups for more redistribution (the two channels considered in Section 3.3). Almås et al. (2020[12]) run a redistributive experiment in a representative survey of 60 countries, in which people have to make real-world choices about reducing, or not, pay gaps between two workers in a real-life situation. Their findings show that people end up reducing them by less when the researchers enforce an aggregate 'efficiency' cost of redistribution, by imposing that only a fraction of the sum taken from the high-wage worker goes to the low-wage worker.[12] Nevertheless, they also find that such "efficiency" considerations are less important than the reasons – i.e. performance or luck – why the wage of the two workers was different prior to any redistribution.

The drivers of trust in public institutions shape demand for redistribution

Even when people are concerned about rising inequality, they may not support redistributive policies because they have limited trust in their government. A stream of observational evidence from the United States – started by Heterington (2006[57]) and Rudolph and Evans (2005[58]) – suggests that low level of trust in government reduces support for redistributive policies. This might explain why, in some countries, demand for redistribution has grown only to a limited extent despite rising inequality (Macdonald, 2019[59]). However, low trust in government does not necessarily spell little support for redistributive policies in all countries at all times. Svallfors (1999[60]) and Edlund (2006[61]) show that Swedish and Norwegian people who are wary of the government do not demand lower redistribution – perhaps because there is strong nationwide support for the welfare state in both countries.

The experimental evidence also yields mixed findings about the association between trust in government and preferences for redistribution. Kuziemko et al. (2015[51]) show that, when individuals receive information about actual levels of income inequality in the United States, their trust in government falls, which might be attributable to the limited – albeit positive – effect of information about inequality on preferences for redistribution. Using an experiment in which they prime respondents to be less confident in the integrity of government, they also show that eroding trust has an independent negative effect on demand for redistribution. Lergetporer, Werner and Woessmann (2020[53]), by contrast, argue that less trust does not explain the limited effect of learning the facts about inequality on redistribution preferences, because the effect is not driven by groups who are usually more trustful of government. In a recent experiment carried out in the United States, Peyton (2020[62]) found that boosting respondents' trust in government by getting them to read an op-ed praising public officials' integrity, did not lead to any sizeable change in demand for redistribution.

Focusing on the public governance drivers of trust in public institutions – responsiveness, reliability, openness, fairness and integrity (OECD, 2017[63]; Murtin et al., 2018[64]) – helps to bring clarity and reconcile the different findings. In fact, the overall "trust in government" is an outcome, shaped by these drivers. The intensity and importance of the different drivers vary extensively across countries (OECD/Korea Development Institute, 2018[65]; OECD, 2021[66]). Furthermore, there are reasons to expect the different drivers to relate differently to demand for redistribution.

Higher levels of satisfaction with government responsiveness, openness and fairness, for example, could be associated with less demand for more redistribution, because people are already satisfied with the current tax and benefit system (see Section 3.3). Edlund (2006[61]) finds that, for a large share of Swedish respondents, "distrust in the capability of the welfare state is an issue of insufficient resources", and therefore people who are not satisfied with the welfare state back increased social spending. Furthermore, people might demand more progressive taxation to make up for being treated unfairly by other policies (Scheve and Stasavage, 2016[67]). Conversely, they might demand less if they feel that the government is very open and fair.

People's beliefs in the integrity of public officials with whom they deal directly also play an important role. Civic-minded citizens are more willing to support a larger welfare state and greater redistribution if they believe that petty corruption is low and are confident that benefits go to those who need them most (Algan, Cahuc and Sangnier, 2016[49]). This dimension of public integrity is therefore likely associated with stronger demand for redistribution.

Integrity at different levels of public institutions may produce different effects. Corruption in the upper echelons of the state – revolving door practices or big business bribes, for example – creates inequalities perceived as unfair and anti-meritocratic. By the same token, when people perceive less top-tier corruption, they may believe that income distribution is fair or more meritocratic to begin with. Consequently, they may demand less redistribution (Alesina and Angeletos, 2005[10]).

Findings from the Trustlab survey (Figure 3.22) confirm the role of some these different drivers of trust in shaping demand for redistribution. People who believe that the government is responsive are less likely to demand more redistribution through progressive taxation. Respondents who see low levels of top-tier government corruption are also less favourable to redistribution. On the opposite, when they perceive low levels of petty corruption they demand more progressive taxation.

Figure 3.22. People demand less redistribution if they believe that the current government is responsive, but demand more if they think petty corruption is widespread

Percentage point change in the preferred level of tax redistribution associated with one standard deviation increase in...

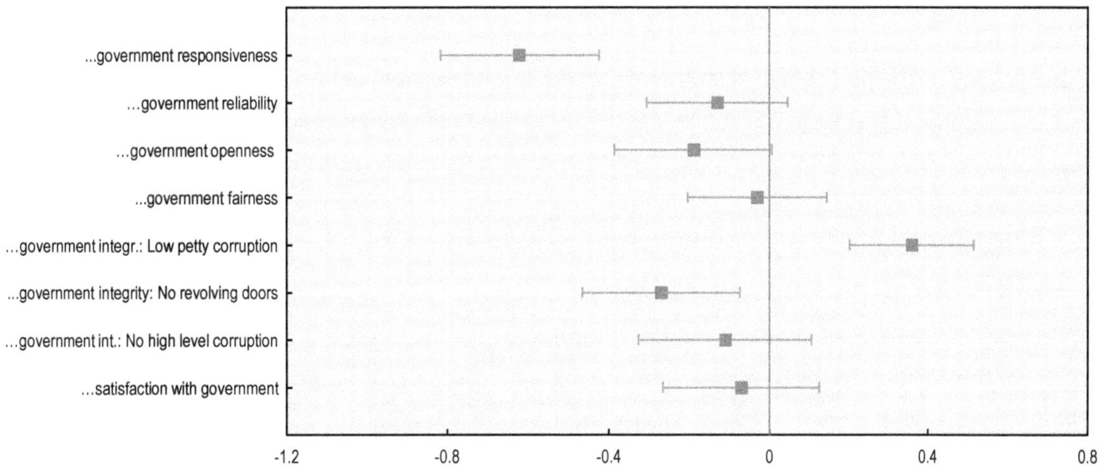

Note: The preferred level of redistribution is calculated as the difference between the Gini index for market income of the country of the respondents minus the respondent's preferred Gini index of post-tax income. The latter is calculated applying the tax schedule indicated by the respondent to the country's market income Gini index. This preferred level of redistribution is higher when the respondent chooses a more progressive taxation schedule. The effect of the single drivers are estimated through a regression that controls for a wide set of respondents' socio-economic characteristics plus country fixed effects. The countries included in the estimates are Germany, Italy, Japan, Slovenia, United Kingdom, United States.
Source: Bonnet et al. (forthcoming[68]) elaboration on the Trustlab survey.

StatLink https://stat.link/kfhm5b

The preferred mix of redistributive policies varies across people and countries

There is a different interpretation of the findings from informational experiment literature on how learning the facts about inequality has little effect on support for redistribution. It is that, while people may agree on the need for some policy action, they disagree on what action. In fact, several experiments into support for certain redistributive policies show that, on average, having information on rising inequality has little effect on support for any one policy. This is in contrast to the observational evidence reported above which finds a more consistent relation between growing inequality and general demand for redistribution.

Settele (2021[16]) exposes respondents to two different estimates of the gender gap in the United States. One is that the gap is wide, with women earning only 74% of what men do. The other is that the gap is narrow, at 94%. She finds that showing respondents evidence of the gender gap has a very strong effect on both perceptions of inequality and general demand for government action to reduce it. The effects on specific policies are also positive, but slight. Zilinsky (2014[69]) shows that supplying information on the extent of inequality increases demand for redistribution, but not for more progressive taxation.

Disagreement about the right policy mix may be prompted by different beliefs about different aspects of inequality. Evidence from Risks that Matter shows that beliefs about income inequality and intergenerational persistence impact policies differently (Figure 3.23). With regard to the general demand for redistribution, they exert similar impacts. However, beliefs about income disparities exert a much stronger effect on boosting demand for progressive taxation, spending on unemployment, and income support. As for the impact of beliefs about intergenerational persistence, it is strong when it comes to expenditure on education and, even more so, on health and long-term care. The explanation might be that people attribute health inequalities to factors beyond individuals' control or inherited from earlier generations (OECD, 2018[70]). Both perceptions of higher income disparities and intergenerational persistence increase demand for state spending on pensions, which underlines the importance of public pension systems in protecting poorer retirees, particularly through the first-tier safety net (OECD, 2017[71]).

Figure 3.23. The preferred mix of redistributive policies depends on different perceptions and combinations thereof

Impact of perceptions on the percentage shares of respondents who demand more…

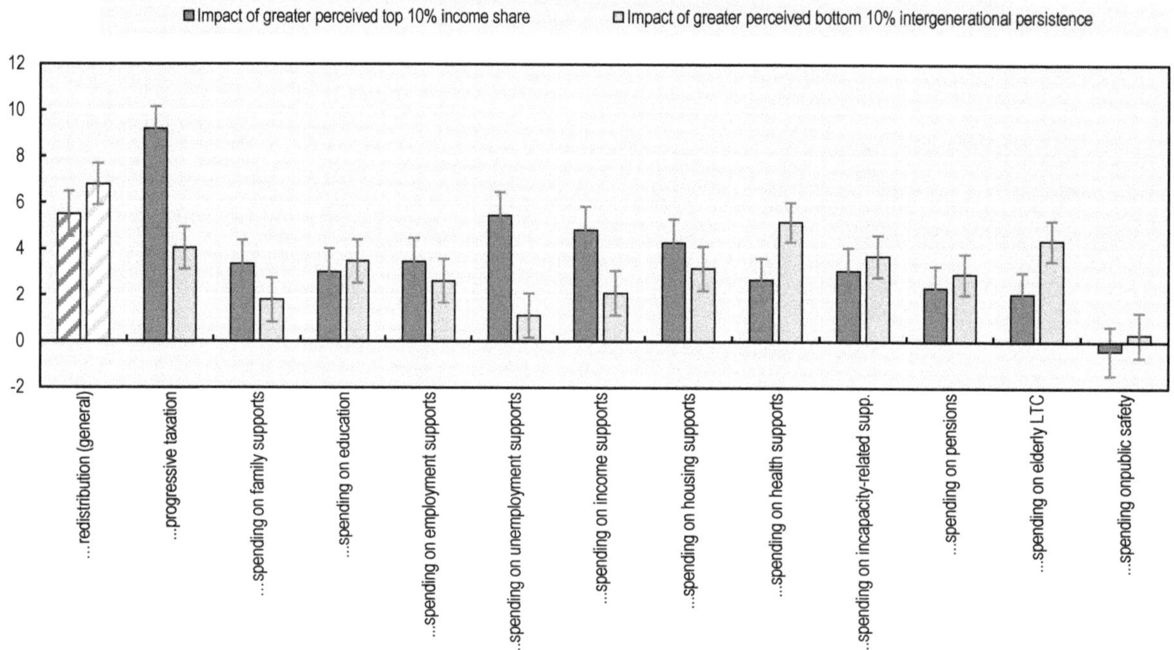

Note: Higher perceptions refer to an increase in either perception by 40 percentage points (approximately a shift from the 25th to the 75th percentile). It is estimated as average marginal effects from a probit regression, conditional on equivalised disposable income decile, gender, education, employment status, age, marital status, size of town, housing situation, and country fixed effects. Effects are not the same as in Figure 3.4 because other perceptions are not accounted for; results accounting for them are similar, however. The general question on demand for redistribution is "In your country, do you think the government should do more or less to reduce income differences?" For progressive taxation, it is "Should the government tax the rich more than they currently do in order to support the poor?" For the other categories, the question is: "Thinking about the taxes you might have to pay and the benefits you and your family might receive, would you like to see the government spend less, spend the same, or spend more in each of the following areas?" LTC stands for long-term care.
Source: OECD calculations from the 2020 Risks that Matter Survey.

StatLink https://stat.link/lj2kat

The general demand for more redistribution masks considerable cross-country differences in the mix of policies which people believe would best reduce income differences. Table 3.7 shows the association between general preferences for more redistribution and the demand for more public spending on different categories of action (relative to the demand for more spending across the board).

On average, across OECD countries, those who demand greater redistribution are most likely to demand more public spending on income support, incapacity benefits, and housing benefits. However, the trend varies from country to country. Although income support is often the category that people associate most readily with redistribution, different countries may also prioritise expenditure on education, unemployment, health, incapacity or pensions.

Table 3.7. People in different countries associate redistribution with different policies

Percentage-point differences in the probability of demanding higher social spending between those who demand more redistribution and those who do not; only top 3 associated categories

	Respondents who demand more redistribution are more likely to demand more social spending in... (percentage point difference shown in the cells)									
	...family	...education	...employ-ment	...unem-ployment	...income	...housing	...health	...incapacity	...pensions	...long term care
OECD					25	22		23		
AUT					31	29		25		
BEL					35				27	24
CAN				25	35			26		
CHE					30	28		33		
CHL		21			19				23	
DEU					27	26		28		
DNK				26	33			25		
ESP				25	25	22				
EST	23			23	32					
FIN					26		27	26		
FRA							25	21	23	
GRC		26			24		23			
IRL					24	30		25		
ISR	29				29			27		
ITA					26	25	23			
KOR					25		27	29		
LTU			24		22		26			
MEX		20		24				22		
NLD						24		25		24
NOR					25		25	25		
POL					31	28		25		
PRT		15	15						14	
SVN	21						26	22		
TUR	31	31	31							
USA					33		37	33		

Note: The higher the value, the more the demand for that specific public spending category is associated with demand for more redistribution with respect to the average category of public expenditure (public safety excluded). For instance, on average across all countries, people who demand more redistribution – i.e. more government intervention in reducing income differences – are particularly more likely to demand more income-related support, followed by incapacity-related and housing support. In details, for each category in each country, the relative association is the difference in the fraction that demand more spending between those who demand more redistribution and those who do not; it is expressed relatively to the average difference across all categories of public spending.
Source: OECD calculations from the 2020 Risks that Matter Survey.

StatLink https://stat.link/3y5cef

Kambayashi and Lechevalier (2021[1]) discuss related evidence for France, Japan and the United States. The three countries differ not only with regard to average levels of support for general redistribution and progressive taxation. They also show different shares of respondents who believe that general redistribution is desirable, but progressive taxation not. Evidence as to preferences for specific policies is crucial for understanding the demand for redistribution, but is rather scarce in cross-national surveys (with the exception of Pontusson et al. (2020[72])).

Different preferences for different policies might also depend on different beliefs in the reasons for top and bottom income inequality. Fong and Poutvaara (2019[73]) draw on data from Germany and the United States to show that the belief in poverty caused by bad luck, rather than lack of effort, generates support for transfers to the poor, while the belief that wealth is due to luck drives backing for taxing high incomes individuals. Several of the respondents who content that poverty reflects bad luck do not, conversely, believe that good luck is the only reason for being rich. Cross-country differences in beliefs as to the root causes of poverty and wealth may be wide, but hard evidence to that effect is limited.

The supply of public policies

A final consideration regards the provision of redistribution. Whether higher demand for redistribution translates into policies depends also on the interaction between citizens' preferences and policy makers. A large body of literature finds that policy makers tend to be more responsive to the opinions of high-income voters (Gilens, 2005[74]; Giger, Rosset and Bernauer, 2012[75]; Bartels, 2017[76]), and are therefore less likely to introduce redistributive reforms. Although analysis of the supply side of redistribution is beyond the scope of this report, it is nevertheless important to highlight that political representation may play a part in shaping people's confidence in the government and demand for redistribution.

Figure 3.24. Countries where more people believe that income disparities are too large are also those where most people perceive the government to be non-responsive

Share of respondents who agree with the statement "People like me don't have any say about what the government does" (y-axis) or that "Income differences are too large" (x-axis)

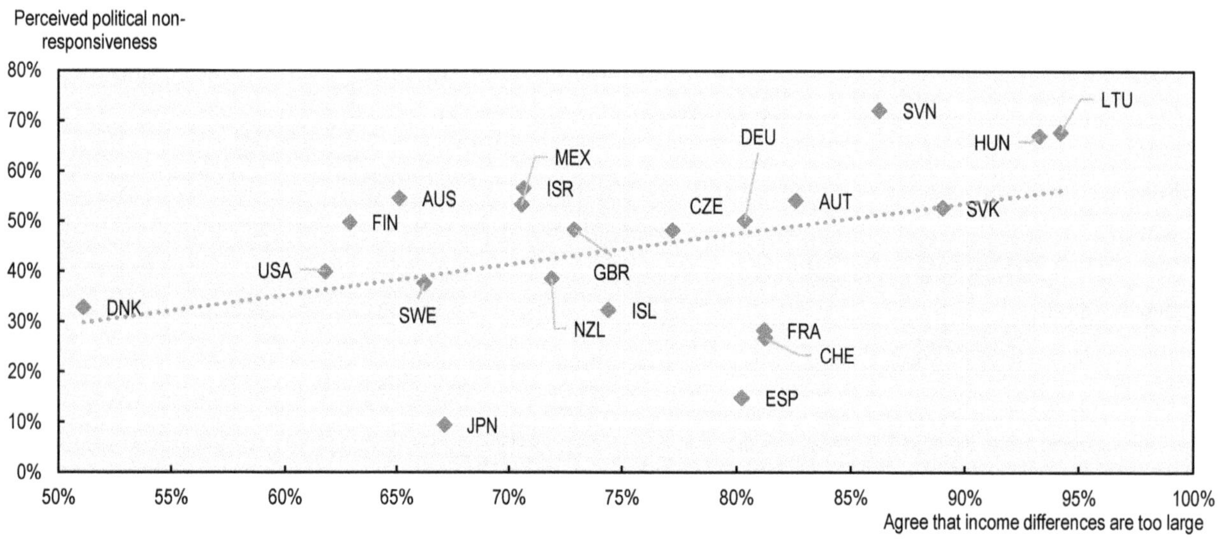

Note: The relation implies that a 1 percentage points increase in the share of respondents who agree that income disparities are too large is associated with a 0.6 percentage points increase in the share of respondents who believe that people like them do not have any say in what the government does. The relation is statistically significant at the 5% level (p value 0.021 with robust standard errors).
Source: ISSP 2017; the sample is different from Figure 2.1 because not all countries included in Figure 2.1 collected information on perceived political representation.

StatLink https://stat.link/o7pgzx

Rennwald and Pontusson (2021[77]) draw on ISSP data to analyse to what extent people believe that the government responds to their preferences. They show that there are stark differences between social classes in perceived political representation, with the working class perceiving the government as less responsive to their need. And gaps have widened over time. Data from the ISSP 2017 wave (Figure 3.24) show that countries where more people believe that income disparities are too wide are also those where most people see the government as non-responsive to their needs. The combination of strong concern over inequality and perceptions of little political representation fuels social resentment.

Round-up

While both perceived and actual inequality influence preferences for redistribution (Sections 3.1 and 3.3), several factors may weaken or offset their impact:

- Rising inequality may increase tolerance for income disparities, therefore lessening demand for redistribution. However, greater tolerance of inequality does not explain why concern over income disparities responds more to growing inequality than redistributive preferences do.
- Lack of confidence in the effectiveness of policies to reduce inequality and raise the living standards of the poor is likely to be an important factor. Informing people about the redistributive impact of policies and their effectiveness in addressing inequalities helps raise support.
- The perceived efficiency costs of redistributive policies, be they behavioural or macro-economic, may lessen support for more redistribution. Nevertheless, experimental evidence suggests that they are less important than the perceived impact of policies, views of the government, and the demand for greater equality.
- Even when people agree that it is the government's responsibility to take action to reduce income differences, they may disagree on the policy mix. Evidence from questions about preferences for general redistribution – which do not collect information on specific policy options – are not enough for the purpose of investigating the policy issue. And cross-country evidence is still limited as to specific redistributive policies and how they relate to perceptions of inequality and beliefs in reasons for inequality.

References

Aksoy, C. et al. (2021), "Calamities, Common Interests, Shared Identity: What Shapes Altruism and Reciprocity?", *CEPR Discussion Paper*, Vol. 16186, https://cepr.org/active/publications/discussion_papers/dp.php?dpno=16186. [83]

Alesina, A. and G. Angeletos (2005), "Fairness and Redistribution", *American Economic Review*, Vol. 95/4, pp. 960-980, http://dx.doi.org/10.1257/0002828054825655. [10]

Alesina, A. and P. Giuliano (2011), "Preferences for Redistribution", in *Handbook of Social Economics*, Elsevier, http://dx.doi.org/10.1016/b978-0-444-53187-2.00004-8. [2]

Alesina, A., S. Stantcheva and E. Teso (2018), "Intergenerational Mobility and Preferences for Redistribution", *American Economic Review*, Vol. 108/2, pp. 521-554, http://dx.doi.org/10.1257/aer.20162015. [31]

Algan, Y., P. Cahuc and M. Sangnier (2016), "Trust and the Welfare State: The Twin Peaks Curve", *The Economic Journal*, Vol. 126/593, pp. 861-883, http://dx.doi.org/10.1111/ecoj.12278. [49]

Almås, I. et al. (2020), *Fairness Around the World: Preferences and Beliefs*, https://www.ifs.org.uk/inequality/wp-content/uploads/2020/11/Fairness-across-the-world-Preferences-and-beliefs.pdf. [12]

Almås, I., A. Cappelen and B. Tungodden (2020), "Cutthroat Capitalism versus Cuddly Socialism: Are Americans More Meritocratic and Efficiency-Seeking than Scandinavians?", *Journal of Political Economy*, Vol. 128/5, pp. 1753-1788, http://dx.doi.org/10.1086/705551. [78]

Amiel, Y. et al. (2014), "Do we value mobility?", *Social Choice and Welfare*, Vol. 44/2, pp. 231-255, http://dx.doi.org/10.1007/s00355-014-0839-2. [8]

Balestra, C. and G. Cohen (forthcoming), "Income Inequality through People's Lenses: Evidence from the OECD Compare your Income Web-tool", *OECD Papers on Well-being and Inequalities*, OECD publishing, Paris. [36]

Ballard, C. and S. Gupta (2018), "Perceptions and Realities of Average Tax Rates in the Federal Income Tax: Evidence from Michigan", *National Tax Journal*, Vol. 71/2, pp. 263-294, http://dx.doi.org/10.17310/ntj.2018.2.03. [82]

Bartels, L. (2017), "Political Inequality in Affluent Democracies: The Social Welfare Deficit", *Centre for the Study of Democratic Institutions*, No. 5-2017, Vanderbilt University, https://www.vanderbilt.edu/csdi/includes/Working_Paper_5_2017.pdf. [76]

Bartels, L. (2005), "Homer Gets a Tax Cut: Inequality and Public Policy in the American Mind", *Perspectives on Politics*, Vol. 3/01, http://dx.doi.org/10.1017/s1537592705050036. [50]

Bechert, L. and L. Osberg (2016), *Social values for equality and preferences for state intervention: Is the USA "Exceptional"?*. [48]

Benabou, R. and E. Ok (2001), "Social Mobility and the Demand for Redistribution: The Poum Hypothesis", *The Quarterly Journal of Economics*, Vol. 116/2, pp. 447-487, http://dx.doi.org/10.1162/00335530151144078. [5]

Benson, R. et al. (2021), *Attituted to inequalities*, Institute for Fiscal Studies. [44]

Bonnet, J. et al. (forthcoming), *Understanding preferences for redistribution: Evidence from the Trustlab survey.* [68]

Bublitz, E. (2020), "Misperceptions of income distributions: Cross-country evidence from a randomized survey experiment", *Socio-Economic Review*, https://doi.org/10.1093/ser/mwaa025. [41]

Buser, T. et al. (2020), "Overconfidence and gender gaps in redistributive preferences: Cross-Country experimental evidence", *Journal of Economic Behavior & Organization*, Vol. 178, pp. 267-286, http://dx.doi.org/10.1016/j.jebo.2020.07.005. [15]

Bussolo, M. et al. (2019), "I Perceive therefore I Demand: The Formation of Inequality Perceptions and Demand for Redistribution", *Policy Research Working Paper*, No. WPS 8929, World Bank Group, Washington, D.C., http://documents.worldbank.org/curated/en/217371561686066298/I-Perceive-Therefore-I-Demand-The-Formation-of-Inequality-Perceptions-and-Demand-for-Redistribution. [21]

Campos-Vazquez, R. et al. (2020), "Perception of inequality and social mobility in Mexico", *AFD Research Papers*, No. 124, https://www.afd.fr/en/ressources/perceptions-inequality-and-social-mobility-mexico. [47]

Cansunar, A. (2021), "Who Is High Income, Anyway? Social Comparison, Subjective Group Identification, and Preferences over Progressive Taxation", *The Journal of Politics*, Vol. 83/4, pp. 1292-1306, http://dx.doi.org/10.1086/711627. [39]

Cappelen, A. et al. (2021), "Solidarity and fairness in times of crisis", *Journal of Economic Behavior & Organization*, Vol. 186, pp. 1-11, http://dx.doi.org/10.1016/j.jebo.2021.03.017. [84]

Ciani, E.; L. Fréget and T.Manfredi (forthcoming), "Learning about inequality and preferences for redistribution: A meta-analysis of in-survey informational experiments", *OECD Papers on Well-being and Inequalities*, OECD Publishing, Paris. [43]

Ciani, E. et al. (forthcoming), *Perceptions of inequality across OECD and EU countries: Long term trends and recent evidence.* [30]

Cingano, F. (2014), "Trends in Income Inequality and its Impact on Economic Growth", *OECD Social, Employment and Migration Working Papers*, No. 163, OECD Publishing, Paris, https://dx.doi.org/10.1787/5jxrjncwxv6j-en. [32]

Clark, A. and C. D'Ambrosio (2015), "Attitudes to Income Inequality", in *Handbook of Income Distribution*, Elsevier, http://dx.doi.org/10.1016/b978-0-444-59428-0.00014-x. [34]

Colagrossi, M., S. Karagiannis and R. Raab (2019), "The Median Voter Takes it All: Preferences for Redistribution and Income Inequality in the EU-28", *Publications Office of the European Union*, No. 2019/6, http://dx.doi.org/doi:10.2760/797251. [25]

Cruces, G., R. Perez-Truglia and M. Tetaz (2013), "Biased perceptions of income distribution and preferences for redistribution: Evidence from a survey experiment", *Journal of Public Economics*, Vol. 98, pp. 100-112, http://dx.doi.org/10.1016/j.jpubeco.2012.10.009. [29]

Durante, R., L. Putterman and J. van der Weele (2014), "Preferences for Redistribution and Perception of Fairness: An Experimental Study", *Journal of the European Economic Association*, Vol. 12/4, pp. 1059-1086, http://dx.doi.org/10.1111/jeea.12082. [11]

Edlund, J. (2006), "Trust in the Capability of the Welfare State and General Welfare State Support: Sweden 1997-2002", *Acta Sociologica*, Vol. 49/4, pp. 395-417, http://dx.doi.org/10.1177/0001699306071681. [61]

Eriksen, K. and L. Fallan (1996), "Tax knowledge and attitudes towards taxation; A report on a quasi-experiment", *Journal of Economic Psychology*, Vol. 17/3, pp. 387-402, http://dx.doi.org/10.1016/0167-4870(96)00015-3. [80]

Fong, C. (2001), *Social preferences, self-interest, and the demand for redistribution*, http://www.elsevier.nl/locate/econbase. [7]

Fong, C. and P. Poutvaara (2019), "Redistributive politics with target-specific beliefs", *ifo Working Papers*, No. 297, ifo Institute – Leibniz Institute for Economic Research at the University of Munich, https://www.ifo.de/DocDL/wp-2019-297-fong-poutvaara-redistributive-politcs.pdf. [73]

Gärtner, M., J. Mollerstrom and D. Seim (2017), "Individual risk preferences and the demand for redistribution", *Journal of Public Economics*, Vol. 153, pp. 49-55, http://dx.doi.org/10.1016/j.jpubeco.2017.06.009. [6]

Gideon, M. (2016), "Do Individuals Perceive Income Tax Rates Correctly?", *Public Finance Review*, Vol. 45/1, pp. 97-117, http://dx.doi.org/10.1177/1091142115615670. [81]

Giger, N., J. Rosset and J. Bernauer (2012), "The Poor Political Representation of the Poor in a Comparative Perspective", *Representation*, Vol. 48/1, pp. 47-61, http://dx.doi.org/10.1080/00344893.2012.653238. [75]

Gilens, M. (2005), "Inequality and Democratic Responsiveness", *Public Opinion Quarterly*, Vol. 69/5, pp. 778-796, http://dx.doi.org/10.1093/poq/nfi058. [74]

Gimpelson, V. and D. Treisman (2018), "Misperceiving inequality", *Economics and Politics*, Vol. 30/1, pp. 27-54, http://dx.doi.org/10.1111/ecpo.12103. [26]

Giuliano, P. and A. Spilimbergo (2013), "Growing up in a Recession", *The Review of Economic Studies*, Vol. 81/2, pp. 787-817, http://dx.doi.org/10.1093/restud/rdt040. [19]

Goerres, A. and M. Jæger (2015), "Why Do Women and Men Differ in Their Preferences Towards Redistribution? An Analysis of Sibling-Parent Data in a Most Gender-Egalitarian Context", *SSRN Electronic Journal*, http://dx.doi.org/10.2139/ssrn.2665122. [13]

Gualtieri, G., M. Nicolini and F. Sabatini (2019), "Repeated shocks and preferences for redistribution", *Journal of Economic Behavior & Organization*, Vol. 167, pp. 53-71, http://dx.doi.org/10.1016/j.jebo.2019.09.016. [20]

Hayes, T. and C. Guay (2020), "Viewing equality as a loss: How highlighting policy costs and benefits influences attitudes", *The Social Science Journal*, pp. 1-15, http://dx.doi.org/10.1016/j.soscij.2019.08.006. [55]

Heterington, M. (2006), *Why Trust Matters: Declining Political Trust and the Demise of American Liberalism*, Princeton University Press. [57]

Hoy, C. and F. Mager (2021), "Why Are Relatively Poor People Not More Supportive of Redistribution? Evidence from a Randomized Survey Experiment across Ten Countries", *American Economic Journal: Economic Policy*, Vol. 13/4, pp. 299-328, http://dx.doi.org/10.1257/pol.20190276. [38]

Hvidberg, K., C. Kreiner and S. Stantcheva (2020), *Social Position and Fairness Views*, National Bureau of Economic Research, Cambridge, MA, http://dx.doi.org/10.3386/w28099. [42]

Kambayashi, R. and S. Lechevalier (2021), "Why do Redistributive Policies Differ across Countries? Analyzing the Multiple Dimensions of Preferences for Redistribution", *Review of Income and Wealth*, http://dx.doi.org/10.1111/roiw.12541. [1]

Karabarbounis, L. (2011), "One Dollar, One Vote", *The Economic Journal*, Vol. 121/553, pp. 621-651, http://dx.doi.org/10.1111/j.1468-0297.2010.02406.x. [28]

Karadja, M., J. Mollerstrom and D. Seim (2017), "Richer (and Holier) Than Thou? The Effect of Relative Income Improvements on Demand for Redistribution", *The Review of Economics and Statistics*, Vol. 99/2, pp. 201-212, http://dx.doi.org/10.1162/rest_a_00623. [40]

Kerr, W. (2014), "Income inequality and social preferences for redistribution and compensation differentials", *Journal of Monetary Economics*, Vol. 66, pp. 62-78, http://dx.doi.org/10.1016/j.jmoneco.2014.03.002. [22]

Klemm, A. and P. Mauro (2021), "Pandemic and Progressivity", *IMF Working Paper*, No. 2021/024, https://www.imf.org/en/Publications/WP/Issues/2021/02/06/Pandemic-and-Progressivity-50030. [18]

Kuhn, A. (2019), "The individual (mis-)perception of wage inequality: measurement, correlates and implications", *Empirical Economics*, http://dx.doi.org/10.1007/s00181-019-01722-4. [24]

Kuziemko, I. et al. (2015), "How Elastic Are Preferences for Redistribution? Evidence from Randomized Survey Experiments", *American Economic Review*, Vol. 105/4, pp. 1478-1508, https://www.jstor.org/stable/43495425. [51]

Lergetporer, P., K. Werner and L. Woessmann (2020), "Educational inequality and public policy preferences: Evidence from representative survey experiments", *Journal of Public Economics*, Vol. 188, p. 104226, http://dx.doi.org/10.1016/j.jpubeco.2020.104226. [53]

Luttmer, E. and M. Singhal (2011), "Culture, context, and the taste for redistribution", *American Economic Journal: Economic Policy*, Vol. 3/1, pp. 157-179, http://dx.doi.org/10.1257/pol.3.1.157. [14]

Macdonald, D. (2019), "Trust in Government and the American Public's Responsiveness to Rising Inequality", *Political Research Quarterly*, Vol. 73/4, pp. 790-804, http://dx.doi.org/10.1177/1065912919856110. [59]

Meltzer, A. and S. Richard (1981), "A Rational Theory of the Size of Government", *Journal of Political Economy*, Vol. 89/5, http://dx.doi.org/10.1086/261013. [3]

Mishagina, N. and C. Montmarquette (2018), "The Demand for Economic Policies, Beliefs, and Willingness-to-Pay: The Case of the Minimum Wage Policy in Quebec", *CIRANO Project Reports*, No. 2018rp-14, CIRANO, https://ideas.repec.org/p/cir/cirpro/2018rp-14.html. [56]

Mollerstrom, J., B. Reme and E. Sørensen (2015), "Luck, choice and responsibility — An experimental study of fairness views", *Journal of Public Economics*, Vol. 131, pp. 33-40, http://dx.doi.org/10.1016/j.jpubeco.2015.08.010. [86]

Murtin, F. et al. (2018), "Trust and its determinants: Evidence from the Trustlab experiment", *OECD Statistics Working Papers*, No. 2018/2, OECD Publishing, Paris, https://dx.doi.org/10.1787/869ef2ec-en. [64]

OECD (2021), *Drivers of Trust in Public Institutions in Finland*, OECD Publishing, Paris, https://dx.doi.org/10.1787/52600c9e-en. [66]

OECD (2021), *Main Findings from the 2020 Risks that Matter Survey*, OECD Publishing, Paris, https://doi.org/10.1787/b9e85cf5-en. [17]

OECD (2019), *Main Findings from the 2018 Risks that Matter Survey*, OECD Publishing, Paris, https://doi.org/10.1787/9266e48a-en. [27]

OECD (2019), *Under Pressure: The Squeezed Middle Class*, OECD Publishing, Paris, https://dx.doi.org/10.1787/689afed1-en. [37]

OECD (2018), *A Broken Social Elevator? How to Promote Social Mobility*, OECD Publishing, Paris, https://dx.doi.org/10.1787/9789264301085-en. [70]

OECD (2017), *Preventing Ageing Unequally*, OECD Publishing, Paris, https://dx.doi.org/10.1787/9789264279087-en. [71]

OECD (2017), *Trust and Public Policy: How Better Governance Can Help Rebuild Public Trust*, OECD Public Governance Reviews, OECD Publishing, Paris, https://dx.doi.org/10.1787/9789264268920-en. [63]

OECD/Korea Development Institute (2018), *Understanding the Drivers of Trust in Government Institutions in Korea*, OECD, http://dx.doi.org/10.1787/9789264308992-en. [65]

Olivera, J. (2015), "Preferences for redistribution in Europe", *IZA Journal of European Labor Studies*, Vol. 4/1, http://dx.doi.org/10.1186/s40174-015-0037-y. [23]

Osberg, L. and I. Bechert (2016), "Social values for equality and preferences for state intervention: Is the USA "Exceptional"?", *Working Paper*, No. 2016-03, Dalhousie University, Department of Economics, https://econpapers.repec.org/paper/dalwpaper/daleconwp2016-03.htm. [45]

Pellicer, M., P. Piraino and E. Wegner (2019), "Perceptions of inevitability and demand for redistribution: Evidence from a survey experiment", *Journal of Economic Behavior & Organization*, Vol. 159, pp. 274-288, https://mural.maynoothuniversity.ie/13719/1/MP_perceptions.pdf. [54]

Peyton, K. (2020), "Does Trust in Government Increase Support for Redistribution? Evidence from Randomized Survey Experiments", *American Political Science Review*, Vol. 114/2, pp. 596-602, http://dx.doi.org/10.1017/s0003055420000076. [62]

Piketty, T. (1995), "Social Mobility and Redistributive Politics", *The Quarterly Journal of Economics*, Vol. 110/3, pp. 551-584, http://dx.doi.org/10.2307/2946692. [9]

Pontusson, J. et al. (2020), *Introducing the Inequality and Politics Survey: Preliminary Findings*, https://archive-ouverte.unige.ch/unige:135683. [72]

Rennwald, L. and J. Pontusson (2021), *A forgotten working class. Perceptions of representation and the role of labour in a comparative perspective*. [77]

Rudolph, T. and J. Evans (2005), "Political Trust, Ideology, and Public Support for Government Spending", *American Journal of Political Science*, Vol. 49/3, pp. 660-671, http://dx.doi.org/10.1111/j.1540-5907.2005.00148.x. [58]

Rueda, D. and D. Stegmueller (2020), "Preferences that Matter: Inequality, Redistribution and Voting", *mimeo*. [35]

Rueda, D. and D. Stegmueller (2019), *Who Wants What?*, Cambridge University Press, http://dx.doi.org/10.1017/9781108681339. [4]

Rueda, D. and D. Stegmueller (2015), "The Externalities of Inequality: Fear of Crime and Preferences for Redistribution in Western Europe", *American Journal of Political Science*, Vol. 60/2, pp. 472-489, http://dx.doi.org/10.1111/ajps.12212. [33]

Scheve, K. and D. Stasavage (2016), *Taxing the rich: A history of fiscal fairness in the United States and Europe*, http://dx.doi.org/10.1177/0094306117705871nn. [67]

Settele, S. (2021), "How Do Beliefs about the Gender Wage Gap Affect the Demand for Public Policy?", *American Economic Journal: Economic Policy*, Vol. forthcoming. [16]

Stantcheva, S. (2020), "Understanding economic policies: What do people know and learn?", *Harvard University Working Paper*, Harvard University, https://www.stefanie-stantcheva.com/research/. [85]

Stantcheva, S. (2020), *Understanding Tax Policy: How Do People Reason?*, National Bureau of Economic Research, Cambridge, MA, http://dx.doi.org/10.3386/w27699. [52]

Svallfors, S. (1999), "Political trust and attitudes towards redistribution", *European Societies*, Vol. 1/2, pp. 241-268, http://dx.doi.org/10.1080/14616696.1999.10749933. [60]

Trump, K. (2018), "Income Inequality Influences Perceptions of Legitimate Income Differences", *British Journal of Political Science*, Vol. 48/4, pp. 929-952, http://dx.doi.org/10.1017/S0007123416000326. [46]

VanHeuvelen, T. (2017), "Unequal views of inequality: Cross-national support for redistribution 1985–2011", *Social Science Research*, Vol. 64, pp. 43-66, http://dx.doi.org/10.1016/j.ssresearch.2016.10.010. [79]

Zilinsky, J. (2014), "Learning About Income Inequality: What is the Impact of Information on Perceptions of Fairness and Preferences for Redistribution?", *SSRN*, http://dx.doi.org/10.2139/ssrn.2485121. [69]

Annex 3.A. Methodological details

Estimates of the effect of inequality on preferences for redistribution by income

The results displayed in Figure 3.16 are predictions from an ordinary probit model estimated on individual microdata, controlling for age, gender, household size, employment status (employed, unemployed, or reference category "other status"), educational level (less than secondary, secondary, or reference category "tertiary"), the log of relative income (with respect to the country average in that point in time), and the Gini index for disposable income from the IDD.

Instead of dropping observations with missing values in the covariates, they are replaced with sample averages (or reference categories) but the covariates include a set of binary indicators, one for each variable, which have the value 1 if that observation was originally a missing value for that covariate. All regressions include country and period (wave) dummies and only countries observed in at least two periods are considered.

The main effects are captured by the interaction between the Gini coefficient and the log of relative income, as in Rueda and Stegmueller (2019[4]). To avoid results driven by spurious patterns over time, relative income (and the missing income indicator) is also interacted with the period dummies. Results are similar if observations with missing income are dropped, or the sample is restricted to the working- age population. Only ISSP is used for consistency in all variables.

Annex Figure 3.A.1. Changes in concern about income disparities and preferences for redistribution in selected countries

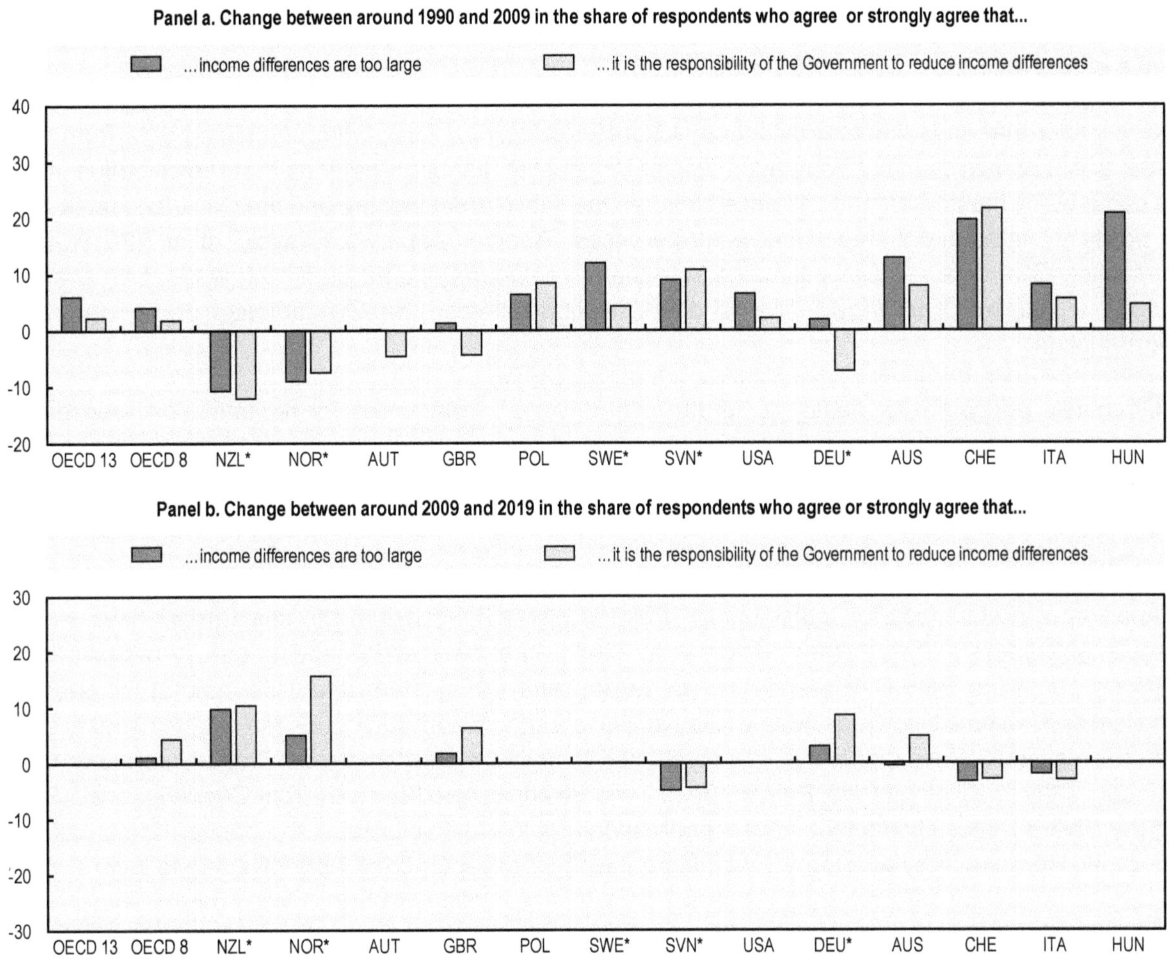

Note: The initial year depends on when countries are observed. For countries marked with * it is 1992-93, for the others 1987-88
Source: OECD calculations on ISSP 1987, 1992, 2009, 2019.

StatLink https://stat.link/0clgdr

Notes

[1] The finding is robust to excluding outliers, either identified by observations with high leverage or by means of the dfbeta statistic.

[2] While university students are not representative of the population, they have the numeracy and logical skills needed to express preferences in abstract comparisons of this type.

[3] Even if people are more willing to compensate inequalities arising because of factors outside the control of individuals (e.g. brute luck), there is evidence that this willingness materializes when those who were

negatively affected by these factors had taken some action to prevent them, even if such action could not have changed the outcome (Mollerstrom, Reme and Sørensen, 2015[86]).

[4] The finding is robust to excluding outliers, either identified by observations with high leverage or by means of the dfbeta statistic.

[5] One paper that finds different evidence is VanHeuvelen (2017[79]), who, combining data from multiple ISSP and ESS waves, finds no relation with net inequality, although he finds that redistribution intensity, as captured by the proportional distance between the Gini market income and the Gini disposable income, is positively related with redistributive preferences. Another paper is Bussolo et al. (2019[21]), who, combining ISSP data and Gini estimates from the *Luxembourg Income Study Database (LIS)* and the "All the Ginis" dataset of Milanovic, find no direct relation between the Gini indicator and preferences for redistribution.

[6] Of course, concern over quality is not the only driver of preferences for redistribution. Concerns and preferences for redistribution might influence each other or they might instead be both related to other unobserved elements, such as general dissatisfaction for the economic conditions. Nevertheless, the results confirm that perceptions of and preferences for inequality are relevant factors in analysing demand for redistribution.

[7] Apart from preferences for redistribution, there is also evidence that the crisis might have increased people willingness to help others. Aksoy et al. (2021[83]) show that influencing survey respondents into thinking about the COVID-19 pandemic (by asking and telling them about its impact) increases their altruism and reciprocity towards people living in their country or abroad, though the effect is weaker towards non-EU residents. The experiments was conducted in nine European countries: France, Germany, Greece, Hungary, Italy, the Netherlands, Poland, Spain, and Sweden. Also the study from Cappelen et al. (2021[84]) on the United States shows that influencing respondent into thinking about the pandemic increases their solidarity. However, they also show that it increases their acceptance of inequality due to luck.

[8] The finding is robust to excluding outliers, either identified by observations with high leverage or by means of the dfbeta statistic.

[9] The evidence is similar, although with larger effects, using lagged inequality and redistribution indicators. However, because of data constraints, using lagged indicators leads to a much smaller, selected sample, and the selection in fact seems to drive the larger results: within this selected sample, even without lagging the indicators, we find similar coefficients, and the one on RS even becomes statistically significant. A fuller evaluation of the relation between actual redistribution and preferences would require disentangling the two side-effects, as well as spelling out the dynamics between policy intervention and changes in preferences. This would require longer time series, which will be available once the next ISSP wave on social inequality is released for a large set of countries. An even more challenging issue is how people gather information about redistributive policies and assess their effectiveness. The evidence in this respect is rather limited, with few exceptions (Eriksen and Fallan, 1996[80]; Gideon, 2016[81]; Ballard and Gupta, 2018[82]; Stantcheva, 2020[85]).

[10] As discussed in Chapter 2, it is important, when assessing relative income "bias", not to neglect that what is referred to as "actual" position is an estimate based on methodological choices. These include a specific definition of income, an adjustment based on an equivalence scale that accounts for household size (but not for other needs), and the choice of using the entire population at a specific point in time as a reference group. As discussed by Hvidberg, Kreiner and Stantcheva (2020[42]), all these choices might not reflect what matters for individuals when they formulate their fairness concerns. So providing them with the "actual" estimate might not change their concerns.

[11] A weak change over time is confirmed by looking at the share who agree or strongly agree, or at the average answer (treating the 5-point Likert scale as cardinal).

[12] In a similar work, but limited to Norway and the United States, Almås, Cappelen and Tungodden (2020[78]) find that efficiency considerations play a very minor role.

4. Has the public opinion become more divided?

This chapter goes beyond country-level averages to look at the entire distribution of people's perceptions of and levels of concern about economic inequalities in different countries. In most, it finds, public opinion is deeply divided with perceptions of inequality widely dispersed from very low to very high. Such dispersion can only be partially explained by standard socio-economic divides across income, education, employment status, gender, age and household size. In some instances, the dispersion of perceptions and concern becomes polarization between groups with starkly different views. Both dispersion and polarization of perceived disparities and concern have grown steeply over time. Higher levels of observed inequality are associated not only with greater perceived disparities and concerns, but with a more divided public opinion.

4.1. The dispersion of perceptions and concern

Perceptions are widely dispersed and polarised

While people OECD-wide perceive high average levels of inequality, public opinion within countries is deeply divided. The distribution of the perceived income shares of the richest 10% in each country (Figure 4.1) reveals that perceptions range widely, from extremely low to extremely high. This dispersion in perceived and preferred disparities points to the scale of disagreement about inequality between citizens of the same country. Analysing it is important, because social tensions can arise not just when large groups of individuals demand more equality, but when people strongly disagree with each other about what current levels of inequality are and should be.

The extent of disagreement, reflected in the dispersion of perceptions, varies from country to country. In only a few is there a relatively strong consensus as to the richest 10%'s share of income – whether perceived to be high as in Greece and Turkey (Figure 4.1, Panel A) or low, like in Denmark and Israel (Panel B). In most countries, sizeable groups view inequality as substantial. But a large minority harbours perceptions of lower inequality (Panels C and D) that are not clustered at particular levels, but scattered across the distribution.

In a smaller subset of countries, there is no single peak in the distribution, but two groups of respondents who agree on either low or high levels of inequality. The presence of distinct groups whose views are far apart but who both show strong internal consensus is a sign of the polarisation of perceptions (Duclos, Esteban and Ray, 2004[1]; Osberg and Smeeding, 2006[2]). Two groups with high and low levels of perceived inequality are to be found in Estonia, France, Finland, the Netherlands, Norway, Poland, and Slovenia (Panels E and F).

Figure 4.1. In most countries, people's perceptions of inequality are strongly dispersed across a wide range of values

Estimated density distributions of the perceived shares of the country's total income that goes to the 10% richest households, year 2020

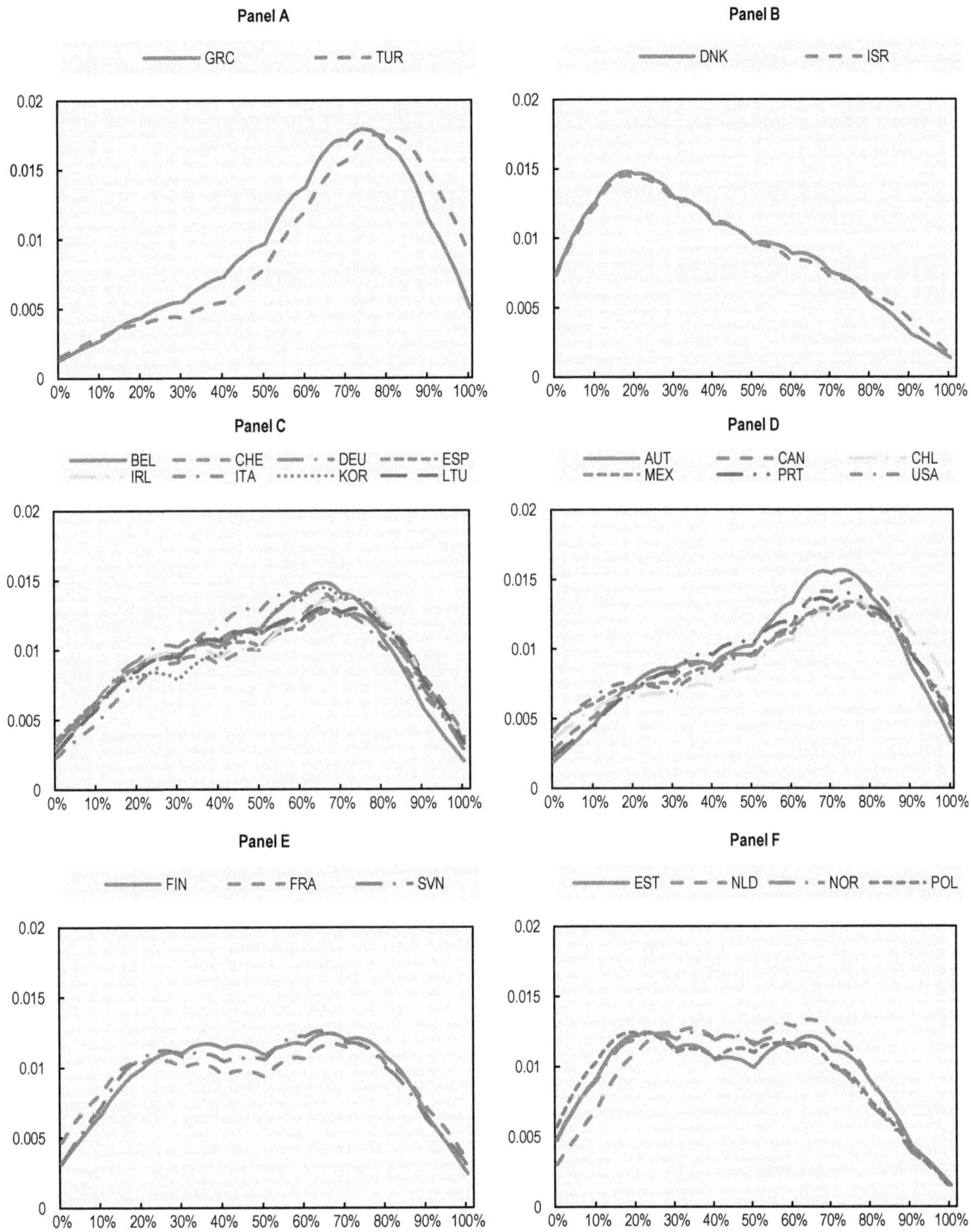

Note: The plots show the probability density functions for the perception of the country's total income going to the richest 10% households, as estimated through the kernel density estimation.

Source: OECD calculations from the 2020 Risks that Matter Survey.

StatLink https://stat.link/gwxm84

Most disagreement is between people with similar socio-economic characteristics

The dispersion in perceptions of inequality can be explained only partly by differences across standard socio-economic groups, as defined by income, education, employment status, gender, age and household size. Indeed, divisions of opinion along these traditional lines are relatively narrow in most countries, even though views of equality are widely scattered. People belonging to the top income tertile believe that the richest 10%'s income share is lower than the poor do, though the difference is quite small – less than 5 percentage points (Table 4.1). In some countries, the rich actually perceive wider disparities, as in Austria, France, Korea, and Turkey. The unemployed, too, tend to think disparities are wider, although employment status matters only in a handful of countries, like Chile, Denmark and Slovenia.

Table 4.1. On average, differences in perceived income inequality across socio-demographic groups are slight

Differences between socio-economic groups in perceptions of richest 10%'s income share

	Education	Income		Employment status	Gender	Age		Household size	
	Tertiary vs lower	Middle vs bottom tertile	Top vs bottom tertile	Not empl. vs empl.	Female vs male	Prime age vs. young	Senior vs. young	3-4 vs 1-2 members	5+ vs 1-2 members
OECD 25	=	-	-	+	-	+	+	-	=
Austria	=	=	+	=	-	++	++	=	++
Belgium	=	=	--	=	=	=	+	=	=
Canada	=	=	-	=	=	=	=	=	=
Switzerland	=	=	=	=	-	=	=	-	=
Chile	-	=	--	++	+	=	=	=	=
Germany	++	=	=	=	--	=	+	=	=
Denmark	=	-	=	++	=	=	=	=	=
Spain	=	=	-	=	=	=	--	=	=
Estonia	=	=	--	=	-	++	+++	=	=
Finland	-	-	=	=	-	++	++	=	=
France	=	=	+	=	--	=	=	-	--
Greece	=	=	-	=	=	++	++	+	=
Ireland	=	=	=	=	--	=	++	-	--
Israel	=	=	--	=	=	+	+	=	=
Italy	=	=	=	=	=	=	=	=	=
Korea	++	=	++	-	---	=	++	=	=
Lithuania	=	=	=	=	-	=	++	-	=
Mexico	=	=	--	=	=	+	=	=	=
Netherlands	=	=	=	=	--	=	=	=	=
Norway	--	-	--	=	=	=	=	=	=
Poland	=	-	=	=	=	=	=	=	=
Portugal	=	=	=	=	=	=	=	+	++
Slovenia	=	-	=	+	=	=	++	-	=
Turkey	++	-	+	=	+	++	+++	=	=
United States	++	=	=	=	=	=	--	=	=

Note: The signs indicate whether the difference between the two groups is positive or negative. "+" (or "-") indicates that the difference is positive (or negative) and less than 5 percentage points; "++" (or "--") if it is up to 10 percentage points; "+++" (or "---") if it is more. "=" indicates differences not statistically different from 0 (less than at the 5% level), regardless of the value of the difference "Prime age" refers to the 30-50-year-olds and "senior" to 50-64-year-olds.

Source: OECD calculations from the 2020 Risks that Matter Survey.

StatLink https://stat.link/tcgmlo

Gender is also a factor. In Germany, Korea, France, the Netherlands and Ireland, women perceive much lower concentrations of income at the top of the distribution than men (by up to 10 percentage points), while the opposite is true in Chile and Turkey. However, in half of OECD countries, women and men generally express similar views on income inequality. Perceptions also vary little with educational attainment. Only in the United States, Turkey, Korea and Germany do respondents educated to tertiary level perceive significantly wider income disparities than the less well educated – again by as much as 10 percentage points. As for age, older respondents generally perceive higher income disparities than the young, with the generation gap especially pronounced in Estonia and Turkey. Only older American and Spanish respondents perceive less income inequality than their younger compatriots (by more than 5 percentage points).

Table 4.2. In some countries, stark divides in perceived intergenerational persistence exist among people with different educational attainment levels

Differences between socio-economic groups in the perceived bottom 10% income intergenerational persistence

	Education	Income		Employment status	Gender	Age		Household size	
	Tertiary vs Lower	Middle vs Bottom tertile	Top vs Bottom tertile	Not empl. vs Empl.	Female vs Male	Prime Age vs. Young	Senior vs. Young	3-4 vs 1-2 members	5+ vs 1-2 members
OECD 25	+	=	+	+	+	+	=	=	=
Austria	++	=	=	=	=	=	--	=	=
Belgium	+++	=	=	-	=	=	=	=	=
Canada	=	=	=	=	=	=	=	=	=
Switzerland	=	=	=	=	=	=	=	=	=
Chile	++	=	++	=	+	--	--	=	=
Germany	=	=	=	=	=	=	=	=	=
Denmark	++	=	=	+	+	=	=	=	=
Spain	=	=	=	=	=	=	=	=	=
Estonia	=	=	=	=	=	=	++	=	=
Finland	=	=	=	=	+	=	=	-	--
France	++	=	=	=	-	=	=	=	=
Greece	=	=	=	=	=	=	=	=	=
Ireland	++	=	++	=	+	=	=	--	=
Israel	++	++	++	=	=	=	=	=	=
Italy	+	=	=	+	=	---	--	+	=
Korea	=	=	=	=	--	=	=	=	=
Lithuania	=	=	=	=	+	=	+	-	=
Mexico	=	=	=	=	=	=	++	=	=
Netherlands	+	=	+	=	=	=	=	=	=
Norway	++	=	=	--	+	+++	++	=	=
Poland	=	=	=	=	=	=	=	=	=
Portugal	+	-	=	=	=	=	=	=	+++
Slovenia	+	=	=	=	+	=	=	=	=
Turkey	+++	=	++	+	+	++	++	=	=
United States	++	=	=	=	=	=	=	=	=

Note: Perceived intergenerational persistence among the poorest 10% refers to the chances that a child from the 10% of lowest-income households will still be living in a poor household once an adult. The signs indicate whether the difference between the two groups is positive or negative. "+" (or "-") indicates that the difference is positive (or negative) and less than 5 percentage points; "++" (or "--") if it is up to 10 percentage points; "+++" (or "---") if it is more. "=" indicates differences not statistically different from 0 (less than at the 5% level), regardless of the value of the coefficient. "Prime age" refers to 30-50-year-olds and "senior" to 50-64-year-olds.
Source: OECD calculations from the 2020 Risks that Matter Survey.

StatLink https://stat.link/xay4mq

Differences between traditional socio-economic groups are slightly wider when it comes to perceived intergenerational persistence. For example, the highly educated (Table 4.2) are particularly pessimistic about intergenerational mobility in the USA, Belgium and Turkey. Women, too, though more moderately so – 5 percentage points less than men. Differences in perception by income group are small and not significant in most countries. There are, however, some exceptions. In Chile, Turkey, Ireland, and Israel the higher income classes express considerably gloomier views of social mobility than poorer respondents. Similarly, although age differences are usually negligible, the under-30s in Chile and Italy have remarkably less faith in social mobility than older respondents – which points to a pervasive sense among the young of lack of opportunity. The opposite is true in Mexico, Turkey, Estonia and Norway.

Overall, differences between traditional socio-economic groups account for a small share of total dispersion in perceptions of inequality and social mobility (Figure 4.2). That share can be measured by breaking down the total variance in perceptions into:

- a between-group component, which captures how much of the total dispersion is due to differences between socio-demographic groups;
- a within-group component, which measures the dispersion of perceptions within classic socio-economic groups (income, education, gender, age and household size).

With some exceptions, the between-groups component explains no more than 5% of the total variance, so perceptions differ widely within groups. In other words, there are high levels of disagreement between people with similar socio-demographic characteristics.

Figure 4.2. Only in a few countries do the differences between socio-demographic groups account for more than 5% of the total dispersion of perceptions

The share of differences in perception between socio-demographic groups to the overall dispersion of perceptions

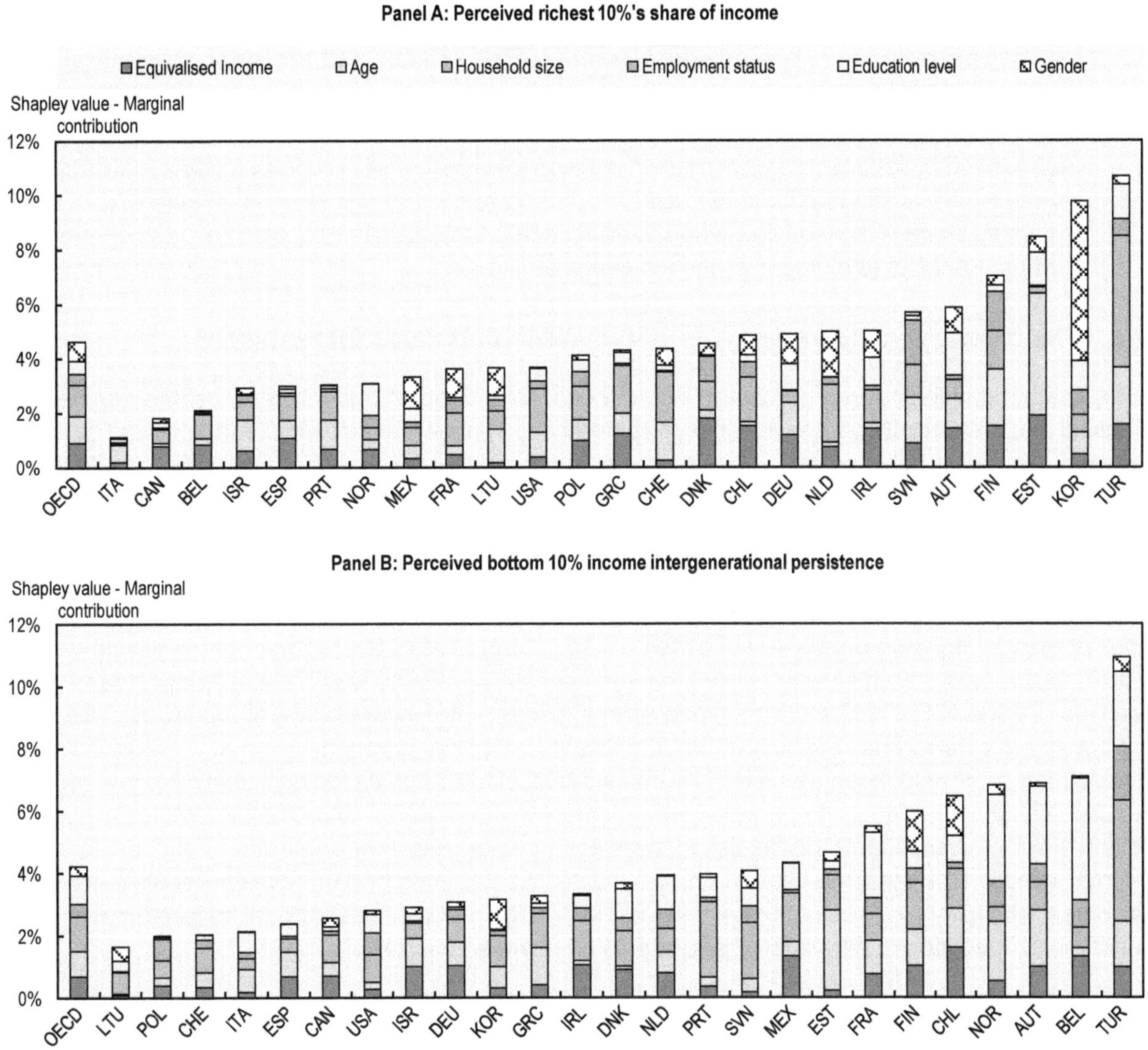

Note: The total in each bar represent the share of the overall dispersion of perceptions – measured by variance – which can be attributed to differences in perceptions over groups defined by socio-economic characteristics. Each segment in each bar refers to the difference between socio-economic groups – for instance, the segment that denotes "Income" refers to contribution of differences in perceptions between rich and poor to the total dispersion of perceptions. The bars' totals represent the total R-squared values for the linear regression of perceived top 10% income share and perceived bottom 10% income intergenerational persistence on socio-demographic covariates in each country. See Ciani et al. (forthcoming[3]) for a discussion of the decomposition.
Source: OECD calculations from the 2020 Risks that Matter Survey.

StatLink https://stat.link/1gaxqi

Only in a few countries do differences between groups account for sizeable shares of the total dispersion of perceptions. Korea's wide gender perception gap, with women believing there is greater inequality, accounts alone for 6% of total dispersion. In Estonia, older respondents consistently take much more negative views of both income disparities and intergenerational mobility. As for household size, it matters in most countries, particularly in Turkey. There, households with 2 members or less and those with more than 5 members perceive high levels of inequality after accounting for other socio-economic characteristics. (Note that this difference by household size is not picked up without accounting for other characteristics, as in Table 4.1 and Table 4.2). One explanation could be that household size correlates with other beliefs and regional factors that are not accounted for.

The conclusion that dispersion within rather than between socio-demographic groups explains the lion's share of country-wide variation in perceptions comes with two possible caveats.

- People in the same group may actually agree with each other but report different figures. In other terms, perceptions are measured with some degree of error and this error contributes to the dispersion. However, the analysis in Section 3.2 shows that differences in perceptions do help explain demand for redistribution on top of socio-demographic differences.
- Self-defined social class status matters in addition to characteristics such as income and education. However, if it is included together with the other variables in calculations (Figure 4.2), the thus explained share of the total dispersion does not rise, because self-defined social class only reduces the importance of other socio-economic characteristics.

The extensive disagreement in perceptions translates into concern

Widely scattered differences of perception do not necessarily indicate that concern, i.e. the gap between perceived and preferred disparities, is widely dispersed, too. If preferred disparities fully mirrored perceived disparities, the gap between the two would be the same for everybody. And there would be no disagreement between people as to the extent of inequality that exceeds their preferences. However, data from Compare your Income (Figure 4.3) show that concern – as it relates to the gap between the perceived and preferred income shares of the richest 10% – is widely dispersed within countries (Balestra and Cohen, (forthcoming[4])).

A look at the country-wide distribution of concern (Figure 4.3) reveals a small but non-negligible group of respondents in most countries who believe that the richest 10%'s income share is actually smaller than it should be (Panels A, B and C and Norton and Ariely (2011[5])).[1] It is followed by a group, whose size varies from country to country and who believe that the level of inequality is very much what it should be. There is then a long tail of respondents who find the current level of top incomes too high. Only in a few countries does the distribution appears to be polarised – Chile, Hungary, Korea and Mexico (Panel D) – with an additional set of respondents distinguished by the very wide gap that separates their perceived and preferred richest 10%'s income shares. The Scandinavian countries and the Czech Republic emerge in this context with fairly cohesive public opinion, as a very large group of respondents believe there is some, but not much, inequality in excess of what it should be (Panels E and F).

Figure 4.3. Concern about the extent of income inequality is also strongly dispersed over a wide range of values

Estimated distribution of the gap in percentage points between perceived and preferred share of the country's total income going to the 10% richest households, 2015-2020

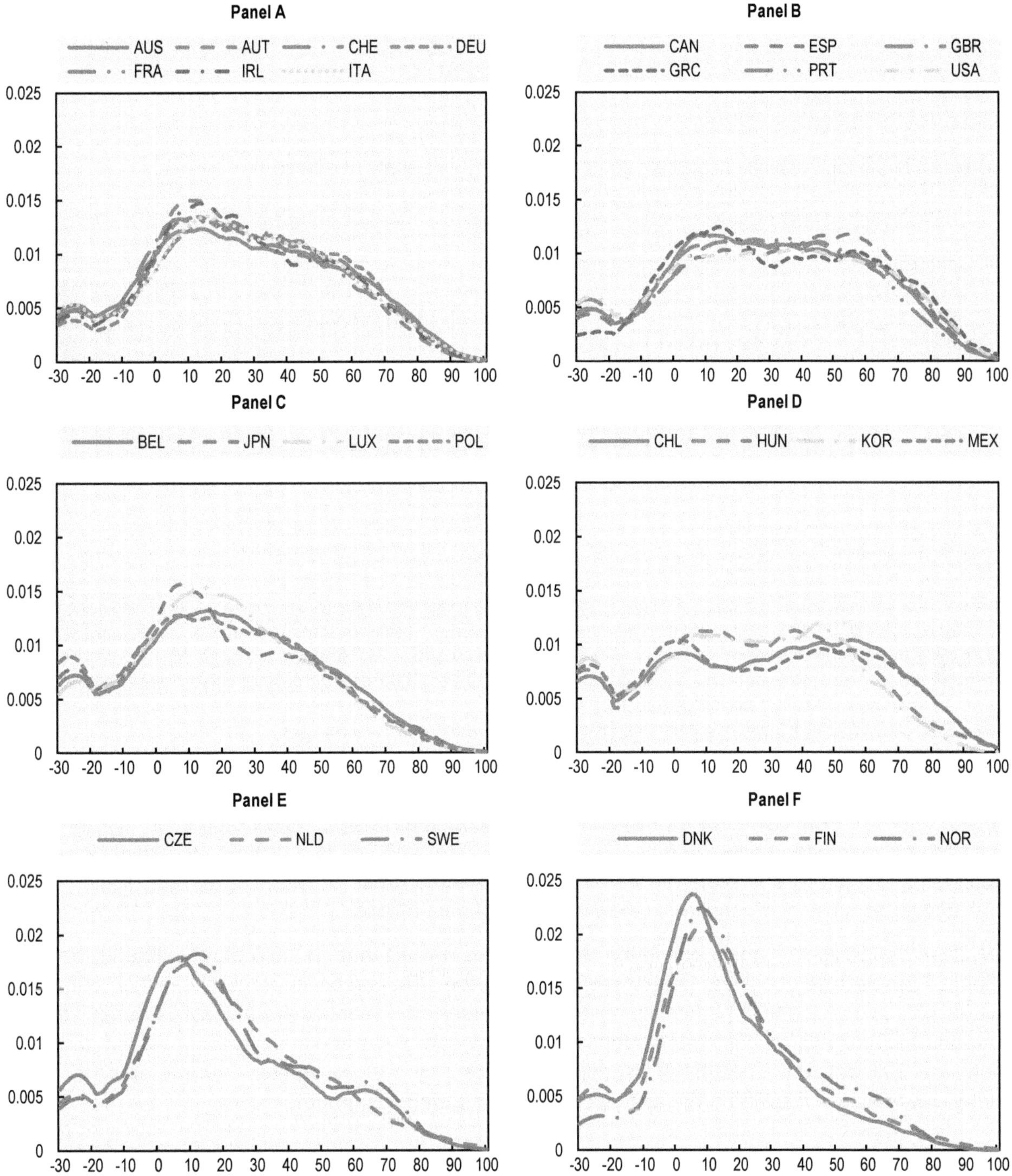

Note: The distributions have been censored at -30 for presentational purposes – those who believe that the perceived top income share is lower than 30 percentage points with respect to their preferred value are included along with the -30. This generates a peak in the distribution at lower values, which is due only to the censoring. The plots show the probability density functions for the perception of total income going to the richest 10% households estimated through the kernel density estimation.
Source: OECD calculations from Compare your Income 2015-20 (Balestra and Cohen, forthcoming[4]).

StatLink https://stat.link/f9lc3d

In all countries preferred richest 10%'s shares of income are less dispersed than perceived ones. The inference is that people tend to be more in agreement as to what income inequality should be, rather than what it currently is. It follows that most of the disagreement in concern (i.e. the gap between perceived and preferred inequality) stems from differences in perceptions across people (Figure 4.4). OECD-wide, the dispersion in perceptions of the richest 10%'s income share contributes to more than two-thirds of the total variance in concern over high income inequality.[2]

Figure 4.4. Most of the dispersion in concern over the income share of the richest 10% share stems from differences in perceptions

Contribution to the total variance of concern about the richest 10%'s share of income

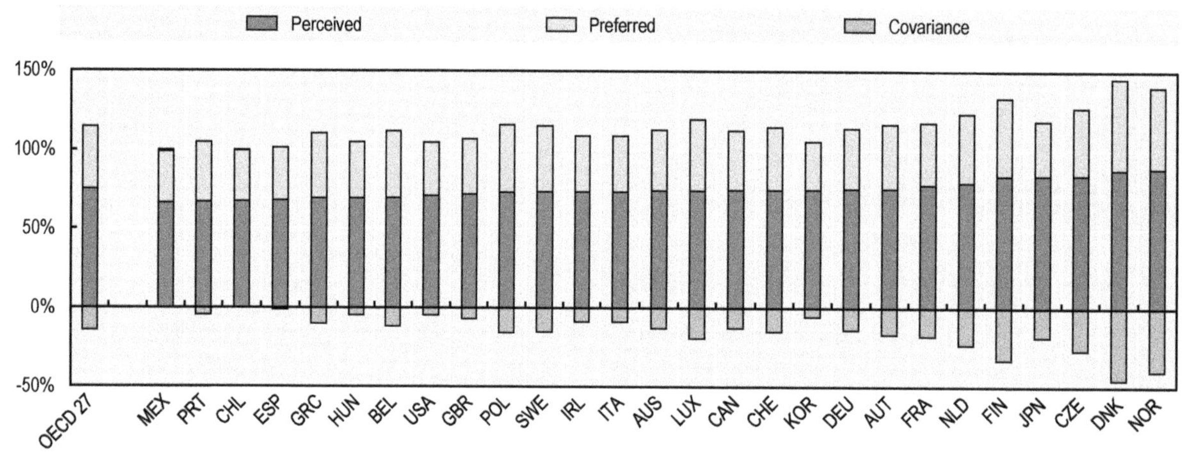

Note: Concern is captured by the percentage point gap between perceived and preferred shares a of country's total income going to the top 10% richest households. The total variance can be broken down into the variance of perceived shares, the variance of preferred shares, minus twice the covariance of perceived and preferred shares. With few exceptions, covariance is close to zero or positive. When it is positive, it means that people who report high perceived shares also report higher preferred shares. This makes the distance between perceived and preferred more similar across people who hold different perceptions.
Source: OECD calculations from Compare your Income, 2015-20 (Balestra and Cohen, forthcoming[4]).

StatLink https://stat.link/xk1oib

Concern over the extent of earnings disparities within countries is also widely dispersed, as the ratio of perception-to-preference shows (Figure 4.5). Countries are split into two groups, according to whether respondents' perceived and preferred earnings are collected gross or net of taxes and social security contributions, as gross and net change the dispersion of perceptions.[3]

Analysis of the gross earnings group in the United States reveals that, for 10% of respondents' earnings, disparities are narrower or equal to their preferences – the 10th percentile of the distribution of concern. Another 10%, above the 90th percentile, believe that perceived disparities are at least 17 times what they deem fair. In Denmark, by contrast, perceptions at each end of the spectrum harbour do not diverge as widely: the 90th percentile perceives disparities that are only 3 times greater than preferences. Cross-country differences in dispersion are also strong in the net earnings group.

Figure 4.5. Concern about the top-bottom earnings ratio is also highly dispersed

Distribution of the perceived top-bottom earnings ratio divided by the preferred ratio: blue dots denote the 10th and 90th percentiles, the rectangle the 25th and 75th percentiles, while the grey dot is the average

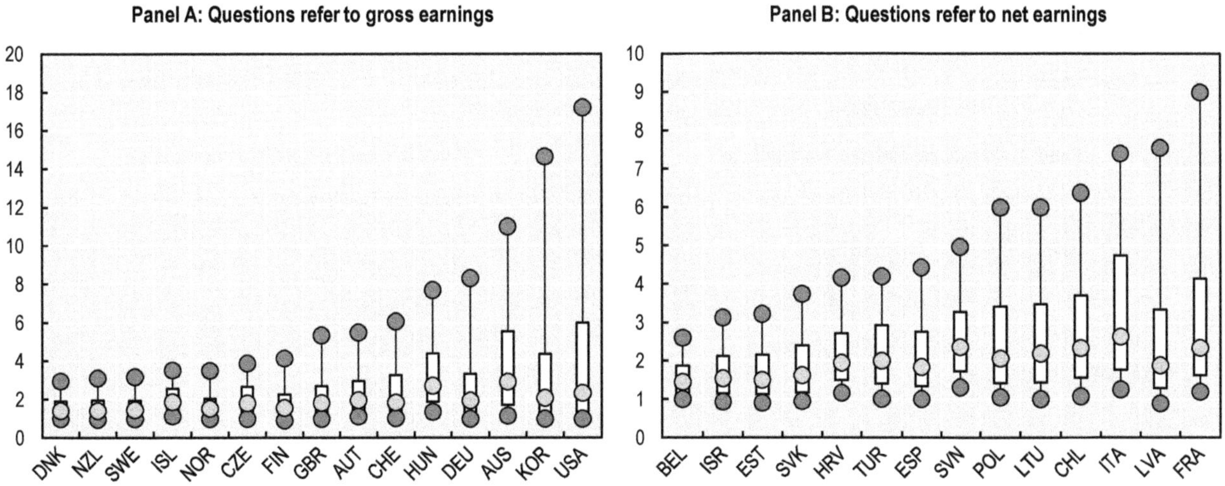

Note: The figure plots how much larger respondents think the current level of earnings disparities is compared to what they believe it should be, at different points across the entire distribution of answers. For instance, in the United Stated the median respondent believes that the top-bottom earnings ratio is twice the one what she would prefer it to be, while the respondent at the 90th percentile believes that it is almost 18 times greater.
Source: OECD calculations from ISSP 2009.

StatLink https://stat.link/71qg56

In all countries, there is a non-negligible group of respondents whose perceptions of disparities are similar to their preferences (Figure 4.6). Countries with the lowest dispersion of perceptions feature large, cohesive groups of respondents who believe that the current level of inequality is wider than their preferences, but not excessively so. In some cases, low-dispersion countries have smaller groups of respondents whose preferences reflect the status quo (e.g. Iceland).

In countries where concerns are more widely dispersed, there is a pronounced gap between proponents of the status quo and respondents who believe inequality is large-scale, and there is a bigger group with a perception/preference ratio of 4 or more. In some instances, particularly in Korea and the United States, there is still a large share of pro-status-quo respondents, which spells wide polarisation.

Figure 4.6. In countries where concern is less dispersed, many believe that earnings disparities are large, but not excessively so

Share of respondents by level of concern over top-bottom earnings disparities, i.e. how much larger the perceived ratio is than the preferred ratio)

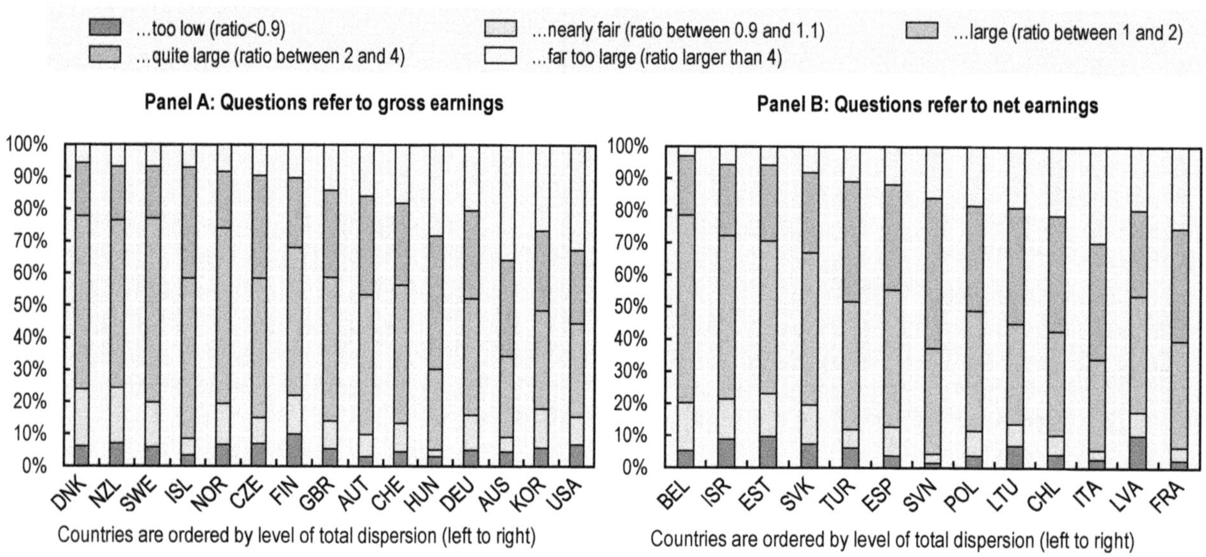

Source: OECD calculations on ISSP 2009.

StatLink https://stat.link/yamwuk

People also disagree extensively about whether top earnings are too high or bottom earnings too low. Disagreement is illustrated by the respondents in different groups who differ in their perception of current levels of top and bottom earnings and what they believe they should be – their preferences (Figure 4.7). The countries analysed are chosen from the bottom, middle and top of the dispersion. The overall cross-country trend points to often strong disagreement about top earnings, which is consistent with previous findings (Kelley et al., 1993[6]). However, different patterns also emerge. In France, for example, most respondents find that the current level of bottom earnings is too low and top earnings too high. In the United States, by contrast, people are more divided over bottom earnings. Compared to other countries, more respondents find them almost fair.

Figure 4.7. People disagree as to whether top earnings are too high or bottom earnings too low

Percentage share of respondents by level of perceived bottom and top earnings (y-axis and x-axis, respectively) compared to preferred levels, selected countries, 2009

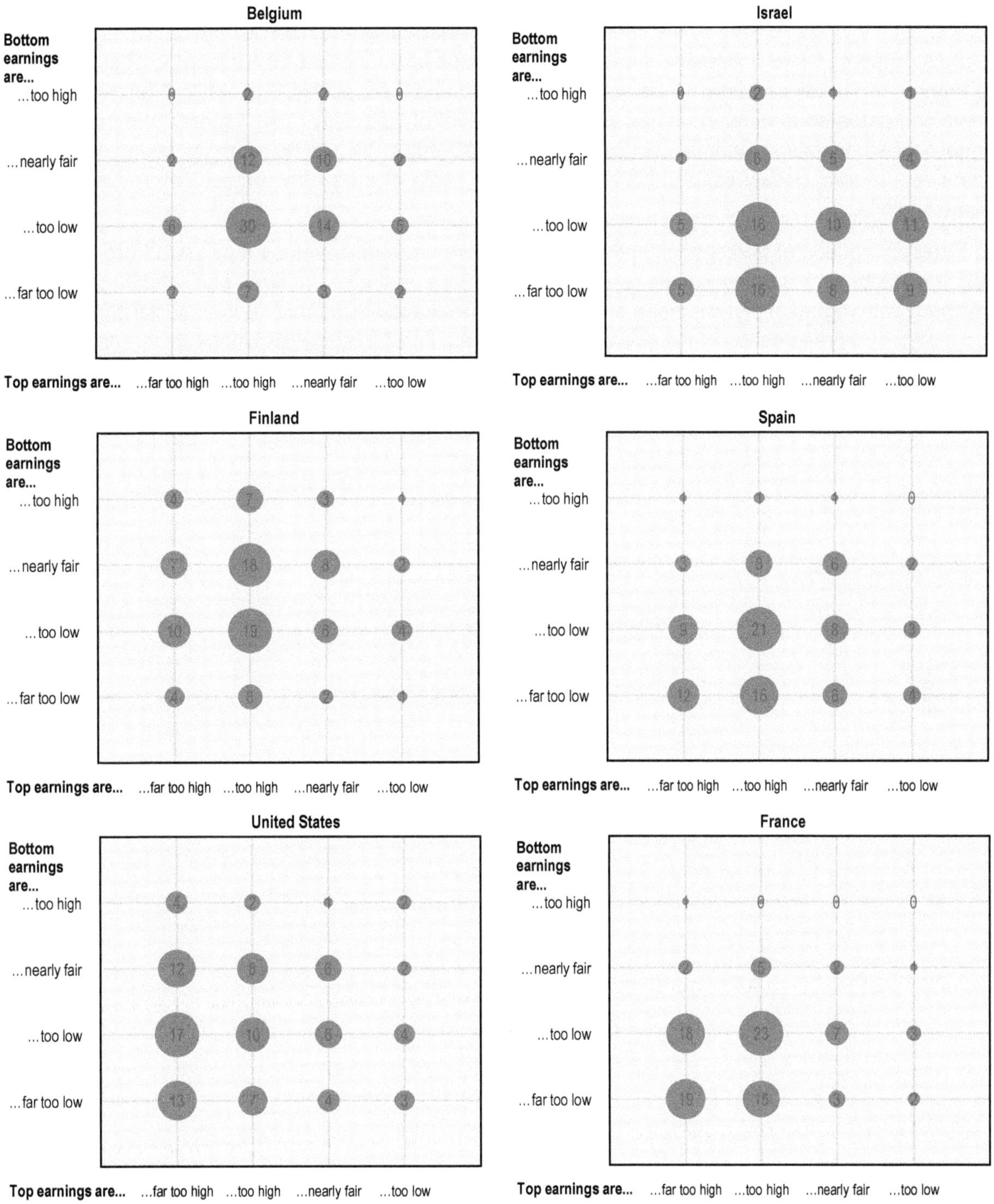

Note: The figure plots on the x-axis the share of respondents who think that top earnings are far too high (they should be 50% less), too high (they should be between 50% and 10% less), are nearly fair (less than 10% from what they should be), or are too low. The y-axis shows the share of respondents who think that bottom earnings are far too low (they should be 50% higher), too low (they should be between 10% and 50% higher), are nearly fair (within 10% from what they should be), or are too high.
Source: OECD calculations from ISSP 2009.

StatLink https://stat.link/dy5n4q

More unequal countries have a more divided public opinion

Perceptions and concern are more widely dispersed where there are higher levels of income inequality (measured by the Gini coefficient for disposable income; Figure 4.8). For perceptions, the correlation is strong with regard to both the perceived richest 10%'s income share and perceived intergenerational persistence. It is driven chiefly by the countries with high inequality and high dispersion (Chile, Mexico and the United States).[4] Two noticeable outliers in perceptions of the richest 10%'s income share are Turkey and France. In Turkey perceptions are weakly dispersed and inequality is high, while France shows wider dispersion compared to other countries with medium level of inequality. The dispersion of concern about inequality of earnings and income – concern being measured by the gap between perceived and preferred disparities – is also closely associated with the actual scale of inequality, particularly in Compare Your Income findings.

The wider distribution of perceptions and concern in more unequal countries may stem from the fact that, when inequality is high, individuals struggle to correctly estimate income and earnings disparities, particularly with regard to high incomes and earnings. The reason might be that their social circle is unlikely to be a perfect representation of the overall income distribution.[5] In societies where social groups mix little there is greater dispersion of outlooks. Groups know little about each other and each other's perceptions. This can also explain why the rich sometimes perceive the top-bottom earnings ratio to be higher than the poor do. Irrespective of the mechanism at work, public opinion is more divided in more unequal societies.

Figure 4.8. Public opinion is more divided in countries with higher income inequality

Dispersion of perceptions and concerns vs. inequality measured by the Gini index

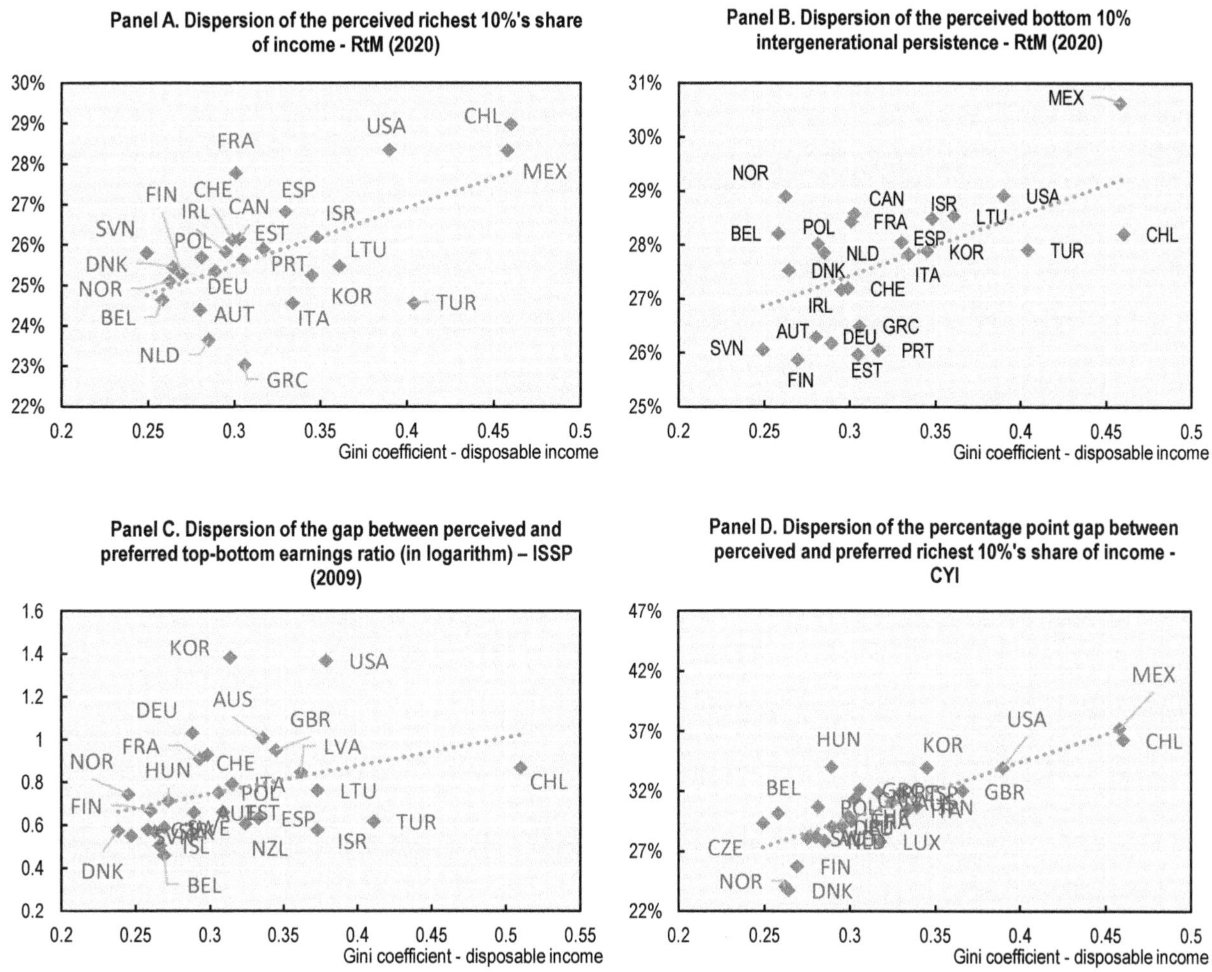

Note: The dispersion of perceptions/concerns is measured as the standard deviation in the sample. The Gini index refers to disposable income and refers to the latest available year for Risks that Matter and Compare Your Income, and to 2008 or 2009 (when available) for ISSP (for years 2008/2009 until 2011 the old income definition for the IDD is used). The standardized slope in Panel A is 0.582 and is statistically significant at the1% level (with heteroscedasticity robust standard errors); for Panel B it is 0.561, significant at the 5% level; for Panel C it is equal to 0.341, significant at the 10% level; for Panel D it is 0.785, significant at the 1% level.

Source: OECD calculations from the 2020 Risks that Matter Survey, ISSP 2009, Compare Your Income 2015-20; *OECD Income Distribution Database* (https://stats.oecd.org/Index.aspx?DataSetCode=IDD) for the Gini coefficient.

StatLink https://stat.link/bhjgvp

4.2. Has the extent of disagreement between people increased?

The distribution of perceptions and concerns has long become more dispersed and polarized

Public opinion has grown more divided over the years. Between the 1990s and the global financial crisis, the increase in perceived earnings disparities (Section 2.2) was not uniform across the population and the gap between people who perceived wide or narrow disparities grew (Figure 4.9 and Giger and Lascombes (2019[7])). As a result, in the countries for which data are available[6], the dispersion of perceptions increased – least in the Nordic countries (Norway and Sweden), and Slovenia and Austria, and most in Australia, Germany and the United States. In fact, dispersion spread most where the average perception of inequality spread most (Annex Figure 4.A.1).[7] This correlation shows that the rise in perceptions, because it was heterogeneous across a country's population, was accompanied by increasingly strong disagreement as to what the level of inequality was.

Although perceived earning disparities shrunk in the most recent decade from 2010-19, dispersion remained the same as during the global financial crisis. It fell somewhat in Italy, Norway, Slovenia and Australia, but was still more widespread than in the late 1990s or late 1980s. It grew in the other five countries observed until ISSP 2019, particularly in Germany.

Figure 4.9. Perceptions of earnings disparities have grown more dispersed over time

90th and 10th percentile of the perceived top-bottom earnings ratio (logarithmic scale)

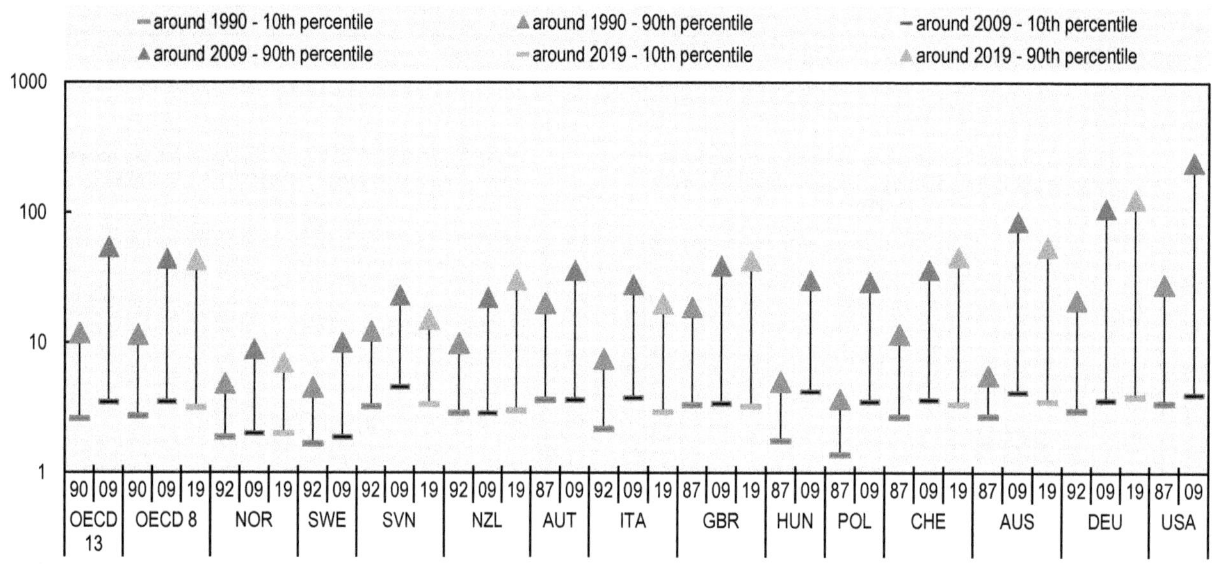

Note: The year refers to the ISSP wave. Countries ordered by change in the 90th-10th distance between late 80s/early 90s and 2009. The lines represent the extent of the differences between the bottom 10% of respondents and the top 10%. For instance in the United States in 2009 the bottom 10 percent of respondents believed that the ratio was lower than 4, while the top 10% believed it was larger than 244. The question on perceptions of the top-bottom earnings ratio relates to gross earnings, apart from Poland and Slovenia (where it refers to net earnings). In Hungary in 1987, neither gross or net earnings were mentioned, perhaps because personal income tax was only introduced in 1988. In Italy the earnings definition used in the ISSP question switched from gross earnings in the first wave to net earnings in 2009: as actual net earnings are usually less dispersed than gross earnings, the change observed in the figure likely underestimates the increase in dispersion.
Source: OECD calculations from ISSP 1987, 1992, 2009 and 2019.

StatLink https://stat.link/2np0rb

Increased dispersion was also associated in some countries with increased polarisation (Osberg and Smeeding, 2006[2]), as the estimated distribution of perceptions attests. Six countries with small (Norway and Sweden), medium-sized (Italy and the United Kingdom) and large (Germany and the United States) changes in dispersion in the two decades up to the global financial crisis illustrate the growing divergence at the time between the 90th and 10th percentiles in perceptions of top-bottom earnings ratios (Figure 4.10). The distributions not only moved towards higher values, but also flattened out considerably over the years, so that the gap between the perceptions of any two respondents increased. Some countries showed signs of rising polarisation. The peaks observed in some countries corresponded to two (or more) groups of respondents clustered around low, medium or high levels of perceived inequality. These values moved away from each other over time, indicating an increase in the extent of disagreement between the groups.

Widening polarization between the early 1990s and the global financial crisis was also apparent in Sweden, despite the limited change in the overall dispersion of perceptions, and Norway. Polarisation nevertheless seemed to ease in the following decade.

Italy and the United Kingdom stand out in that they started from a narrow range of perceptions, before they dispersed increasingly in the two decades up to the global financial crisis. Dispersion eased only mildly in the following decade, while polarisation across different groups persisted. Both in Germany and the United States the distribution in late 1980s and early 1990s was already dispersed and polarized. Disagreement grew even stronger in the following two decades and perceptions moved further apart. The strong level of disagreement has continued in Germany.

Figure 4.10. The distribution of perceived top-bottom earnings ratios has become more dispersed and polarised

Estimated density distribution (y-axis) for each possible top-bottom earnings ratio (x-axis, logarithmic scale), selected countries, the year refers to the ISSP wave

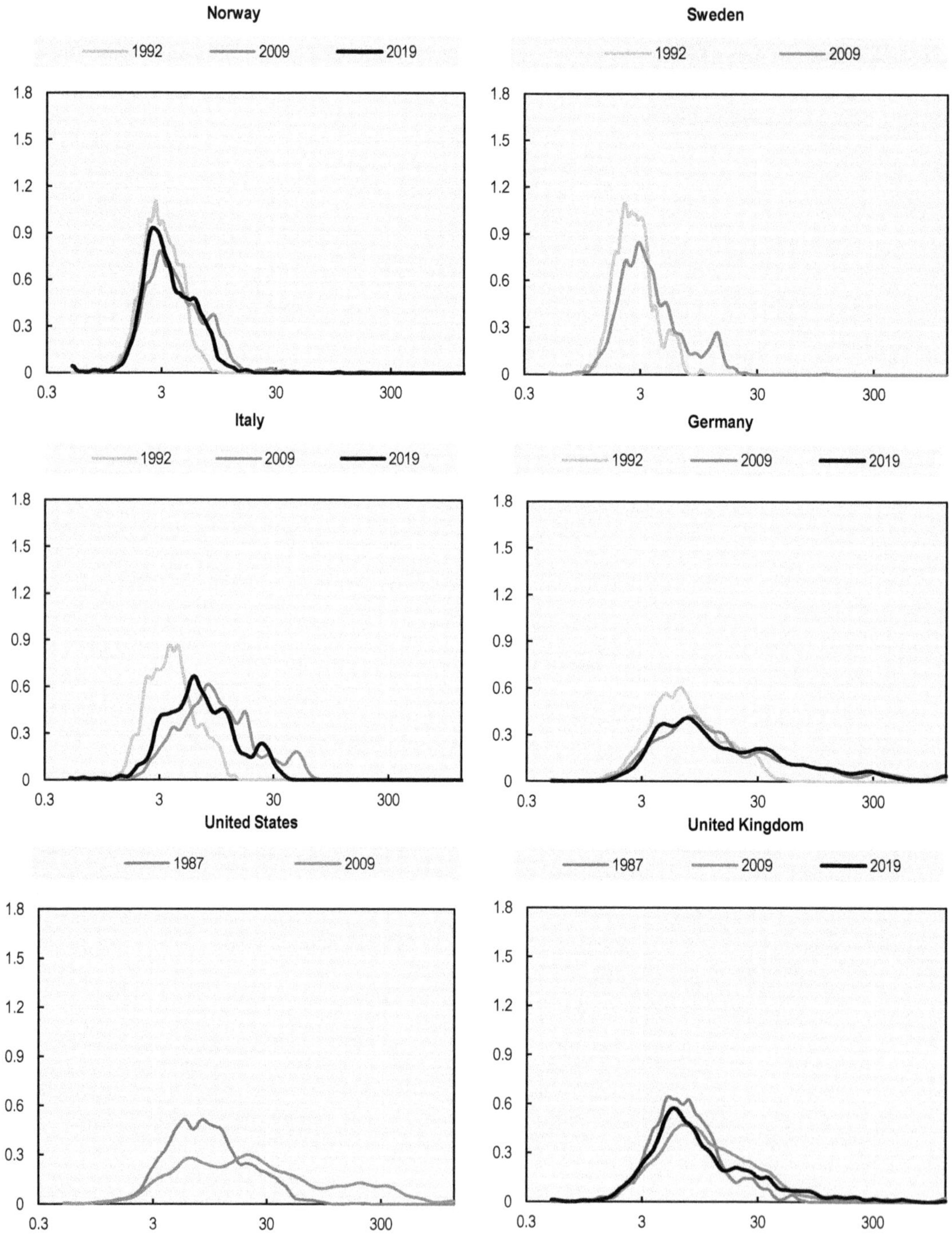

Note: The graphs plot the density of responses; respondents' answers are more frequent around the points where the values are higher. For instance, in the United States in 1987 most respondents believed that the ratio was between 3 and 30, while in 2009 there was more dispersion, with an increase in the number of those who believed it was much larger than 30. The density is estimated using kernel regressions with Gaussian kernel. The x-axis is in log scale.
Source: OECD calculations on ISSP 1987, 1999, 2009.

StatLink https://stat.link/1vx2le

The rise in the dispersion of perceptions over time has been due mostly to the rise in disagreement over levels of top earnings (Figure 4.11 and Osberg and Bechert (2016[8])). Australia, the United Kingdom, Norway and the United States saw sizeable increases in disagreement over levels of bottom earnings.[8] Top earnings nevertheless fuelled far stronger disagreement, probably because most people had limited experience or knowledge of highly paid occupations (the benchmark being the pay of doctors or CEOs of a national corporation). Respondents probably received different, wide-ranging information about top incomes, which rose fast in most OECD countries. As a result, people changed their perceptions of them in very different ways.

Figure 4.11. The increased disagreement about the level of disparities is mostly due to the increased dispersion of perceived top earnings

Change in the dispersion of the logarithm for the perceived top-bottom earnings ratios between around 1990 and 2009

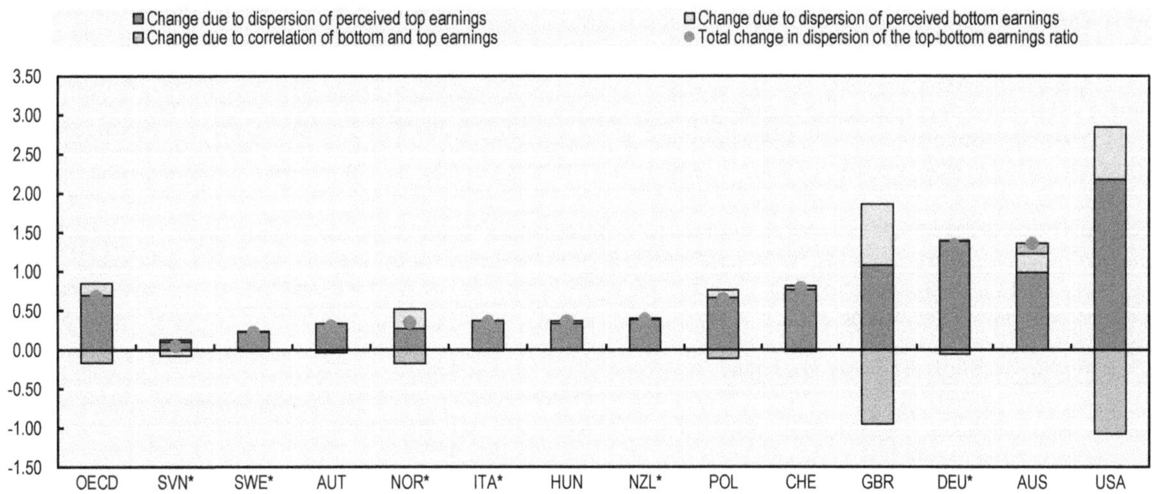

Note: The dispersion of the top-bottom earnings ratio is captured by the variance of its logarithm. It is broken down into the dispersion of beliefs about the level of top-earnings and bottom-earnings. For instance, the increased dispersion of beliefs across the population in Germany is entirely due to the rise in dispersion of beliefs about top-earnings, while the level of disagreement over the current level of bottom earnings has remained stable over time. The component due to correlation is the opposite of twice the covariance between perceived bottom and top earnings. It is negative in the United Kingdom and the United States because, in both countries, respondents who report higher top earnings also report higher bottom earnings, and this correlation has increased over time. Countries denoted by * are observed from 1992.
Source: OECD calculations from ISSP 1987, 1992, 2009.

StatLink https://stat.link/qprnta

The increasing dispersion in perceptions has given rise to growing disagreement over what people think the earnings differentials should be and what they think they are (Figure 4.12). In most countries, there has been increasing divergence between:

- people who believe that perceived current earnings differentials are acceptable,
- those whose preferred level of disparities is far from what they think the current level is.

The increasing dispersion of concern is mostly attributable to growing disagreement over the scale of current earnings differentials, rather than to the rise in the top-bottom ratio that individuals deem acceptable (Ciani et al., forthcoming[3]).

Figure 4.12. Increasing disagreement relates not only to perceptions, but to concerns

10th and 90th percentile of the gap between people's perceived and preferred top-bottom earnings ratio; the year refers to the ISSP wave

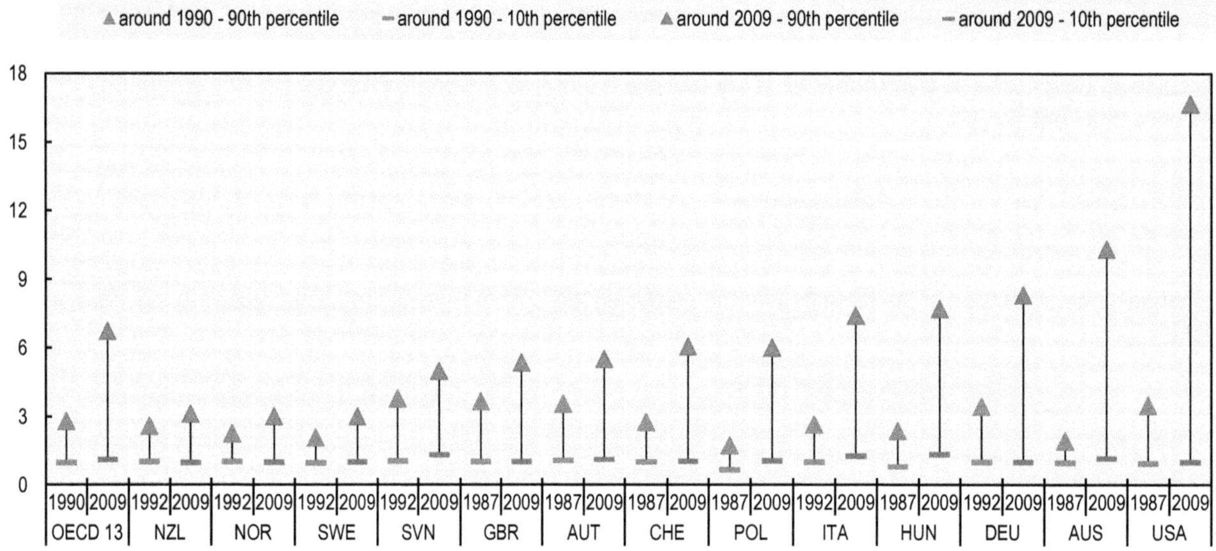

Note: The gap is calculated as the ratio between perceived and preferred top-bottom earnings ratios and can be interpreted as an alternative measure of concern over earnings disparities. For instance, in 2009 in Australia, 10% of respondents (the bottom 10% in the distribution of concerns) thought that the top-bottom earnings ratio is at most only slightly larger – 1.2 times – than it should be. At the opposite spectrum, 10% of respondents (the top 10%) thought that it is more than 10 times what it should be. In 1987 the difference between the two groups was smaller.

Source: OECD calculations from ISSP 1987, 1992, 2009.

StatLink https://stat.link/tzd70n

Most of the increased dispersion of perceptions of and concern over earnings disparities is among people with similar socio-economic characteristics

The long-run increase in the dispersion of perceptions of and concern over earnings disparities might be due to compositional changes. For instance, the increase in educational level might have changed the relevance of educational divides in explaining overall dispersion, as some groups become more relevant in size. However, compositional changes in terms of education, relative income, employment status, gender, age and household size explain little to nothing of the change in dispersion of perceptions and concerns about the top-bottom earnings ratio (Figure 4.13, Panel A).

The increased dispersion in perceptions and concern can stem from higher levels of disagreement between people with different socio-economic characteristics (i.e. *between* socio-economic groups dispersion), but also from disagreement among people with similar characteristics (i.e. *within* socio-economic groups dispersion). Differences between socio-economic groups – as defined by gender, age, education, household size, employment status and relative income – increased over time, and these growing differences explain part of the overall increase in the dispersion of perceptions and concerns (Figure 4.13, Panel B). For the United States, Germany, the United Kingdom, Switzerland and Australia, where the rise in dispersion was stronger, a non-trivial share of the change in the levels of disagreement about levels of income inequality can be attributed to changes in between-group variation. Nevertheless, within-group variation remains responsible for the lion's share of the surge in dispersion observed between 1987/1992 and 2009, both for perceptions and concerns.

Figure 4.13. The dispersion of perceptions of and concern over earnings disparities rose mostly within

Decomposition of the change in the dispersion of perceptions and concerns between 1987/1992 and 2009

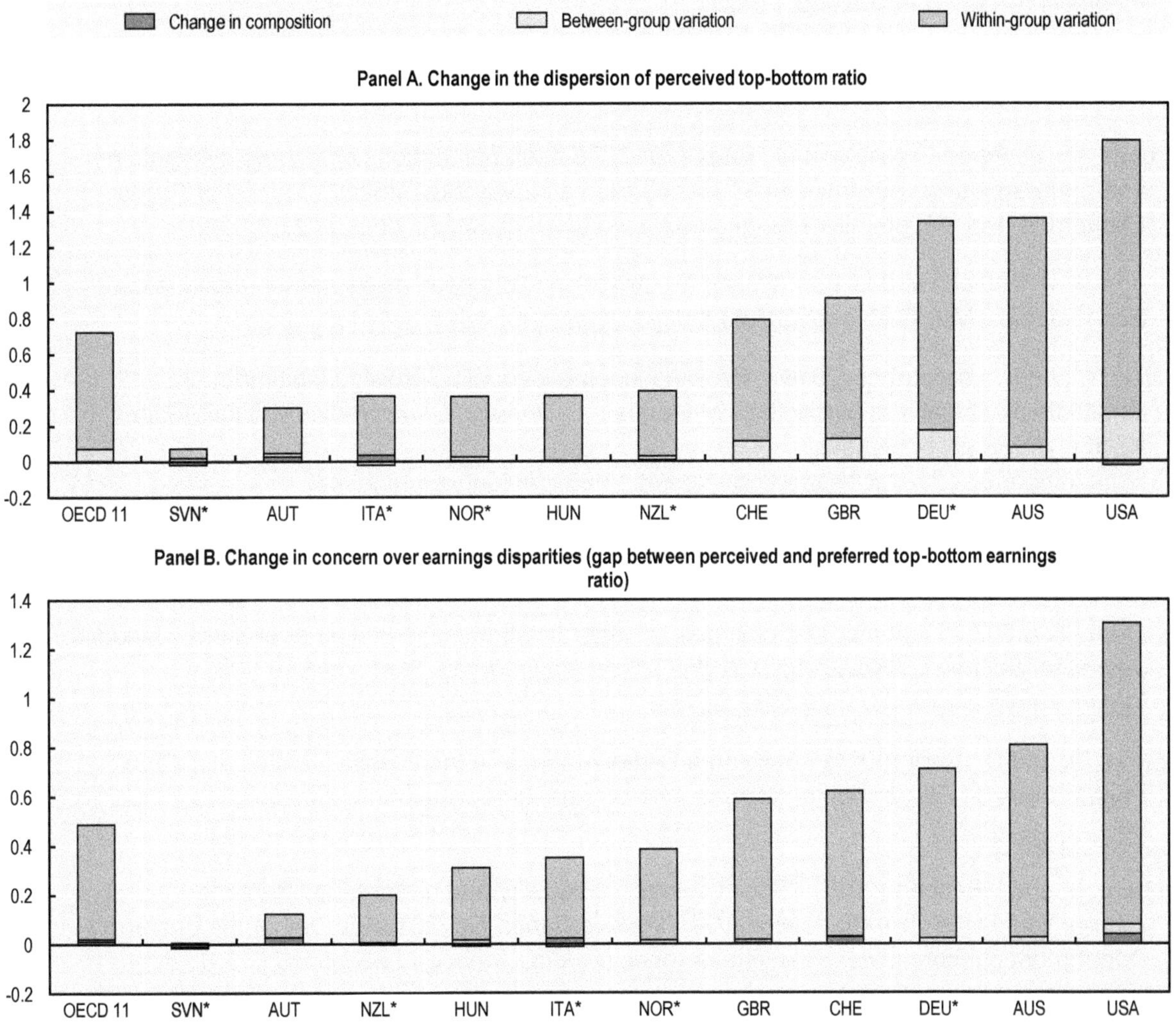

Note: The dispersion refers to the variance of the logarithm of the perceived ratio in the upper panel and to the variance of the logarithmic difference between the perceived and preferred ratio in the bottom panel. The decomposition was obtained through the creation of counterfactual distributions (see Annex 4.B). An asterisk (*) indicates that 1992 was the first wave used for the country. Sweden and Poland were dropped because of the absence of available income data for the two first waves.
Source: ISSP 1987, 1992, 2007.

StatLink https://stat.link/me5q4h

References

Balestra, C. and G. Cohen (forthcoming), "Income Inequality through People's Lenses: Evidence from the OECD Compare your Income Web-tool", *OECD Papers on Well-being and Inequalities*, OECD Publishing, Paris. [4]

Ciani, E. et al. (forthcoming), *Perceptions of inequality across OECD and EU countries: Long term trends and recent evidence.* [3]

Cruces, G., R. Perez-Truglia and M. Tetaz (2013), "Biased perceptions of income distribution and preferences for redistribution: Evidence from a survey experiment", *Journal of Public Economics*, Vol. 98, pp. 100-112, http://dx.doi.org/10.1016/j.jpubeco.2012.10.009. [10]

Duclos, J., J. Esteban and D. Ray (2004), "Polarization: Concepts, measurement, estimation", *Econometrica*, Vol. 72/6, http://dx.doi.org/10.1111/j.1468-0262.2004.00552.x. [1]

Giger, N. and D. Lascombes (2019), "Growing income inequality, growing legitimacy: A longitudinal approach to perceptions of inequality", *Unequal Democracies Working Paper*, No. 11, University of Geneva, https://unequaldemocracies.unige.ch/files/4515/9370/6124/wp11final.pdf. [7]

Kelley, J. et al. (1993), *The Legitimation of Inequality: Occupational Earnings in Nine Nations1*, http://www.journals.uchicago.edu/t-and-c. [6]

Lemieux, T. (2002), "Decomposing changes in wage distributions: a unified approach", *Canadian Journal of Economics/Revue Canadienne d`Economique*, Vol. 35/4, pp. 646-688, http://dx.doi.org/10.1111/1540-5982.00149. [9]

Norton, M. and D. Ariely (2011), "Building a Better America—One Wealth Quintile at a Time", *Perspectives on Psychological Science*, Vol. 6/1, pp. 9-12, http://dx.doi.org/10.1177/1745691610393524. [5]

Osberg, L. and I. Bechert (2016), "Social values for equality and preferences for state intervention: Is the USA "Exceptional"?", *Working Paper*, No. 2016-03, Dalhousie University, Department of Economics, https://ideas.repec.org/p/dal/wpaper/daleconwp2016-03.html. [8]

Osberg, L. and T. Smeeding (2006), ""Fair" Inequality? Attitudes toward Pay Differentials: The United States in Comparative Perspective", *American Sociological Review*, Vol. 71/3, pp. 450-473, http://dx.doi.org/10.1177/000312240607100305. [2]

Annex 4.A. Additional figures

Annex Figure 4.A.1. Where perceived inequality grew the most, perceptions became more dispersed

Change in the average and dispersion of the perceived top-bottom earnings ratio, 1990 and 2009

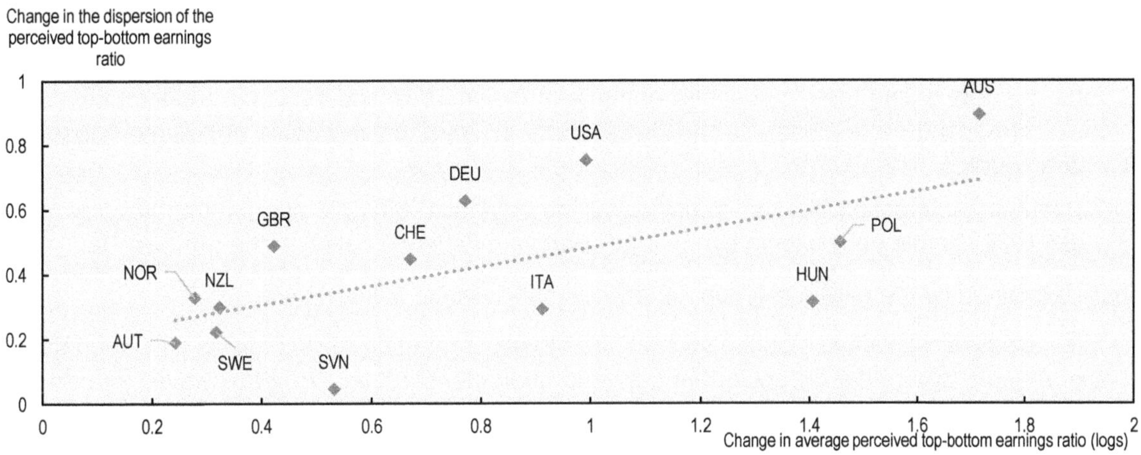

Note: The dispersion refers to the standard deviation of the logarithm of the top-bottom earnings ratio, the average top-bottom earnings ratio is the average of the logs of the ratio.
Source: OECD calculations from ISSP 1987, 1992, 2009.

StatLink https://stat.link/mehupj

Annex 4.B. Methodological details

Decomposition of changes in dispersion into compositional effects and between-groups variance

The decomposition for Figure 4.13 was obtained through the creation of counterfactual distributions, as in Lemieux (2002[9]). In details, the share of the change in dispersion due to compositional effects was obtained as follows:

- First, by reweighting the distributions of the samples in 1987 and 1992 for each country so that they correspond more closely to the distributions of 2009, on the basis of common observable characteristics.
- Second, by subtracting the total variance for the original 1987/1992 sample from the reweighted 1987/1992 sample and dividing by the total change in variance between the two periods.

The share explained by the between-group variation is obtained the following way:

- First, a counterfactual distribution for 1987/1992 was created by (i) running an OLS regression of the variable of interest on socio-demographic characteristics on the 2009 wave; (ii) using it to calculate fitted values for the 1987/1992 observations; (iii) adding to the fitted values the residuals from an OLS regression conducted on 1987/1992. These values use between-groups differences as in 2009 (the fitted part) but within group variation (the residuals) from 1987/1992. This exercise was conducted using the weights calculated to account for compositional effects.
- The total variance of the reweighted 1987/1992 was then subtracted from this counterfactual distribution and divided by the total change in variance between the two periods.
- The share explained by within-group variation (the unexplained part of our models) is obtained after subtracting the total variance of the reweighted counterfactual distribution for 1987/1992 from the original 2009 distribution, and then dividing by the total change in variance between the two periods.

Notes

[1] This group appears to be grouped around the -30 value, but this is only due to the fact that the value had to be censored for presentational reasons. In fact, the group is widely dispersed over the [-100, 0) range.

[2] Note that a negative contribution to the overall variance comes from the fact that preferred and perceived disparities are correlated, i.e. people who believe the income share of the top 10% is higher also tend to report a higher preferred share. However, the correlation is generally weak and therefore this contribution is small, on average.

[3] If income (or payroll) taxes are progressive, net earnings are less dispersed than gross earnings. The reason is that individuals are likely to form their beliefs by observing the earnings of a sample of some workers around them. Their concerns are therefore less likely to be more dispersed if these earnings are more dispersed, which depends on whether the object is gross or net earnings.

[4] A more elaborate analysis of outliers, based on each observation leverage and dfbeta, shows that the relations are not driven by specific outliers.

[5] Individuals form their expectations by observing a subset of the entire population composed, for example, of relatives, friends and co-workers (Cruces, Perez-Truglia and Tetaz, 2013[10]). Even if this subset was a random draw from the entire population, there are still chances that it would not be truly representative of the entire population and that the individual estimates of inequality would contain some "sampling" error, exactly as happens to statisticians working with a small sample. The more dispersed the earnings and income distributions are, the higher the individual sampling error is, and the greater the dispersion of perceptions.

[6] Norway, Sweden, Slovenia, New Zealand, Austria, Italy, Great Britain, Hungary, Poland, the Czech Repubic, Australia, Germany and the United States.

[7] All the figures analysing the change in distribution over time (Section 4.2) account for the fact that, for some countries, the initial wave involved a certain degree of censoring of the questions about chairman's earnings, while no censoring was applied to 2009. To this aim, for countries where there was at least 1% censoring in the first wave, the same level of censoring was applied to the final wave. See Ciani et al. (forthcoming[3]) for more details.

[8] However, in these countries (apart from Australia), the tendency of people who report higher top earnings to also report higher bottom earnings has increased over time, reducing the dispersion of the ratio between the two.

5. Implications for policy

Reforms to reduce deep-seated economic inequalities in outcomes and opportunities require wide public support. This chapter outlines how measuring and analysing perceptions of and concern about inequality can help to design more effective policies. It highlights how, behind the strong demand for greater economic equality, there are widely diverse perceptions and concerns – both between and within countries – which policy makers need to address when designing redistributive reforms. Such perceptions and concerns have important implications for the demand for policy intervention, but the perceived effectiveness of policies is also crucial for public support: people do not just demand more redistributive policies, they want to see them reducing inequality and creating more opportunity. Addressing those policy considerations calls for greater effort in collecting high-quality, large-scale evidence about people's perceptions and their concern over economic inequalities. The chapter concludes with a brief examination of the crucial evidence gaps that new data could fill.

5.1. Implications for gathering public support for redistributive policies

The COVID-19 crisis has exposed the wide-ranging inequality that characterises OECD societies (OECD, 2020[1]). Indeed, the shocks to the labour market that it has caused have had highly asymmetric effects across the income distribution. Preliminary evidence suggests that, without the swift intervention of ad-hoc state action, the shocks would have seriously worsened existing disparities (Brewer and Gardiner, 2020[2]; Chetty et al., 2020[3]; Almeida et al., 2020[4]; Clark, D'Ambrosio and Lepinteur, 2020[5]; European Commission, 2020[6]; Carta and De Philippis, 2021[7]).

The planned recovery packages are a tremendous chance to introduce reforms that address structural disparities and widespread lack of opportunity(Boone et al., 2020[8]; OECD, 2020[1]; OECD, 2020[9]). Such reforms require public support wide enough to guarantee their sustainability over time and help them achieve their long-term objectives. However, and often to the surprise of policy makers, support for redistributive government intervention has not risen significantly over the last three decades (Section 3.4). Yet income and earnings disparities have risen considerably, particularly between the 1990s and early 2000s (OECD, 2011[10]), and current levels of inequality and intergenerational persistence remain high (OECD, 2018[11]).

One recurrent interpretation of the limited increase in demand for redistribution over the last decades is that people are "unaware" of the true levels of inequality around them, or are unable to process the information to that effect from researchers and the media. The evidence presented in this report does not lend support to that view. OECD-wide, most people do express strong concern about the scale of income disparities. Indeed, average levels of concern have increased over time, particularly where conventional indicators of inequality, such as the Gini index, have also increased (Section 2.1). Perceived earnings disparities have also risen significantly over time (Section 2.2). Recent data from the Risks that Matter survey show that people perceive high income inequality and low social mobility, particularly if they have experienced hardship during the COVID-19 crisis.

Taken together, all this evidence does not square with the claim of widespread unawareness. On the contrary, it shows that people have incorporated into their concern and perceptions rising inequality and low social mobility. And most people in most countries are strenuously calling for greater equality of economic outcome and opportunity.

Measuring and interpreting people's perceptions of and their concern about inequality is critical if policy makers are to build sustainable reforms. Perceived disparities and the concern over inequality are important drivers of demand for redistributive policies, overshadowing in some instances the importance of socio-economic characteristics like own income (Section 3.1). Growth in actual inequality – as measured by conventional indicators – leads to an increase in redistributive preferences only insofar as people's concern also increases accordingly (Section 3.2). Collecting information about perceptions and concern is therefore crucial to designing and implementing reforms to reduce inequality.

However, the evidence presented in the previous chapters also shows that strong demand for equality does not always translate into country-wide support for redistributive policies (Section 3.4). Understanding why not is necessary if policy design is to take people's concern about inequality into consideration. Against that background, four key policy issues emerge:

- The interconnectedness between income inequality and intergenerational persistence.
- How policy design can respond to the heterogeneous nature of perceptions of inequality and demand for redistribution.
- How policy effectiveness matters to people.
- How a divided public opinion complicates policy action and how information can help.

Perceptions of income inequality and intergenerational persistence are closely bound up

Long-term policies to tackle inequalities are often designed on the assumption that there is a simple trade-off between inequality of resources and intergenerational persistence, so that greater equal opportunity at birth would make current inequality more acceptable. Previous evidence and policy analysis argued that such trade-off is not straightforward. Indeed, as inequality in economic and social outcomes today shapes access to opportunities in education and the labour market, it produces unfair advantages and disadvantages that are passed on to the next generation (OECD, 2015[12]; Atkinson, 2015[13]).

The evidence provided in this report shows that also individuals do not imply a simple trade-off. They view intergenerational persistence and income inequality as closely bound up, perceiving one when they perceive the other (Section 2.2). Moreover, perceived income inequality drives demand for more redistribution even when intergenerational persistence is perceived to be low, and vice-versa (Section 3.1). Although the importance accorded to income inequality and intergenerational persistence differs from one society to the other, policy makers need to consider that people want inequality-reducing action that addresses both outcomes and opportunities.

Perceptions of inequality and demand for redistribution are highly heterogeneous and lead to support of different policy mixes

Although people care about inequality of both outcomes and opportunities, concern over and perceptions of economic inequality are highly heterogeneous along different aspects. There are wide differences between countries and people about which side of income disparities is more relevant (whether bottom incomes are too low or top incomes are too high), which obstacles to intergenerational mobility (e.g. parental education or wealth) are more challenging (Chapters 2 and 4), and what are the sources of disparities (e.g. the role of hard work in getting ahead in life). Perceptions of income inequality and intergenerational immobility may combine differently, so calling for different policy mixes, which could give either more weight to policies that directly affect outcomes, like unemployment benefits, or to those that promote opportunity, such as educational policies (Section 3.4). People in different countries also associate redistribution with different interventions, ranging from progressive taxation and income support to housing and healthcare policies. Neglecting the many diverse factors in designing reform packages might lead to a puzzling situation in which, despite high demand for more equality, reforms fail to gather sufficient public support.

Policy effectiveness determines policy support

Both observational and experimental evidence (Section 3.4) show that people's support for redistributive policies depends on whether they expect them to be effective. Demand is lower if people believe, correctly or incorrectly, that policies have only a limited impact on people's economic conditions – because, for instance, most benefits do not go to those who really need them. Information campaigns about inequality-reducing policies increases support for them and can strengthen the link between perceived inequality and preferences for redistribution. Designing effective policies is, therefore, not only a concern for economists, policy makers and advisors, but key to public support. People do not only demand more redistributive policies, they want to see them actually reducing inequality and increasing opportunity.

Policy makers must also rise to the challenges of policy evaluation and communication. Governments need to collect data on policy outcomes and analyse them transparently, as recommended by the OECD's Council on Open Government (OECD/LEGAL/0438). However, because of its independence from policy makers, the research community has a crucial role to play in scrutinizing the evidence and preventing non-rigorous results from sapping confidence in findings on which the experts agree.

Governments should also communicate robust evidence as to the effects of policies. Doing so requires gaining people's trust and successfully conveying messages to a non-expert audience. Useful guidance on how to reach out to people may be drawn from this report's analysis of how people form their perceptions.

A strongly divided public opinion challenges reforming action, but information can help

Although people generally call for greater equality, public opinion is strongly divided in OECD countries, as shown by the widely divergent perceptions of inequality within most countries, which fuels disagreement between people from the same country. Such dispersion is an additional challenge to reform, as any proposal, even if supported by the majority, is likely to face strong opposition from some groups.

The dispersion of concern is due in part to the heterogeneous range of people's preferences for equality (Chapter 4). However, much of it also stems from different perceptions of current levels of inequality and intergenerational persistence. Experimental evidence shows that providing people with factual information about inequality changes their perceptions (Section 2.2), even if it does have only a minor effect on redistributive preferences (Section 3.4). Facilitating communication and discussion of sound evidence on inequality could help provide meeting points in the national debate, even if it did not necessarily narrow differences of opinion about policies. A first important step would be to clear up the confusion between disagreement about what the level of inequality is – facts on which people should be able to agree – with disagreement about what it should be – which speaks to people's preferences and principles.

Several initiatives seek to raise awareness of income distribution and inequality of opportunity in order to lay some common ground for public debate. For instance, the OECD's Compare Your Income webtool allows people from OECD member countries to assess where they stand in their national income distribution according to the best available estimate from the *OECD Income Distribution Database (IDD)*. People may also use it to compare their perception of the poverty line with a statistical estimate from the *IDD*. The Opportunity Atlas, built by the US Census Bureau together with Raj Chetty, Nathan Hendren and John Friedman, maps the economic outcomes of children born in different neighbourhoods across the United States. However, more information does not necessarily broaden agreement. Indeed, revealing the profound divide between rich and poor may actually reinforce differences of opinion across the income distribution. Furthermore, as there are many possible reasons why people's perceptions differ from objective measures (Section 2.2), governments should be transparent and clear when communicating empirical evidence to avoid conflict between their, expert, view and people's views. Contextualising evidence can help prevent such conflict and help individuals to take in information and, possibly, update their perceptions.

5.2. Implications for interpreting and analysing people's perceptions of inequality

The discussion of subjective evaluations of economic inequality often starts with analysis of the extent to which perceptions are distorted views of reality. This report follows a different approach. Instead of identifying whether people's estimates are fully comparable with conventional estimates, it seeks to understand what can be learnt about the way people form their perceptions and concerns, and how that influences their demand for redistributive policies.

The report finds that people's perceptions of inequality are not an artificial construct. Although they may not correspond to statistical estimates, international differences in perceptions correlate well with international differences in conventional indicators (Section 2.2), which suggests that people incorporate evidence of economic inequality into their own views. Nevertheless, such perceptions vary from person to person and country to country beyond the differences in actual measures, so painting a complex picture.

These perceptions matter for demand for redistribution (Section 3.1) and convey crucial information as to what matters to people, which policies need to take into account.

People's concern about inequality should not be taken as their personal description of reality. As argued in Chapter 2, concern is a normative assessment that people build not only from their perceptions of the current level of inequality, but also from their preferences. Even if every member of a society perceived the same level of income inequality, concern would vary because different individuals have different views of what a fair level of inequality would be.[1] In that respect, people's concern cannot be taken as "right" or "wrong", inasmuch as it reflects their preferences. Separating the two components – perceptions and preferences – is crucial for understanding how concern about inequality changes over time and across countries.

The report shows that preferred level of (earnings) inequality rose over time, but by less than perceived disparities (Section 2.3). The distinction between preference and perception is also relevant to any policy discussion that tries to find support for reform across different groups and people, as it is clearly fruitless to contend that perfect information would lead to perfect agreement.

Interpreting the available evidence on subjective views of inequality requires careful methodological consideration. The reports offers several insights into the definition and measurement of the different aspects that form these subjective views. However, their ambiguity requires further methodological discussion, given the multidisciplinary nature of the research into subjective views of inequality, which combines analysis from economics, political science, psychology and sociology. Developing clear guidelines is necessary for any systematic collection of data on perceptions of and concern about economic inequality. The OECD Expert Group on New Measures of the Public Acceptability of Reforms aims at contributing to this effort. The discussion from previous chapters highlights four important areas of further research:

- More granular data on the entire distribution of perceptions and concern;
- Preferences for concrete policy options;
- Perceptions of the effectiveness and functioning of redistributive policies;
- How perceptions and concern evolve over time.

More granular data on the entire distribution of perceptions and concern

It is important to analyse the entire distribution of perceptions and concern and to collect data that allow for more granular analysis. Going beyond the average level of concern and support for policies helps to understand how the policy debate can become divided and polarized, so predicting disagreement and tension over the introduction of redistributive reforms. As Chapter 4 shows, the dispersion of perceptions and concern increased in most OECD countries. Socio-economic divides, like income and education, explain only a slight share of the total dispersion of perceptions and concern, and a very small share of increased dispersion over time. Measuring and analysing the distribution of perceptions and concern among people in a country can prove valuable in understanding new forms of social conflict.

There is also limited knowledge about the variability of perceptions at a more granular level. Although the aggregate perceptions of different socio-economic groups do not differ strongly, little is known about their target-specific beliefs and their perceptions of certain patterns of inequality. For instance, drawing on a large dataset, Hviedberg, Kreiner and Stantcheva (2020[14]) find that Danish people view income disparities within their own educational or occupation reference group as the least fair.[2] Furthermore, most current surveys are not representative at sub-national level and do not, therefore, allow proper analysis of differences in perceptions and concern in local areas. A more granular analysis would require considerable effort in collecting data on perceptions – through large-scale representative surveys, for example.

Preferences for concrete policy options

There is limited evidence as to people's preferences for concrete policy options and their views of the role of other actors, such as trade unions and firms. Evidence from the previous chapters shows that people have different preferences for different policy mixes (Section 3.4), partly because their perceptions and concern vary so much from one aspect of inequality to another, such as top or bottom income inequality and intergenerational persistence. Yet, little is known about the relation between perceptions and demand for specific policies.

The evidence is also rather limited about preferences for predistribution policies that focus on market income disparities, such as minimum wage and gender quotas. Some national surveys, often carried out as part of informational experiments (Kuziemko et al., 2015[15]; Stantcheva, 2020[16]), focus on the relevance of analysing concrete policy options – which include predistributive action – both because people might favour specific policy mixes and because much of the disagreement might arise when it comes to discussing concrete options. However, most of the cross-country surveys focus on general "preferences for redistribution" questions, with the exception of the recent Inequality and Politics Survey conducted by Pontusson et al. (2020[17]). More comparative evidence can help shed light on what drives preferences for specific policies, including regulation and pre-distributive policies, and in what conditions different policy mixes have more chance of wide supported. The OECD Risks that Matter survey, and the new wave of Compare Your Income are concrete steps in this direction, as they collect people's concerns on a wide range of different social and fiscal policies – from detailed tax rates to specific social benefits.

Following the literature on preferences for redistribution, this report has focused on people's views about the role of government in tackling income inequality. However, concern about inequality might also increase demand for the intervention of other actors, such as trade unions, firms and civil society. Collecting people's opinions about a wider range of alternative interventions might prove valuable in understanding the cases in which concern about income disparities does not translate into demand for redistribution.

Perceptions of the effectiveness of redistributive policies

There is still limited evidence as to people's understanding of redistributive policies. The evidence discussed in Chapter 3 shows that people's views of the functioning and effectiveness of policies play a key role in shaping support for redistribution as a response to rising inequality.

Recent work by Stantcheva (2020[16]) on the United States uses a combination of survey and experimental methods to consider people's widely varying views of the government and the redistributive impact of tax policy. Following a similar approach in a comparative framework might prove useful both for understanding differences across countries and for guiding reform action within each country.

How perceptions and concern evolve over time

Chapter 2 shows that tracking how perceptions and concerns evolve over time affords important insights into how people form their views and respond to changes in inequality. Yet, few national surveys do any such tracking, re-interviewing respondents in multiple waves.[3] Consequently, there is little analysis of whether people's perceptions and preferences change or stay the same over time.

One exception is Fong, Kauppinen and Poutvaara (2021[18]), who use data from the German Socio-Economic Panel to show that people change their opinions about growing transfers to the poor and taxes on the rich. One way to fill the evidence gap would be to include questions about subjective factors of inequality in existing longitudinal household panel surveys, possibly co-ordinating the effort so as to have the same questions across different countries.

References

Almeida, V. et al. (2020), "Households´ income and the cushioning effect of fiscal policy measures during the Great Lockdown", *JRC Working Papers on Taxation and Structural Reforms*, No. 06/2020, European Commission, Joint Research Centre, Seville, https://ec.europa.eu/jrc/sites/default/files/jrc121598.pdf. [4]

Atkinson, A. (2015), *Inequality: What can be done?*, Harvard University Press, Cambridge, MA, https://www.tony-atkinson.com/new-book-inequality-what-can-be-done (accessed on 2021 October). [13]

Boone, L. et al. (2020), *Building back better: enhancing equal access to opportunities for all*, https://oecdecoscope.blog/2020/07/21/building-back-better-enhancing-equal-access-to-opportunities-for-all/. [8]

Brewer, M. and L. Gardiner (2020), "The initial impact of COVID-19 and policy responses on household incomes", *Oxford Review of Economic Policy*, Vol. 36/Supplement_1, pp. S187-S199, http://dx.doi.org/10.1093/oxrep/graa024. [2]

Carta, F. and M. De Philippis (2021), "The impact of the COVID-19 shock on labour income inequality: Evidence from Italy", *Occasional Papers (Questioni di Economia e Finanza)*, No. 606, Bank of Italy, https://www.bancaditalia.it/pubblicazioni/qef/2021-0606/QEF_606_21.pdf?language_id=1. [7]

Chetty, R. et al. (2020), *The Economic Impacts of COVID-19: Evidence from a New Public Database Built Using Private Sector Data*, National Bureau of Economic Research, Cambridge, MA, http://dx.doi.org/10.3386/w27431. [3]

Clark, A., C. D'Ambrosio and A. Lepinteur (2020), "The Fall in Income Inequality during COVID-19 in Five European Countries", *ECINEQ Working Papers Series*, No. 565, Society for the Study of Economic Inequality, http://www.ecineq.org/milano/WP/ECINEQ2020-565.pdf. [5]

European Commission (2020), *Employment and Social Developments in Europe 2020*, Luxembourg: Publications Office of the European Union, http://dx.doi.org/10.2767/478772. [6]

Fong, C., I. Kauppinen and P. Poutvaara (2021), "Economic Experiences, Target-specific Beliefs and Demands for Redistribution", *mimeo*. [18]

Hvidberg, K., C. Kreiner and S. Stantcheva (2020), *Social Position and Fairness Views*, National Bureau of Economic Research, Cambridge, MA, http://dx.doi.org/10.3386/w28099. [14]

Kolm, S. (1976), "Unequal inequalities. I", *Journal of Economic Theory*, Vol. 12/3, pp. 416-442, http://dx.doi.org/10.1016/0022-0531(76)90037-5. [20]

Kuziemko, I. et al. (2015), "How Elastic Are Preferences for Redistribution? Evidence from Randomized Survey Experiments", *American Economic Review*, Vol. 105/4, pp. 1478-1508, https://www.jstor.org/stable/43495425. [15]

OECD (2020), *Building back better: A sustainable, resilient recovery after COVID-19*, https://www.oecd.org/coronavirus/policy-responses/building-back-better-a-sustainable-resilient-recovery-after-covid-19-52b869f5/#section-d1e45. [9]

OECD (2020), *Enhancing equal access to opportunities for all in G20 countries*, OECD Publishing, http://www.oecd.org/economy/enhancing-equal-access-to-opportunities-G20/. [1]

OECD (2018), *A Broken Social Elevator? How to Promote Social Mobility*, OECD Publishing, Paris, https://dx.doi.org/10.1787/9789264301085-en. [11]

OECD (2015), *In It Together: Why Less Inequality Benefits All*, OECD Publishing, Paris, https://dx.doi.org/10.1787/9789264235120-en. [12]

OECD (2011), *Divided We Stand: Why Inequality Keeps Rising*, OECD Publishing, Paris, https://dx.doi.org/10.1787/9789264119536-en. [10]

Pontusson, J. et al. (2020), *Introducing the Inequality and Politics Survey: Preliminary Findings*, https://archive-ouverte.unige.ch/unige:135683. [17]

Rueda, D. and D. Stegmueller (2019), *Who Wants What?*, Cambridge University Press, http://dx.doi.org/10.1017/9781108681339. [19]

Stantcheva, S. (2020), *Understanding Tax Policy: How Do People Reason?*, National Bureau of Economic Research, Cambridge, MA, http://dx.doi.org/10.3386/w27699. [16]

Notes

[1] The same, in fact, is also true of the experts' view. As put by Kolm (1976, p. 416[20]): "I can take (…) any two countries and prove that inequality is higher in the one or in the other, by choosing different inequality measures." To take this into account, the Atkinson index explicitly incorporates a parameter that captures aversion towards inequality, and therefore its value changes with the level of aversion.

[2] The authors use a sample of 9 415 respondents aged 45-49. This sample size is more than 9 times the usual sample in surveys like ISSP or Risks that Matter.

[3] The German Socio-Economic Panel and the British Household Panel Survey collect people's preferences with respect to some redistributive policies (see Rueda and Stegmueller (2019[19]) for a discussion).

www.ingramcontent.com/pod-product-compliance
Ingram Content Group UK Ltd.
Pitfield, Milton Keynes, MK11 3LW, UK
UKHW051503290926
15471UKWH00008B/1383

9 789264 775954